Social Welfare in Canada Revisited

SOCIAL

WELFARE

IN CANADA

REVISITED

FACING UP TO THE FUTURE

ANDREW ARMITAGE

OXFORD
UNIVERSITY PRESS

70 Wynford Drive Don Mills Ontario M3C 1J9

Oxford New York
Athens Auckland Bangkok Bombay
Calcutta Cape Town Dar es Salaam Delhi
Florence Hong Kong Istanbul Karachi
Kuala Lumpur Madras Madrid Melbourne
Mexico City Nairobi Paris Singapore
Tapei Tokyo Toronto

and associated companies in
Berlin Ibadan

Oxford is a trade mark of Oxford University Press

Canadian Cataloguing in Publication Data

Armitage, Andrew
    Social welfare in Canada revisited

3rd ed.
Previous eds. published under title:
Social welfare in Canada.
Includes bibiographical references and index.
ISBN 0-19-541204-4

1. Public welfare – Canada.   2. Social service – Canada.   3. Charities – Canada.
I. Title.   II. Title: Social welfare in Canada

HV105.A7 1996   361.971   C95-932803-3

This book is printed on permanent (acid-free) paper

Printed in Canada

CONTENTS

*To my wife Molly and to our sons, daughters-in-law, and grandchildren: Mark,
Karen, Nicholas, and Spencer;
Paul; Timothy and Mary Jane – that we may all live
our lives in a peaceful and just society.*

ACKNOWLEDGEMENTS

The opportunity to write *Social Welfare in Canada Revisited* was provided by the University of Victoria through an administrative leave. Members of the School of Social Work, both faculty and students, have had a major influence on my understanding of social welfare since I joined them in 1987. In particular I want to acknowledge the influence of Marilyn Callahan, Brian Wharf, and Michael Prince and of our First Nations colleagues, Elizabeth Hill, Laurie Gilchrist, and Kathy Absolon.

McClelland & Stewart remained an excellent publisher. *Social Welfare in Canada* has now been in print for twenty years. They encouraged me to write again on this occasion, and provided assistance in the transition to Oxford University Press Canada.

FOREWORD

When the first edition of *Social Welfare in Canada* was published in 1975 one could say with confidence that "a more just, tolerant, and humane Canadian society is possible. . . . social welfare measures have a major and inescapable contribution to make towards attaining such a society."[1] The underlying assumption was that further growth was desirable and expected. The book recognized some of the problems of bureaucratization and power differentials that characterized social welfare; but in the end, faith remained that expansion, more social workers, more programs, and more resources would lead to a society in which the values that characterize social welfare would be fulfilled: that we would, through steady growth, move toward a more just and compassionate society.

In 1988, when the second edition was published, the account given in 1975 still seemed relevant, as "the major programs and institutions of the welfare state have remained intact from the early 1970s." At the same time the tone was much more cautious, as "Resources were initially [in the 1970s] expanded, then cut back [in the 1980s], and today they remain restrained. Periodic interest in reform has often faded rather than culminated in change, leaving unanswered questions for some future policy agenda." In addition, "The high ideals of the welfare state remain beyond the grasp of the welfare institutions that have been developed."[2]

In 1995 all the fundamentals and, with them, the programs are immersed in change. It is time to "revisit" social welfare in Canada in order to understand the nature of the dilemmas that now have to be faced in policy, planning, and participation in the institutions that we have inherited, whether we intend to work for them or against them.

The second edition was a rewrite and updating of the first, but this text is a new one. It uses the same structure as the earlier editions and makes limited use of parts that remain current, but the appraisal and the conclusions are different. We are not producing a "more just and tolerant" Canadian society. Some major programs have already disappeared and others are threatened. The "deficit" is a major stimulus to change, but the problems of social welfare are also internal and are reflected by a loss of confidence in the provisions that have been enacted and by a search for radical alternatives. In the mid-1990s the radical alternatives of the conservatives are being enacted, while the left is deeply divided between the original liberal mainstream and the alternative approaches to social structure and social programs provided by a Marxist/socialist analysis and by the social movements.

In addition, Canada must contend with the uncertainty created by the 1995 Quebec referendum. The referendum result – 49.4 per cent for separation, 50.6 per cent for remaining in Canada – reduces the capacity of the federal government to maintain the flow of funds needed to finance the deficit and increases, through higher interest rates, the size of the deficit. In the short term, both factors increase the pressure on government expenditures and hence the pace and extent of the restructuring process. In the longer term Canada will need a social vision of its own if it is to resist the political and economic drift toward complete integration with the United States.

This book remains an "introduction." The literature of the social welfare field is rich, varied, and critical, a significant change from 1975 when the first edition was published. A major purpose of this book is to introduce the student to the differing perspectives on social welfare that have been developed. In introducing ideas with which I do not agree, I have tried to be as fair as I can to the writers' arguments and intent. The end notes are designed to point the way for further reading so that the student can develop an understanding and establish a personal point of view. I remain a liberal, and in the last chapter you will find out why.

Notes

1. Andrew Armitage, *Social Welfare in Canada: Ideals and Realities* (Toronto: McClelland and Stewart, 1975), p. vi.
2. Andrew Armitage, *Social Welfare in Canada: Ideals, Realities and Future Paths* (Toronto: McClelland and Stewart, 1988), pp. 7-14.

Chapter 1

SOCIAL WELFARE

What is social welfare? Today, in common parlance, "social welfare" is defined by the social services and in particular by the services directed toward income security and personal and family life. This book uses this common understanding as a boundary for the discussion of specific services that follow.

However, the *concept* of social welfare is much broader and can be defined as a major component of the organized pursuit of social justice in modern societies. It is an understanding of this broader definition of social welfare, and in particular its application in Canada, that is at the heart of this book.

This view of social welfare, based in the pursuit of social justice, is often referred to as the "liberal" view. This is not a reference to the Liberal Party or to any particular government. Instead, the term "liberal" is used to distinguish a school of philosophical thought and understanding. As such, the "liberal" view is one of the five major viewpoints that have influenced popular and academic understandings of social welfare, the others being the conservative, socialist, feminist, and anti-racist points of view.

The conservative point of view is illustrated by a recent social policy publication from the C.D. Howe Institute:

Canada's social programs need repair. They are too elaborate. They are too expensive. And they may not be good for the people they are supposed to help. They may not have caused Canada's current huge debt problem, but they are too large a component of public expenditure not to be part of the solution.[1]

The socialist viewpoint is illustrated by Bob Mullaly's *Structural Social Work*:

It [the social welfare state] can be used as a stepping stone toward a socialist society. Because social welfare programs and services represent a break with the free market doctrine of distribution, social democrats believe that the advantages of such a system would be seen by the general public as preferable to that of the free market, thus aiding in the transformation from a capitalist to a socialist society.[2]

The feminist perspective is not based in an ideology *per se* but in a separate experience of social welfare.

> Perhaps the most striking claim in feminist analysis of social policy is that it is impossible to understand the Welfare State without understanding how it deals with women. . . . What we should have at the end of such an investigation of social policy is a new understanding, not only of the way the Welfare State deals with women, but also of social policy itself. To suggest that there is such a thing as a 'feminist social policy' to put in the place of the other traditions would be to claim too much. For one thing, it would do violence to the variety of perspectives held by women working and writing in this area; for another, it would suggest a completed task.[3]

Although the task may be incomplete, two main lines of contribution from feminism are having a major impact on social welfare. One is to demand a re-examination of all aspects of social welfare through a "gender lens." The second is to recognize the emergence of fields of social welfare provision that have been created as a result of women's experience and action to date. Among the latter are such fields as child and elder care, employment equity, sexual assault and family violence, and abortion and birth control services.[4]

An anti-racist critique of social policy has also been developed on the basis of a distinct experience of social welfare. In the experience of First Nations, blacks, South Asians, and other visible minorities, the policies and provisions of the welfare state have features that make them part of the institutional racism of Canadian society. Racism in this sense does not mean personal racial slurs and discrimination; instead, as Naidoo and Edwards define the term, "Racism results from the transformation of race prejudice, ethnocentrism, or both through the exercise of power against a racial group defined as inferior by individuals and institutions with the intentional or unintentional support of the entire culture."[5] Thus the families and children of First Nations were the subjects of institutional racism when the young people were sent to residential schools for education in a culture and religion seen by the ruling majority as superior to that of their parents.

The decision to give the liberal point of view a central place in this text may strike the reader as being arbitrary or premature. However, whether or not one agrees with the liberal perspective, it makes a good place to anchor the text as the writers from the other four points of view are agreed that liberalism is (or was) the driving force behind the institution of social welfare. It has also been the driving force behind the aspirations and commitment of the majority of professionals in social welfare institutions. The other points of view are having a major impact on social welfare in Canada, and on the development of critical thinking about social welfare, but do not yet appear to have so changed the institution as a whole that any one of them could claim to represent its mainstream values and objectives.

The contribution to understanding and policy formulation of each viewpoint is found throughout this text. Chapter 8 provides a more thorough treatment of the ideas, research, and knowledge base that inform each.

The Liberal Values

The liberal point of view, as applied to social welfare, ascribes particular importance to the following shared values: (1) concern for the individual; (2) faith in humanity; (3) equity; (4) equality; (5) community; (6) diversity; and (7) democracy.

1. *Concern for the individual.* All liberal conceptions of society place high value on the individual. The literature of social welfare illustrates this concern. In their interpretation of the role of social welfare in industrial society Wilensky and Lebeaux[6] find a distinguishing characteristic in its "direct concern with human consumption needs." By this is meant that if government activities are placed on a continuum from activities directed to maintenance of the social system as a whole, such as national defence, monetary policy, and the administration of justice, to activities directed to providing benefit to individuals, for example, schools, recreational facilities, and health services, then social welfare must be classified among those activities organized primarily with respect to the needs of the individual.

In the profession of social work, the concern with the individual finds expression in the commitment of the code of ethics to the principles of client-centredness, confidentiality, self-determination, and advocacy. It also finds negative recognition in the charge that social workers are "do-gooders" or "bleeding hearts," persons, that is to say, whose concern for human suffering and desire to help others exceed what others might expect to accomplish. At the international level the United Nations Universal Declaration of Human Rights expresses the concern thus:

> Article 22. Everyone, as a member of society, has the right to social security, and is entitled to realization through national effort and international co-operation, and in accordance with the organization and resources of each State, of the economic, social and cultural rights indispensable for his dignity and the free development of his personality.[7]

2. *Faith in humanity.* Concern for the individual is matched by a high degree of faith in the individual. This finds expression in social welfare programs and social work activities directed toward change in both institutions and individuals. In the former case, the basic thesis is that people are restricted and prevented from the fulfilment of their potential by ignorance and by ill-designed and inhumane social institutions. If these factors are changed, then people will achieve not only greater happiness and greater realization of potential but will be able to contribute to and receive more from their peers. When change in individuals is considered, the same basic thrust emerges. People can be helped to liberate themselves from their self-constructed prisons of ignorance, fear, and anger and thereby obtain greater personal fulfilment. The 1971 Senate Committee on Poverty expressed the value thus:

> A recent development in Canadian social philosophy is the emergence of the more positive human resource development approach. This philosophy recognizes the inherent value of the literate, educated and trained population. . . .

Development of human resources to their greatest potential is regarded as a desirable objective in itself.[8]

The value is expressed, too, in the rejection of the basically suspicious thrust of normative economic theory. The rejection of the idea that productivity depends on economic rewards and penalties is captured in the following quotation:

> that man is by nature greedy, lazy, etc.; that money incentives are required to make him work; and that it is perhaps an unfortunate necessity for industry to have a pool of unemployed and therefore miserable people from which to draw the energy (manpower) to work the machines, or to do the 'dirty work' of a society. . . . the 'market mentality' [is not only] seen as corrosive of human dignity and identity, it is increasingly seen as inefficient, even in its own terms, for society as a whole.[9]

Here, a high degree of faith is held in the positive aspects of our humanity. Failure to obtain these high aspirations is usually interpreted as representing failure in institutions, socialization patterns, or opportunities. Such failures can be prevented or corrected. Failure to obtain the best is regarded as an unfortunate and correctable aberration.[*]

3. *Equity.* The commitment to equity indicates a willingness to listen to, search for, and reduce, if not eliminate, those features of the social condition that create relative differences of power and privilege, and hence of advantage and disadvantage. Examples of such differences include the relationships between children and adults, the relationships between men and women, the relationship between those who are able bodied and those who have different physical or mental capacities, the differences that visibly or culturally distinguish people from one another, and the relationship between people of differing sexual orientation.

The liberal Oxford philosopher John Rawls has suggested two principles of social justice that are sufficiently broad to provide a beginning point for discussion of equity in this wide range of social relationships:

> First: each person is to have an equal right to the most extensive basic liberty compatible with a similar liberty for others. Second: social and economic inequalities are to be arranged so that they are both (a) reasonably expected to be to everyone's advantage, and (b) attached to positions and offices open to all.[10]

Applying these principles to the relationship between a child and his or her parents permits some inequality of status and freedom between parent and child, but only to the extent that such inequality can be reasonably expected to be to everyone's advantage. Thus a parent has no right to mistreat, exploit, or neglect

---

[*]This statement would provoke sharp disagreement from the welfare conservative, who would hold that financial incentives and penalties are essential and that the disregard of this fact by liberal welfare theory is one of the principal problems that social welfare has to address.

a child while still holding to the right to parent. A moral basis thus exists for a social welfare function that aims to protect the welfare of children. An analysis of how children are treated in our society, including how they are treated by social welfare, is an important corollary.

Applying these principles to the differences between men and women requires that men and women be treated equally in employment, marriage, divorce, inheritance, ownership, and civic life while permitting women to advance differing claims based on their exclusive role in child-bearing. It also requires that social policy be subject to a feminist analysis that examines how the welfare state deals with women.

Applying these principles to race and ethnic relationships would exclude any consideration of differences based on appearance while permitting an ethnic group to articulate its right to resist cultural practices that acted to its disadvantage. An analysis of the role of social welfare is also necessary.

It should not be supposed that the principle of equity is easily applied. For example, between parents and children the words "reasonably expected to be to everyone's advantage" require interpretation, and frequently interpretations differ among parent, child, and social welfare authorities. A teenager who needs an abortion or who lives with a gay companion may hold that her liberty in no way infringes on the liberty of others, but not all would agree. Some parents and social groups would consider that they, or the state, had a right to intervene. In recent years there have been differences of view on these matters within Canadian society, and much wider differences of view exist between societies.

4. *Equality.* A strong egalitarian thrust is a central feature of social welfare values and is a particular expression of the general concern with equity. The value finds expression in two related concerns: a general concern with the extent of inequalities and a particular concern with poverty. The concern with the extent of inequalities directs attention to the relative standards of living of different groups of persons. The concern with poverty directs attention to the minimum standards of living that are to be tolerated in the society, regardless of the individual poor person's financial contribution to the society. In both cases, there is a clear rejection of the idea that the income distribution resulting from inheritance, property, productivity, bargaining, and the like should be allowed to stand.

Beginning with Rawls's principles of justice the social policy analyst W.G. Runciman approaches the subject of inequalities from a point of departure that assumes that economic equality between persons should be the beginning point from which discussion of difference should proceed.

> Starting, therefore, from the assumption that all social inequalities require to be justified it can, as a minimum, be shown that rational persons in a state of nature would agree on three broad criteria, or principles, in the light of which, subsequent inequalities of reward could be claimed to be just.[11]

These three principles are need, merit, and contribution to the common good. Of the three, *need* is regarded as the most basic. A person who is sick needs additional resources to obtain the most basic type of equality with others in the society. *Merit* is accepted as a criterion only to the extent that it equates with the willingness of individuals to do things that are difficult to do, involving demonstrable hardship and sacrifice to the doer. *Contribution to the common good* is accepted because everyone stands to benefit. It follows that the extent of financial advantage should be proportionate to the extent of the general benefit obtained for all. Thus the ideal world would be characterized by those differences in wealth and income that all had agreed are justified, rather than by wealth and income being privately determined. In particular, in Runciman's approach to inequality and equity, there would be sensitivity first to the situation of those who were least well off.*

5. *Community.* The values of community are attentive to the need of individuals for a social context for their lives. Community values take the form of assertions that people should have the opportunity to fulfil themselves through their relationships with others. Ideally, people should live in a community from which they draw satisfying social relationships, which provides adequate developmental opportunities for their children, and in which participation, in deciding how the collective welfare is to be obtained, is open to all.

The concept of community includes the geographic local community but also includes communities based on any common tie, such as age, interest, employment, leisure, or ethnic origin. Community is seen as providing the primary means of social control and socialization and the first level of collective support to the family. The community is also the site of such organized measures of support as family life education, day care, homemaker services, and mental health services.

In addition, the community has increasingly been seen as a source of employment and economic development through such activities as community development, community economic development, and community social services. All of these activities have a goal of improved relationships among people, less alienation, less class separation, and less racial or ethnic conflict.

6. *Diversity.* Earlier statements[12] of the goals of social justice failed to recognize that differences arise not only between individuals but also between religions, cultures, and social groups. Rawls refers to these differences of world view as "reasonable comprehensive doctrines" in the following manner:

> Thus, it is not in general unreasonable to affirm any one of a number of reasonable comprehensive doctrines. We recognize that our own doctrine has, and can have, for people generally, no special claim on them beyond our own view of its merits. Others who affirm doctrines different from ours are, we grant, reasonable also, and certainly not unreasonable.[13]

In the discussion of equity and equality we noted that the application of these principles differs with individual situations. Recognizing diversity as a value requires

---

*The "conservative" view of the welfare state differs radically from the liberal conception on this point, holding that the right to wealth and income lies primarily with individuals, who have the right to determine its use and hence set the minimum levels of assistance.

that respect be shown as well to differences of peoples' collective historical and cultural experience.

An example is provided by the relationship between First Nations and general Canadian society. Let us grant that the inequality between persons of Native origin and others cannot reasonably be expected to be to everyone's advantage. Until the 1970s it was generally assumed that the welfare of First Nations peoples lay in their full integration into the general society. This view was rejected by First Nations and the view now is that they should have the opportunity to form their own societies and govern their own affairs. There are many questions about how such a separation can be made and sustained, but the need to recognize a separate Aboriginal presence is now entrenched in the Canadian constitution.

Opening the discussion of social welfare to issues of diversity has led to major changes in the scope of that discussion and requires us to see social welfare as it has developed as an historical expression of Western culture rather than as a universally applicable institution. In particular, the impact on First Nations has to be part of any liberal analysis of social welfare.

7. *Faith in democracy.* The example of the change in First Nations policy illustrates another important feature of the values of social justice, which is that their application is fallible and subject to change. Kymlicka, in his discussion of liberalism and individual freedom, notes that:

> [The] assumption that our beliefs about the good life are fallible and revisable is widely endorsed in the liberal tradition from John Stuart Mill to the most prominent contemporary American liberals. . . . As Rawls puts it, individuals 'do not view themselves as inevitably tied to the pursuit of the particular conception of the good and its final ends which they espouse at any given time'. Instead they are 'capable of revising and changing this conception'. They can 'stand back' from their current ends to 'survey and assess' their worthiness.[14]

In practical terms, the revision of public policy lies within the boundaries of the political process. Hence, the importance of the attachment to, and confidence in, democracy. "Democracy," meaning rule by the people, is an extension of faith in humanity, from the individual to the collective. In ideal terms, democracy is the participation of all affected parties in processes of decision-making to an extent proportionate to how much they are affected by the results. Decisions are expected to be on the basis of rational argument, respect for difference, and negotiated compromise rather than being imposed through the assertion of differences of power.

Realistically, it must be conceded that such is not the real state of Canadian political affairs or of any other political jurisdiction, and there is a search for more participatory and consensual ways to make public choices. However, until better ways can be devised a basic commitment to the typical form of democracy found in liberal societies generally and in Canada in particular (a universal adult electorate, a choice of political parties, periodic elections) remains. The accepted instruments of change are thus persuasion, argument, protest, publicity, organization, interest group politics, and alliances. On the other hand, subversion, intimidation, violence, and personal attack, not to mention revolution, are considered unsuitable and unethical means to the ends of social welfare.*

The Context of Social Welfare

Social welfare, as we know it, is the product of a particular time and culture. The fact that it has been established within the last 100 years and is a creation of Western developed societies provides it with a familiarity that would be lacking if it had occurred in another time and place. This familiarity can distract us from understanding the context in which social welfare both was developed and now exists. The importance of seeing social welfare in context cannot be overemphasized, for the principal reason that social welfare is changing is that the context in which it arose has changed. Some of these changes are affecting all Western developed societies, while some are distinct to Canada.

1. *The global economy and the information age.* The global economy is not a new phenomenon. There was international trade in rare objects from the earliest time, and by the nineteenth century a global economy of sorts was founded on colonialism and on European military and technological supremacy. During the twentieth century America and developed post-colonial societies, including Canada, Australia, and South Africa, became full members of this colonially based international economy. It was a global order characterized by great inequalities and it was managed to the benefit of the Western developed societies as a matter of military, financial, and economic policy. During this period the institutions of social welfare were developed.

The current global economy has undergone major changes from this earlier pattern. One change was marked by the OPEC oil cartel in the 1970s. The cartel showed that a determined group of non-Western countries could take control of a critical commodity and manipulate its price and supply to their benefit. However, a more profound change was the development of a much more complex manufacturing and trading world in which major growth in the proportion of production took place outside the Western developed market economies, first in Japan and in Southeast Asia and increasingly in India, Latin America, North Africa, and the Middle East. Now, in the 1990s, the centrally planned and managed economies of Eastern Europe and Russia are becoming full participants in a global economy that is no longer completely dominated by the Western developed societies and, in the future, will become less so.

Concurrent with the development of this many-centred world has been the development of transnational corporations (TNCs) and financial systems that lie

---

*The socialist/Marxist writers differ from the liberal conception of both democracy and change process on this point. For example, Mullaly calls into question the efficacy of representative democracy and pluralism (pp. 68-69) and endorses change through subversive acts (p. 179). Revolutionary Marxists go further, opposing all forms of participation in welfare institutions as only serving to support the continuation of a fundamentally flawed social order.

outside the control of any national government and are only loosely regulated through international conventions and agreements. Thus, the manufactured goods we buy in our stores come from all parts of the world and are frequently made through production processes that occur in more than one country and often on more than one continent.

The development of the latest form of the global economy and its associated financial systems has been made possible by a new technology – the computerized information systems on which we now depend. The speed with which information can now be processed and communicated anywhere in the world has produced fundamental changes in the way the world does business, organizes its affairs, and understands itself. Furthermore, we are still in the early stages of this revolution in our collective affairs. We do not know where it will take us, but the changes that have already occurred are such that we know the world of the twenty-first century will be as different from our own as the world of the nineteenth century was from ours.

Already, as a result of these changes, the Western developed societies can no longer unilaterally determine the terms of trade or retain income and wealth developed by the transnational corporations within their boundaries.[15] In 1958 the Swedish economist and welfare state architect Gunnar Myrdal wrote:

> We will never be able to come to grips with the international problems of today and tomorrow if we do not squarely face the fact that the democratic Welfare State in the rich countries of the Western world is protectionistic and nationalistic.[16]

The nature of the welfare state was recognized in 1958 but the change to a different world order is having consequences that could not then have been foreseen.

2. *Capitalism.* The capitalist free market economy provides the economic context of social welfare. The economic historian Robert Heilbronner points out that there have been only three mechanisms for the exchange of goods and labour between people and societies in the history of mankind. The first is tradition: the sharing of goods and labour on the basis of cultural expectations as occurred (and continues to occur) in First Nations communities (e.g., through ceremonies like the potlatch). The second is command: the authoritative distribution of goods and labour as occurred in the building of the pyramids and in the command economies of Eastern Europe prior to the 1990s and as occurs today in the government sector of our economy. The third form of distribution is through the market economy in which goods and labour are exchanged at a price. The capitalist form of the market economy has developed since the eighteenth century as a mechanism that encourages the private ownership of the means of production and distribution and hence the accumulation of wealth by individuals and corporations.

The capitalist form of the market economy has many problems. It is exploitative, unstable, and environmentally insensitive, creates extremes of wealth and poverty, and is devoid of any moral character. However, it has provided a mechanism for a dynamic series of social and economic revolutions that have transformed all societies that have participated, whether they wanted to or not.

The first of these was the industrial revolution of the late eighteenth and nine-teenth centuries that brought with it the cotton mill and the steam engine along with mass child labour; a second revolution brought with it the railway, the steamship and along with them a new form of economic instability – business cycles; a third brought electrification . . .; a fourth introduced the automobile . . .; a fifth has electronified everything. . . . Over the entire period of humanity children had lived lives that were essentially the same as their parents. . . . From the mid-nineteenth century on that sense of continuity was ever more noticeably displaced by a sense of change.[17]

With each revolution has come, too, an increase in individualism, freedom, income, health, and longevity of life not only for the wealthy but for most but not all members of society. The affluence and advantage enjoyed by participants in cap-italist market economies have exercised an attraction wherever they have become known. Where they have had the choice people have, more often than not, chosen the market economy over having their affairs organized by either tradition or command. Once such a choice has been made it has never been permanently reversed. Furthermore, the alternative that was developed under socialist auspices in Eastern Europe and the Soviet Union has disintegrated and been replaced by new capitalist systems. For the foreseeable future there is no alternative to capi-talism in sight.

In this capitalist economic order individuals are expected to provide for them-selves. The pages of Canadian government statements of social policy are filled with obeisance to the goals of economic growth and with exhortations as to the values of economic self-reliance and independence. Further, these values have been increasingly emphasized as insecurity about the future of Western society has grown. The society's rhetoric entrusts its future to the private initiative of indi-viduals rather than to institutions – whether unions, governments, or corporations. Social welfare provision is closely related to this capitalist view of economic freedom and responsibility.

As a result, many of our social welfare policies can be viewed as the secondary consequence of this series of social and economic revolutions and as a reaction to the amoral character of capitalism. Based on a varying mixture of concern at the unfairness of the capitalist economic order, human sympathy for the unfortunate, recognition of the claims advanced by those who have been disadvantaged by change, and fear that organized opposition might disrupt the market economy, social welfare measures have been developed. The large field of income security policies can be viewed as a response to the problems of social dislocation caused by unplanned changes in demand for different types of labour and the consequent impossibility of private citizens providing for themselves in all circumstances. The large field of personal and community social services can be viewed as a response to the dislocation of community and family life caused by urbanization.

In the early years of capitalist economic growth there was little or no attempt to mitigate the social effects of continuous change. The social costs of social change were allowed to lie where they fell. Latterly, there has been more understanding that economic change creates both winners and losers and that losers should receive some compensation or adjustment assistance from the state. Thus, a case was made that the James Bay Cree should be compensated for lost lands due to hydro development, that a workman dispossessed of usable skills by technological change should be compensated by the society, and that an elderly renter, whose neighbourhood is to be destroyed for new construction, should be rehoused. We have also come some way toward recognizing that there should be a settlement of changes that occurred in the past. Examples here include First Nations who were dispossessed of their land without compensation during the process of settlement and victims of poor industrial working conditions. Finally, the claims of farmers and fishermen to compensation has been partly recognized where they have lost their livelihood due to change in either international prices or environmental conditions.

Some parts of our social welfare policies can be seen as necessary activities to the market economy but are undertaken outside it. Examples include universal education, public health systems, and the criminal justice system. Moreover, the need for social welfare is also a product of the positive achievements of capitalist society: people live longer and hence need more care. They live more by their brains and hence need more sophisticated education and training.

With each change in the market economy has come a change in the social environment, in the demand for labour, in the types of education that are relevant, and in the disparities of wealth and income that are generated. Each of these changes has made some features of our social welfare systems less relevant than they were while creating new issues that need a response. One indicator of these changes is the proportion of the Canadian work force in various types of employment. Table 1 provides an overview of these changes. The change in the proportion of the working population in the blue-collar (manufacturing), primary, and transportation occupational groups is particularly significant, as these groups represented the majority source of employment when the social welfare systems were developed. Our unemployment insurance provisions were designed in the 1940s for an economy dominated by male workers in blue-collar and primary industries who were assumed to be the primary source of family income. It is not surprising that they did not anticipate the 1990s distribution of employment and gender roles.

3. *The nation-state and international relationships.* The national state remains the fundamental political unit of society, but its power to control its affairs has been

TABLE 1: *Distribution of the Labour Force, 15 years and Over, by Occupation Division, 1941-1991 (numerical distribution by 000s)*

Occupation Sector	1941		1961		1981		1991	
	No.	%	No.	%	No.	%	No.	%
All	4,183	100	6,458	100	12,267	100	14,220	100
Blue-collar	1,058	25	2,446	38	3,465	28	3,017	21
Primary	1,134	27	830	13	929	8	867	6
Transport	266	6	496	7	939	7	1,060	7
White-collar and Service	1,496	36	3,246	50	6,864	56	9,829	69

SOURCE: *Census of Canada*, various years.

reduced by the advent of the new form of the global economy. The transnational corporations have proved to be difficult to regulate, control, or tax. Each country wants and needs the employment that the TNCs generate, but as the TNCs can choose where they operate the individual countries are placed in a situation of competing with one another to offer the most favourable, meaning profitable for the TNCs, operating conditions. Taxation of TNCs has also been difficult, partly because when production and trade processes are distributed globally it is difficult to establish where profit has been generated. In addition, countries with high rates of corporate tax risk driving away new TNC investment.

Social welfare remains an internal jurisdiction of each country. State actions may range from inactivity through support to such institutions as churches, philanthropic groups, and the family, to the active conduct of programs of state provision. Indeed, one of the strengths of social welfare is that each country has been able to devise the system that expresses its own need and social character.[18] This same strength, however, can lead to each country being involved in a competition aimed at minimizing the costs of welfare in order to provide a more profitable and attractive environment for international investment. The European Community has recognized this danger and agreed on a series of conventions governing the regulation of industry, working conditions, and social benefits. Although European proponents of the welfare state see many limitations of what has been accomplished,[19] the European example provides more support for the welfare systems of each member state than is available in North America.

In North America, Canada is partnered with the United States and Mexico in the North American Free Trade Agreement (NAFTA). As neither of the other partners has had as strong a social welfare system as has Canada, there is no support through NAFTA for Canadian welfare provisions. This is not to say that Canada cannot have its own social welfare system, but it has to be designed, financed, and managed in a manner that supports, or at least does not harm, Canada's external economic competitiveness.

In some circumstances nations have had to ask for international assistance to develop or support their internal economies. Where this has happened, as was the case in New Zealand in 1988, international bodies have played a more active role in requiring changes in social welfare as a condition of assistance. For New Zealand, this included adopting policies of financial restraint that influenced social welfare expenditures through such effects as creating unemployment and limiting the government revenues available to finance programs. To date, Canada has not been in the situation of asking for such assistance, but with the growth of federal and provincial deficits the possibility of Canada requiring such assistance at some point in the future has materially increased. Thus, one reason why it is important to control the growth of the deficit is that doing so supports the preservation by Canada of sufficient independence to protect its social welfare system from external influences and demands.

4. *Ethnonationalism and cultural pluralism.* The post-war social welfare service state was founded in the aftermath of the Holocaust at a time when racism was seen as an extremely dangerous force in social policy. It also occurred during a period in

which the leadership of Western societies, in matters of governance, was taken for granted. As a result, social welfare was developed on the basis of a policy of state-cultural separation and a principle that common social services would be available to all citizens, regardless of culture or ethnic origin. However, these principles were themselves based on another assumption – that "modern" Western institutions would be or could be made appropriate for all peoples, and, sooner or later, would displace traditional ones. The approach to social policy favoured treating people as individuals with human rights rather than as ethnic groups with collective rights.

In the 1990s it is apparent that the issues of ethnicity, culture, and race have not been dealt with to people's satisfaction, and this paradigm now is seen as constituting a form of institutional racism. Instead, there has been a reawakened understanding that the nation-state has to accommodate a variety of claims to different types of collective identity within its boundaries. The name being given to one of these newly recognized identities is ethnonationalism, which occurs where there is more than one nation within a state, occupying lands of their own and sharing a distinct historical and cultural tradition. Levin defines both the objectives and the dilemma of ethnonationalism:

> The demand of a state for every people is the strong sense of ethnonationalism, the extreme political expression of cultural identity. Reconciling the strong version of this ideal with the institutional realities of a state for every people is, however, a practical impossibility. That there are far fewer states than ethnic groups makes the depth of the attachment to the ideal and the sense of deprivation in its frustration all the more poignant. The politics of ethnonationalism worldwide draws its importance not from this disproportion of numbers, but from the fact that more than half the governments of these independent states must deal with political claims made on an ethnic basis where there are few if any workable solutions. . . .
>
> Acceptance of the right to self determination – the weak sense of ethnonationalism – also presents problems, since it leaves unattended the question of what forms of institutional autonomy can meet the aspirations of 'people' for autonomy. . . . New political forms which offer autonomy without sovereignty are difficult to imagine. Furthermore, any new solution bears the burden of achieving acceptance without a history to give it legitimacy.[20]

Canada faces two major ethnonational forces, the recurrent issue of establishing Quebec as a separate state (the first sense of ethnonationalism) and the issue of Aboriginal government (the second sense of ethnonationalism).[21]

In addition, Canada, along with all other developed states, has become, through immigration, a polyethnic multicultural state in which Aboriginal peoples and peoples of French, British, other European, Asian, and African origins live together using common social institutions. The changes taking place in this mix of peoples of different origins are substantial. For most of the century peoples of French and British origins dominated all others by a wide margin. This is no longer the case. Table 2 shows the historic pattern and the recent change.

TABLE 2: *Population of Canada by British, French, and "Other" Origin, 1901-1991 (000s)*

Ethnic	1901		1921		1941		1961		1971		1981		1991	
Origin	No.	%	No.	%	No.	%	No.	%	No.	%	No.	%	No.	%
British	3,063	57.0	4,869	55.4	5,716	49.7	7,997	43.8	9,624	44.6	9,674	40.2	7,595	28.1
French	1,649	30.7	2,453	27.9	3,483	30.3	5,540	30.4	6,180	28.6	6,439	26.7	6,146	22.7
Other	659	12.2	1,466	16.7	2,308	20.0	4,792	25.8	5,764	26.7	6,370	26.4	7,429	27.5
Multiple*	-	-	-	-	-	-	-	-	-	-	1,600	6.7	5,810	21.5
Total	5,371		8,788		11,507		18,238		21,568		24.084		26,994	

*Until the 1981 census respondents could only report one ethnic origin determined by their paternal ancestry.
SOURCE: *Census of Canada*, various years.

Until the 1970s the assumption of Canadian social policy was that immigrants (and Aboriginal peoples) would assimilate to either the English or French majorities. This is clearly no longer the case. First, there are the many peoples of neither French nor British origin. Then there are those of multiple origins who do not consider themselves to be in any one ethnic group. For most of the century, too, "Other" represented people of principally European origin. This is rapidly changing. At the time of the 1981 census, 70 per cent of the "Other" were of European origin, but by 1991 only 56 per cent of these were European. The rapid growth in the numbers of people of non-European origin is also apparent when the 1986 and 1991 censuses are compared (see Table 3).

TABLE 3: *Peoples of Non-European Ethnic Origin, Canada, 1986 and 1991 (000s)*

Ethnic Origin	1986	1991	% increase
Aboriginal peoples	373	470	26
Arab/West Asian	75	144	92
South Asian	260	420	61
Chinese	360	585	62
Filipino	93	157	69
Korean	26	44	69
Other East and Southeast Asian	73	114	56
African	5	26	420
Caribbean	48	94	96
"Black"	170	224	32
Latin America	32	85	165
Other	342	787	130

SOURCE: *Census of Canada*, 1986, 1991.

It is now apparent that the origins of the peoples in Canada are complex and that the old British/French paradigm and even the later British/French/Other European paradigm no longer represent the basis on which social policy can be developed. The challenge is to build, or rebuild, social institutions that serve all peoples with equity. Genuinely common institutions have to be developed. Assimilation was too simplistic and spoke only of a one-way street toward integration. Instead, we are finding that Canadian social policy and its administration have to change to provide for a society of many peoples.[22]

5. *Feminism.* European culture was (and is) not only racist but also patriarchal. Women were denied the vote until long after voting had been extended to all men.

A woman's property rights were limited and on marriage were lost to the man. Women were subject to discrimination in employment both by being denied access to some types of employment and by being paid less in all employment. Roles performed by women, particularly caring roles, were taken for granted and not valued at all. As late as the 1950-60 period the common wisdom was that "a woman's place is in the home," where she would provide for the care of children, prepare the meals, keep a clean and tidy house, and remain faithful to her husband. The man, on the other hand, was expected to be a "breadwinner," bringing home a wage from which he would give his wife what was needed for the household; he would be part of the children's lives but on a more limited basis, with work taking precedence; he was also free to use the balance of his income for his interests and there was to some degree a "double standard" of fidelity.

These cultural assumptions were the understanding of men's and women's roles that were held by men. Dissenting women's voices were not heeded, or were treated as marginal or extreme points of view. As a result, social welfare was based on patriarchal assumptions and upheld male privilege. By most women and some men, these assumptions are now regarded as wrong, but the institutions that were established on these assumptions and the male privilege that they created continue. Changing the institutions to provide for equity between men and women has been proceeding for the last two decades. The process is by no means complete and the privilege that resulted (and results) from their unreformed character remains. There are also reactions to uphold male privilege by resisting, or reversing, those modest actions that have been taken, for example, to provide greater equity in the workplace.

In addition, feminism as a reforming and reframing influence on social welfare poses a deeper challenge than correcting androcentrism. The deeper challenge is to look at what the pursuit of social welfare means based on the life experience of women, as is seen, for example, in the Baines, Evans, and Neysmith text, *Women's Caring: Feminist Perspectives on Social Welfare*.

6. *Social spending and the deficit.* All developed countries devote a substantial portion of national revenues to social welfare measures. However, major variations exist in the percentage of various countries' economies devoted to social spending (see Table 4). Social spending is defined to include public expenditures on pensions, unemployment insurance, education, health care, and families (including family allowances).

TABLE 4: *Social Spending among G-7 Countries, 1960, 1980, and 1990, as a Percentage of Gross Domestic Product*

	1960	1980	1990
Canada	12.1	17.5	20.2
France	13.4	24.7	26.7
Germany	20.5	24.6	22.0
Italy	16.5	21.2	26.3
Japan	8.0	14.3	14.4
United Kingdom	13.9	18.0	16.9
United States	10.9	13.1	12.4

SOURCE: OECD Economic Survey, Canada, 1994

The variations between countries can be partly accounted for by differences in the number of beneficiaries and the age structure of the population. Table 5 shows the major differences that exist. Canada's relatively low proportion of expenditure on pensions, it should be noted, is largely the result of the age structure of the population.

TABLE 5: *Social Expenditure Programs, in G-7 Countries, as Percentages of Total Government Expenditure, 1990*

	Education	Health	Pensions	Unemployment	Total
Canada	12.5	13.0	13.0	6.8	45.3
France	10.5	14.4	25.2	3.0	53.1
Germany	8.8	12.9	23.3	2.8	47.8
Italy	10.0	12.2	27.0	0.7	49.9
Japan	13.4	17.3	20.4	0.8	51.9
U.K.	10.7	11.1	14.0	1.4	37.2
U.S.A.	12.7	2.5	19.1	0.8	35.1

SOURCE: OECD Economic Survey, Canada, 1994

These differences also represent variations in the priority given to social welfare, value choices made through democratic electoral processes in each country. The figures support the case made by Linda McQuaig[23] and other social welfare writers that Canada's social spending is not out of line with that of other OECD countries or out of control. Indeed, there appears to be the opportunity to increase levels of social expenditure without damaging Canada's economic competitiveness. Unfortunately for the advocates of increased social spending, Canada's public finances are now operating under a constraint asserting enormous pressure to lower program expenditures. This pressure comes from the size of the federal and provincial debt servicing costs.

Since the 1970s Canada has incurred an unbroken succession of annual public expenditure deficits. Each year more has been spent than has been raised by taxation, and each year the difference has been financed by borrowing (Table 6). In the period up to 1983 Canada's public debt was similar to that of other OECD countries, at around 50 per cent of gross domestic product (GDP); it is now (1994), at 95

TABLE 6: *Trends in Public Revenue and Expenditure, 1961-1992, as Percentage of GDP*

	1961	1975	1981	1985	1992
Revenue					
Federal	15.9	18.5	18.3	17.4	20.0
Provinces	12.0	18.9	21.5	22.6	24.8
Total	27.9	37.4	39.8	40.0	44.8
Expenditure					
Federal	14.3	16.3	16.4	19.5	19.5
Provinces	16.2	23.6	24.9	27.3	31.9
Total	30.5	39.9	41.3	46.8	51.4
Deficit	1.8	2.5	1.5	6.8	6.7
Expenditure by type					
All programs	27.5	36.1	35.0	38.4	42.0
Debt service	3.0	3.8	6.3	8.4	9.4

Note: Federal expenditures are net of transfers to the provinces.

SOURCE: John Richards, *The Case for Change* (Ottawa: Renouf, 1994), p. 41.

per cent, substantially higher.[24] As a result Canada has had to devote an increasing proportion of public expenditure each year to paying debt servicing costs.

At 9.4 per cent of GDP (21 per cent of all government revenues) the costs of debt servicing are exercising an enormous pressure on all other public expenditures. Canada has to reduce government deficits to a much lower proportion of GDP; ideally, they would be completely eliminated. Even when deficits are reduced, governments will have to pay the existing level of debt service costs for the foreseeable future. The 9.4 per cent of GDP represented by these costs is the reason why Canada cannot afford a higher level of social spending.

Furthermore, Canada owes 40 per cent of its GDP to foreigners.[25] As a result, the continued financing of the deficit and the associated debt depend on Canada's ability to borrow funds internationally, and Canada is vulnerable to international exchange rate changes and the interest rate it must pay on its debt varies with the opinion of international bond rating agencies on how well the government is managing its fiscal affairs. While the effects of other changes in the context of social welfare are affecting all Western developed societies, the deficit (and the effect it is having on social spending) is a "made in Canada" problem. This problem is exacerbated by uncertainty about the continued unity of the country and the difficulties that would result from the need to apportion the debt between Quebec and Canada.

7. *The aging of Canada's peoples.* Social welfare was developed at a time when the "baby boomers" were children. They are now in the middle of their working lives, with those born earliest in the post-war years now reaching their fifties. They will soon be leaving the labour force, pushed out by globalization and the information age, into a "retirement" that is a euphemism for unemployment.[26] Table 7 shows the rapid aging of the Canadian population.

TABLE 7: *Population Projections by Age Groups*

Year	Population by age (000s)			Percentage by age		
	0-17	18-64	65+	0-17	18-64	65+
1991	6,616	16,986	3,155	25	63	12
1996	6,525	17,701	3,579	23	63	13
2001	6,172	18,445	3,934	21	65	14
2006	5,653	19,115	4,279	19	66	15
2011	5,072	19,466	4,800	17	66	16

SOURCE: Statistics Canada, *Projections for Canada and the Provinces 1989-2011*, Catalogue 91-520 (Ottawa: Supply and Services, 1990).

There will be many more retired people in the years ahead and most will not have been able to organize their lives and personal affairs so as to retire in comfort at age fifty-five. Instead, they will depend on the provisions of the public-sector social welfare system.

Values and Social Context

When the liberal values of social welfare are related to the social context there are many obvious sources of conflict. The value of concern for the individual is in conflict with global economic processes and values that see all transactions in purely financial terms.[27] The value of equality conflicts with the propensity of capitalist societies to create and maintain inequality through such mechanisms as inheritance, private ownership, and the resolution of scarcity through competitive bidding. The values of maintaining viable communities conflict with the processes of change that disrupt them in the course of technological and environmental change, industrial development (or decline), and urbanization. The values of equity and diversity are in conflict with established positions of privilege and power and with the rights of private ownership, which always favour the status quo.

One view of the relationship between social welfare values and economic processes is that there has been a progressive shift in the relationship with the passage of time and the development of social welfare institutions. Eric Trist held this view:

> The relationship of welfare and development takes three principal forms: when development is a function of welfare; when welfare is a function of development; when welfare and development are interdependent functions.[28]

The first of these represents the circumstances of pre-industrial society, in which welfare is conserved by such traditional structures as the family, stable social classes, religion, and community. The study of First Nations and other Aboriginal peoples shows what such a society was like. The "development" brought by contact with capitalist society was an overwhelming threat to welfare. When it gained ascendancy First Nations and Aboriginal peoples suffered a loss of cultural and social institutions, and at the same time lost much of the ability to manage their own affairs or provide for the welfare of each other.

The second form, where economic growth (development) takes precedence over welfare, typifies capitalist society. Economic growth is the major focus of attention, and welfare (i.e., social welfare) is identified with those special situations that require attention because of unmet human needs. These "special situations" lead first to what Wilensky and Lebeaux define as a "residual" conception of social welfare that "holds that social welfare institutions should come into play only when the normal structures of supply, the family and the market, break down."[29] As society's understanding of the endemic nature of its needs has grown, it is held, so have the depth and continuity of commitment to social welfare measures. Wilensky and Lebeaux use the term "institutional" to refer to this second concept of social welfare,

> [which] implies no stigma, no emergency, no abnormalcy. Social welfare becomes accepted as a proper, legitimate function of modern industrial society in helping individuals achieve self-fulfilment. The complexity of modern life is recognized. The inability of the individual to provide fully for himself, or to meet all his needs in family and work settings is considered a "normal" condition; and the helping agencies achieve "regular" institutional status.[30]

In the writings of Alfred Kahn these ideas are identified with the "social planning phase of the welfare state,"[31] and in the works of Romanyshyn such ideas are linked with the concept of "social development":

> Social welfare as social development recognizes the dynamic quality of urban industrial society and the consequent need to adapt to change and to new aspirations for human fulfilment. It goes beyond the welfare state to a continuing renewal of its institutions to promote the fullest development of man.[32]

These ideas begin to approach a third concept of the relationship of welfare to development, where both are planned for together in a manner that is environmentally sustainable. The National Welfare Grants division of Health and Welfare Canada sponsored a series of projects in the early 1990s to explore these ideas more thoroughly. One product of this work was the publication by the Roehr Institute of the booklet *Social Well-being*, in which the concept of well-being is introduced in the following manner:

> One weakness of the post-war framework for well-being was the incapacity of social, economic and political institutions to fully grasp the interdependence among people, their communities, their society and the environment. The promotion of individual well-being came to be seen as achievable independent of investments in the social and economic development of communities and independent of the establishment of social entitlements. Social investments and entitlements have been withdrawn in the name of economic restructuring and budgetary deficit, without due recognition of the impact on individual well-being. In the name of societal well-being global economic integration has been pursued, but in a manner that has resulted in the loss of economic and social security for households and communities. . . . *A new framework for well-being must take into account the interdependence of various levels within society.*[33]

This concept of the relationship between social welfare values and economic processes represents a plea for a balanced integration of one with the other.

A second, conservative, view of the integration required between social welfare values and economic processes is provided by Courchene and Lipsey:

> In their view [that of Courchene and Lipsey], the social contract must change to complement the nature of the economy on which it rests. In other words, the welfare state should complement the underlying economy, and should not – and probably cannot – be used in the long run merely to offset the fundamental changes happening there. Key symptoms of this inability to reconcile changed economy with an entrenched social contract are growing transfer dependency, persistent and unsustainable public sector budget deficits, growing mismatches between economic opportunities and available skills and growing inequality in the distribution of income.[34]

In this view the institutionalized social welfare measures that Canada has established have only served to delay processes of inevitable social change. The costs of this delay are now mounting and have reached the point where they can no longer be paid. Social welfare has to be changed, not only in scale but in form, and, by this view, must be integrated with (i.e., dominated by) economic policy. The liberal values it represents can only be preserved (and then in a reduced form) by making them subordinate to financial imperatives. This requires major changes in social welfare programs.

A third view of the relationship is provided by socialist writers of the political economy school of analysis. Writers from this perspective support resistance to any reduction in the scope or form of social welfare but are increasingly pessimistic as to whether such resistance will achieve anything useful. Their analysis of social welfare in capitalist society is that it arose out of:

> the attempt by government to contain intractable conflict arising from the contradictory interests of the subordinate and ruling classes, and to implement redistributive or "averaging" mechanisms as a response to resistance by working classes to intolerable conditions surrounding the reproduction of their labour. Such reforms are a compromise response to the outcomes of the contradiction between labour and capital in a system with no inherent mechanism for addressing such conflicts.[35]

Today, with the establishment of the global economy and the weakening of the nation-state, the capitalist economic system appears to be an overwhelming and uncontrollable force for the deepening of social inequalities and the establishment of hegemonic power.

As Canada enters the late 1990s and prepares for the twenty-first century, the conservative view has become the Canadian ruling discourse. The practical consequence of this predominance is that social welfare institutions are preparing for a period of unprecedented change to which, understandably, established providers of service and consumers of services are opposed. At the same time equity demands that space be found in the process of restructuring for the interests of those groups (women, Aboriginal peoples, the disabled, etc.) who were not at the table when the existing services were developed. The effects will be seen in a decade of contention in which issues of social policy will often be high on the agenda of issues with which governments must deal. Chapters 2, 3, and 4 deal with the theory and practice of redistribution. Chapters 5 and 6 focus on the theory of community and the role of community social services. Chapter 7 deals with the political economy of welfare. Finally, in Chapters 8 and 9 the discipline of social policy studies and the future of social welfare are considered.

Notes

1. William Watson, *The Case for Change: Reinventing the Welfare State* (Toronto: C.D. Howe Institute, 1995), p. 1.
2. Robert Mullaly, *Structural Social Work* (Toronto: McClelland & Stewart, 1993), p. 94. Mullaly

writes from the socialist viewpoint, which he divides into two different forms, social democracy and Marxism. He agrees (p. 79) that liberalism is the defining force in Canadian social welfare and that this book has a liberal point of view.

3. Gillian Pascal, *Social Policy: A feminist analysis* (London: Tavistock Publications, 1986), p. 1.

4. For an introduction to the range of contributions that feminism is making to the development of social welfare services, see Carol Baines, Patricia Evans, and Sheila Neysmith, *Women's Caring: Feminist Perspectives on Social Welfare* (Toronto: McClelland & Stewart, 1991); *Canadian Social Work Review* (Women and Social Work: Celebrating Our Progress), 10, 2 (Summer, 1993).

5. Josephine Naidoo and R. Gary Edwards, "Combatting Racism Involving Visible Minorities," *Canadian Social Work Review*, 8, 2 (1991), p. 212.

6. H.L. Wilensky and C. Lebeaux, *Industrial Society and Social Welfare* (New York: Free Press, 1965), p. 145.

7. United Nations, *Universal Declaration of Human Rights* (New York, 1948), Article 31.

8. Senator David Croll, *Poverty in Canada: Report of the Special Senate Committee on Poverty* (Ottawa: Queen's Printer, 1971).

9. David Woodsworth, *Social Policies for Tomorrow* (Ottawa: Canadian Council on Social Development, 1971), pp. 7-8.

10. John Rawls, *A Theory of Justice* (London: Oxford University Press, 1972), p. 60.

11. W.G. Runciman, *Relative Deprivation and Social Justice* (London: Pelican Books, 1972), p. 310.

12. See the first two editions of *Social Welfare in Canada* or any comparable text written before the 1990s.

13. John Rawls, *Political Liberalism* (New York: Columbia University Press, 1993), p. 60.

14. Will Kymlicka, *Multicultural Citizenship: A liberal theory of minority rights* (Oxford: Clarendon Press, 1995), p. 81.

15. For a full discussion of the global economy, see Peter Dicken, *Global Shift: The internationalization of economic activity* (London: Paul Chapman Publishing, 1992).

16. Gunnar Myrdal, *Beyond the Welfare State* (London: Duckworth, 1958), p. 119.

17. Robert Heilbronner, *Capitalism in the Twenty-First Century* (Concord, Ont.: Anansi Press, 1992), p. 19.

18. Allan Cochrane and John Clarke, *Comparing Welfare States: Britain in International Context* (London: Sage Publications, 1993), show how each welfare state incorporates significant features of the national society in its benefits and organization.

19. *Ibid.*, pp. 253-55.

20. Michael D. Levin, ed., *Ethnicity and Aboriginality: Case Studies in Ethnonationalism* (Toronto: University of Toronto Press, 1993), pp. 3-4.

21. For a fuller discussion of the issues of Aboriginal self-government and its relationship to social policy, see Andrew Armitage, *Comparing the Policy of Aboriginal Assimilation: Australia, Canada, New Zealand* (Vancouver: UBC Press, 1995).

22. For a fuller discussion of the issues of ethnonationalism and multiculturalism, see Kymlicka, *Multicultural Citizenship*.

23. Linda McQuaig, *The Wealthy Banker's Wife: The Assault on Equality in Canada* (Toronto: Penguin Books 1993), pp. 15ff.

24. OECD Economic Survey, 1994: Canada, p. 44.

25. Thomas Courchene, *Social Canada in the Millennium* (Toronto: C.D. Howe Institute, 1994), p. 40.

26. Grant Schellenberg, *The Road to Retirement* (Ottawa: Canadian Council on Social Development, 1994), pp. 40ff.

27. See Gloria Geller and Jan Joel, "Struggle for Citizenship in the Global Economy: Bond Raters

versus Women and Children," Seventh Conference on Canadian Social Welfare Policy, Vancouver, June, 1995.

28. Eric Trist, "The Relation of Welfare and Development in the Transition to Post-Industrialism," Ottawa: Canadian Centre for Community Studies, 1967, p. 12.

29. Wilensky and Lebeaux, *Industrial Society and Social Welfare*, p. 138.

30. *Ibid.*, p. 140.

31. Alfred J. Kahn, *Theory and Practice of Social Planning* (New York: Russell Sage Foundation, 1969), p. 50.

32. John Romanyshyn, *Social Welfare: Charity to Justice* (New York: Random House, 1971), p. 380.

33. The Roehr Institute, *Social Well-being: A paradigm for reform* (North York, Ont.: The Roehr Institute, 1993), p. 40; emphasis added.

34. David M. Brown, "Economic Change and New Social Policies," *The Case for Change* (Ottawa: Renouf, 1994), p. 116.

35. Gary Teeple, *Globalization and the Decline of Social Reform* (Toronto: Garamond Press, 1995), p. 21.

Chapter 2

REDISTRIBUTION

Social welfare is designed to mitigate the inequalities in income and wealth that capitalism creates. As a result, the redistribution of money, goods, and services is a central function of social welfare.

Redistribution as an Economic Institution

Redistribution serves the basic purpose of decreasing inequalities. People are able to obtain goods and services for themselves that they could not have afforded on the basis of their incomes or wealth. Redistribution contradicts the most basic tenets of "market" economic ideology.

First, the "market" exchange is viewed as being a "free" exchange while social welfare operates in the command economy. In the market economy, no one is forced to accept employment, to purchase particular goods, to give money or service to others. Instead, all decide which economic exchange they wish to engage in and the totality of their "free" actions establishes the values of the contributions of each. This ideology neglects the effects of monopoly, differences in knowledge of opportunities, etc.; it nevertheless remains a fundamental part of normal economic exchange expectations. In contradistinction, the "welfare" exchange is compulsory. The attempt to attain welfare purposes on the basis of the voluntary contributor and the independent, self-determining beneficiary failed in the nineteenth century.[1] Instead, social welfare in its origins was made compulsory, on the givers by taxation and on the beneficiaries in the form of either social rights or social sanctions carried out under the authority of the courts.

Second, the market exchange is viewed as being based on a *quid pro quo*. That is, there is a *real* exchange. The worker contributes labour and in return receives wages. The consumer uses money to obtain goods and services. The owner obtains a rent for another's use of his property. In each case, the exchange is a mutual one. In the case of welfare, however, no true exchange occurs. The more appropriate term for the transaction is transfer. This basic affront to the values of economic ideology is one reason for the continuing demand that the able-bodied "work for welfare." Surely, it is thought, the community should get some positive contribution in return for the payments it is making.

Lastly, the market exchange of capitalist societies is fundamental to the creation of inequalities. The exchange is not, in fact, an equal one, but favours those who, through their position in the market, are able to create the terms on which others work and for this service obtain part of the return from others' labour for themselves. The labour market exchange is thus effectively a partial transfer of the profit from workers' efforts to those who have control of economic processes of production or distribution or who possess real property or capital. A major reason for the welfare transfer is to correct in part this unequal exchange and the poverty and inequality it creates. There are, however, limits. C.B. Macpherson draws to our attention the fact that:

> ... the offsetting transfer within the welfare state can never, within capitalism, equal the original and continuing transfer. This is fully appreciated by the strongest defenders of capitalism, who point out, quite rightly, that if welfare transfers got so large as to eat up profits there would be no more incentive to capitalist enterprises, and so no more capitalist enterprise.[2]

Thus the welfare transfer is always a secondary one in capitalist economic processes.

Much of the economic literature identifies social welfare as constituting a burden on economic processes, an item of unproductive expense the economy has to sustain. At best, social welfare is justified by the need to secure social stability. Welfare economics is the study of the application of economic theory to well-being. In welfare economics individuals are discouraged from maximizing their financial situation without consideration of the effects of their choices on others. Thus, those that are better off are provided with a reason to help the poor, as they derive benefits in such forms as a healthier general population, stronger workers, greater financial stability, and greater acceptance of those inequalities that remain.[3] However, this means that the disadvantaged only exercise influence to the extent that their lives impinge on the privileged. The welfare economics approach leaves open the possibility that the privileged may choose to use their resources to keep the poor away from them rather than correcting the underlying inequality. This formula for examining inequality is therefore clearly less powerful than the social justice formula, and it leads to different conclusions on the extent of equalities that should exist. In particular, it does not raise or answer the moral question as to whether the extent of poverty and/or inequality is just.

These views are shared by the socialist critics of the welfare institutions of capitalist societies, who view them as being "a central element in the framework of repression under which men live in market-dominated societies . . . a historical freak between organized capitalism and socialism, servitude and freedom, totalitarianism and happiness."[4] Recent socialist commentators have gone further, pointing out that this modest role for social welfare neglects:

> the possibility that capitalism without reforms might not spur a working class

into revolution but instead simply reduce it to poverty, destitution and fear of itself – and thereby break its will to resist. Second, they take for granted that in times other than extreme crisis and social breakdown the working classes could be an effective opposition to a trained and disciplined modern army or police force. The evidence would strongly suggest otherwise.[5]

This example of socialist analysis leads to a discouraging conclusion. It also does not recognize the role of liberal values in contributing to where a specific balance is struck with capitalism between coercive social control and control through welfare measures of relief and accommodation.

Nevertheless, the analysis reinforces the important observation that there is nothing inherent in capitalism that supports social welfare. In each case the welfare transfer requires both ideological and political justification. The assertion of this justification has a direct effect on the form of social welfare programs and, hence, on the recipients of social welfare benefits. There have been five principal arguments used to justify the welfare transfer: need; insurance against risk; compensation for loss; investment in human potential; and economic growth. Each, in turn, when translated by legislation into a program, has a determining effect on eligibility criteria for program benefits. The effects of the need to frame the social welfare distribution of income within the capitalist economic discourse have also led to recurrent concerns with universal versus selective transfer mechanisms, stigma, workfare, and maintaining public support.

Need

The concept of "need" is a central one in social welfare thought and, indeed, in everyday life. Nevertheless, the concept has some subtleties worth exploring. Foremost of these is the distinction that must be drawn between "needs" and "wants." "Want" implies a purely private assertion by a person; "need" adds the notion of necessity and hence obligation on the part of others to respond. However, the "others" are free to allow or reject the need. Rejection in effect converts the alleged "need" back to the category of being a "want" because no one has agreed on its necessity or accepted any obligation. Allowing the "need," on the other hand, legitimizes it. Thus, "needs" are the subjects of social and not private or individual definition.

Where the justification for a program is the need of the intended beneficiaries, it follows that eligibility will be determined by whether or not the need exists; the simplest case is where a need is assumed to exist. This was the original basis for the universal, non-means-tested Old Age Security and Family Allowance programs. Such programming, in its original form, no longer exists. Old Age Security continues as a "demogrant," but benefits are subject to tax and clawback provisions of the Income Tax Act, limiting the receipt of benefits on the basis of income. Family Allowances have been terminated and replaced by the Child Tax Benefit.

The more typical approach to the determination of eligibility based on need is to conduct an inquiry or *needs test* into the individual's circumstances to determine whether, within the meaning given to need by the program in question, need exists for this individual. Such inquiries are characteristic of public assistance, public housing, and student aid programs. The determination of need at the level of the individual inevitably requires consideration not only of his or her financial circumstances, but also of his or her dependencies. More need has to be recognized in the circumstances of a man and woman living separately than in the case of a man and woman living together because in the latter case they share a roof. The inquiry to determine need thus is necessarily extensive, involving the review of matters that most people treat as being their private affairs. Furthermore, an element of discretion is desirable in such reviews because of the variability of individual circumstances; one teenager might be expected to live in his parents' house as a dependant while for another this arrangement might not be appropriate. Discretion also increases the authority of the granting agency in the lives of the recipients.

A distinction is sometimes drawn between a *means test* and a needs test. The means test is perceived as being a more arbitrary form of the needs test in that attention centres only on the individual's resources, e.g., income, assets, etc., and not on his requirements. However, for the purpose of this discussion, the distinction is not an important or significant one. Both types of test involve a similar type of process to determine eligibility, and they have a similar impact on applicants.

A variation of the needs test is used where income alone is considered and assets are disregarded. An *income test* is used in the Old Age Guaranteed Income Supplement program. An income test is also applied where social welfare benefits are conveyed in the form of tax deductions or refundable tax credits. Examples are the deductions for pension plan contributions, medical expenses, child care, tuition fees, and disability, and the refundable tax credits for the GST and the Child Tax Benefit. In these cases the annual income tax return is used to establish eligibility for these welfare benefits.

Finally, in some social welfare programs, the financial circumstances of applicants are not the most relevant aspect of need determination. Particularly where programs, such as probation and child protection, are thrust upon their beneficiaries by force of law, the process to determine need becomes clearly one in which the society makes a judgement (a formal legal judgement) that the person is in need of special attention. A similar situation often exists in the admission process to such institutions as mental hospitals and children's treatment centres. The need of the adult or child is determined by an assessment process that seeks to identify the form of the risks to life or health and the alleged pathology and whether aid can be given by the treatment centre. These tests are no less tests of need than the financial tests discussed earlier. Their distinguishing characteristic is that they use social-psychological rather than social-economic criteria for the decision.

Needs tests of one form or another have characterized social welfare from its earliest origins in the Elizabethan Poor Law. They remain a central feature of social welfare. In the 1990s their use is increasing as a way to target social welfare programs more closely to the need of beneficiaries.

Insurance

The concept of insurance as justification for welfare transfers has been taken over from the ideology of the economic market, but with major changes. The market use of the concept of insurance implies that the chance of a foreseeable risk, fire, accident, or death is assessed. On the basis of the assessed chance, and on the value of the loss incurred, a premium is charged to all who wish to protect themselves. If the foreseen contingency occurs, the insurer pays a settlement to the insured. The system is usually (auto insurance is an exception) a voluntary one in that neither insurer nor insured is forced to enter into a contract. It is designed in such a way as to be financially viable or the insurer goes bankrupt. There are no welfare transfer functions in private insurance for, although some receive benefits that others have paid for, the deliberate intention is to group insured policy-holders according to the nature of their risk so that each pays a fair premium for the protection bought.

Social insurance uses some of these ideas but modifies them in significant ways to obtain a welfare transfer effect. The four best-known Canadian social insurance programs are Unemployment Insurance, the Canada Pension Plan, medicare, and hospital insurance. The principal ways in which social insurance differs from private insurance are as follows.

1. *Compulsion rather than free contract.* Government programs typically demand universal coverage. This ensures the maximum distribution of the risk and that no one will have to seek assistance from other government agencies because they decided not to seek insurance. It also prevents the growth of private-sector insurance plans offering reduced premiums to low-risk clients.

2. *Lack of "group experience" ratings.* While private insurance plans seek to relate benefits and risk closely to the individual insured's situation, government insurance plans typically average all risks. Payment of premiums thus becomes a form of taxation, not particularly related to the chance of the individual becoming a beneficiary, and thereby produces a welfare transfer effect between those at risk and those not at risk.

3. *"Subsidy" elements.* While private insurance plans have to be actuarially sound, government insurance plans usually contain provision for subsidies. Thus, until recently, if unemployment exceeded some anticipated rate (4 per cent in the 1970s), the Unemployment Insurance fund was subsidized from general government revenue. The Canada/Quebec Pension Plan remains heavily subsidized through an internal transfer from current contributors to current beneficiaries, the extent of which is raising current pensions to four times the level justified on the basis of contributions and fund investments.[6]

4. *Increased range of "risks" accepted.* Unemployment is uninsurable as a "private" risk, partly because it is difficult (as the Unemployment Insurance Commission is aware) to control persons who are "unemployed" by choice and partly because the risk of massive unemployment, resulting from recession, would threaten any private scheme with bankruptcy. Social insurance accepts these risks because a social purpose is to be obtained by protecting people against unemployment. In

practice government underwrites payments, preventing bankruptcy of the plan and ensuring that beneficiaries receive their entitlements.

5. *Benefits/contributions relationship.* In both private and social insurance a record of the contributions of those covered is kept and benefits are paid in foreseen circumstances. Eligibility for benefits is created by having an acceptable contributions record and by the occurrence of the foreseen contingency. In these circumstances, the applicant's right to benefit is contractually assured. Hence, no inquiry into other aspects of his personal or financial circumstances is necessary. The difference from private insurance is that in social insurance an acceptable contributions record is determined by social policy rather than by actuarial considerations.

Social insurance has provided social welfare benefits on a contractual basis without the need for a review of individual or family circumstances. However, this has resulted in some unintended consequences that have attracted increased attention.

(a) Regressive distribution of subsidies. For example, the Canada/Quebec Pension Plan provides a large subsidy to current beneficiaries. This subsidy increases with the beneficiaries' contributions, thus, those who have made higher contributions (and incomes) get the most benefit.

(b) Lack of equity in coverage. Social insurance was developed as a response to two principal problems of industrialism, occasional unemployment and retirement income. An assumption was made that these were the problems of all independent earners and particularly of heads of households. Benefits and conditions of receipt were generous as compared to benefits distributed on the basis of needs tests. At the same time other risks, for example, the risks of family separation or chronic underemployment, were not considered. The result has been the creation of a two-tier income support system that works to the disadvantage of women.

> First, there are the benefits available to individuals as 'public' persons by virtue of their participation and accidents of fortune in the capitalist market. . . . Second, benefits are available to the 'dependants' of individuals of the first category, or to 'private' persons, usually women.[7]

(c) System manipulation. Because benefits are determined by pre-stated eligibility conditions it is possible to extract benefits from social insurance by organizing one's affairs in order to qualify. For example, Unemployment Insurance benefits have been paid to workers in manufacturing during layoffs for refitting and to fishermen and loggers during periods of unemployment due to seasonal conditions. Provincial governments have introduced temporary employment programs that provide just sufficient employment to qualify for Unemployment Insurance. Lastly, individuals can organize their affairs to leave employment on terms that permit them to qualify for benefits. They can also maximize their income by retaining benefits while returning to work in the "underground" economy.

All of these are examples of system manipulation to maximize benefits or minimize contributions. Thus, the existence of social insurance gradually becomes built into peoples' lives and plans in ways that were not foreseen or intended. Indeed, the incentives to maximize social welfare income will, in marginal situations, displace employment income because the social welfare income is guaranteed by government while employment income is not. These effects are of considerable concern to economists as they are seen as having raised Canada's unemployment rate and reduced the efficiency of the Canadian economy and hence its global competitiveness.[8]

As a result of these criticisms social insurance programs of all types are under close scrutiny and may not survive the policy reforms of the next decade.

Compensation

The concept of *compensation* as providing a justification for welfare transfers has also been taken over from the marketplace and from the British common law. Under common law if one suffers a loss through either the deliberate or careless act of another, one is entitled to sue and obtain compensation through the courts. Examples of the use of the concept of compensation in social policy include: (1) treaties and comprehensive settlements with Aboriginal peoples; (2) programs of compensation, for example, Workers' Compensation and victim compensation; and (3) court-ordered financial settlements for separated families.

Most of the historic treaties made with Aboriginal peoples contain provisions for goods, money, or services in return for the release of land for settlement or development. A lot of controversy surrounds this practice of compensation. The treaties were often entered into at times when Aboriginal communities were being overwhelmed, the terms of treaties were more often imposed than negotiated, and current conditions are very different from the historical ones. Nevertheless, the principle of a negotiated settlement between peoples as a way of providing compensation for rights they have lost and as a basis for their management of their own welfare has not been set aside. Indeed, it is in the process of being revisited as part of the exploration of how to provide Aboriginal peoples with an appropriate settlement of outstanding land and treaty claims and contemporary rights of self-government.

Workers' Compensation provides the clearest example of the use of the concept of compensation in establishing a major social program. The principle underlying the program embodies an historic compromise, first enacted in Canada in 1914 in Ontario, between the right of employees to sue for industrial injury and their need to prove employer negligence as a condition of receiving a settlement.[9] Workers' Compensation has stayed closer to its market roots than social insurance. Although the compensation contract is required of both employer and employee as a condition of employment and is thus not voluntary, other features of Workers' Compensation operate on market principles. Thus insurance premiums are based on industry accident records; premiums are paid by employers and are not subsidized from general revenues; and benefits are tied to lost employment income rather than to need.

However, Workers' Compensation, like Unemployment Insurance, is under pressure due to changed conditions. The theory that industry premiums would pay for benefits assumed the continuity of industrial activity. When an industry declines or ceases to exist the costs of compensation to its former employees become a charge on all employers. Also, the process of submitting and processing compensation claims is becoming more litigious, with increases in costs to both Workers' Compensation plans and claimants. Finally, the determination of the extent of injury places physicians in the position of being adjudicators rather than patient advocates.

There has been some looser use of the concept of compensation in the establishment of specific programs devoted to population groups that have suffered some general types of disadvantage. Thus, part of the argument for special services for veterans is that their military service has resulted in an effective loss of earning power, seniority, etc., not to mention the specific losses resulting from identifiable injuries. In addition, in recent years there has been increased recognition of the right of victims of certain types of crime, e.g., sexual abuse while a child, to compensation.

Court-ordered settlements as a basis for welfare remain the primary means whereby family dependency and welfare issues are settled. The continued dominance of a common law tradition in this field is testimony to the lack of attention in social welfare to internal family relationships and risks. Women, of course, are the principal caregivers. As they have performed this role by choice or ascription rather than as employment, it has been free. The consequence of this gift of skill, time, and labour is that, on divorce or separation, the courts, too, attach no monetary value to caring work within the home. As a result, on divorce, men's incomes and women's incomes diverge sharply. Ross Finie, in *The Economics of Divorce*, shows that:

> . . . in the first year after divorce after-tax family income declines to 0.72 and 0.45 of the pre-split level for men and women respectively. . . . Over one third of the women . . . fall into poverty at divorce, compared to just 9% of the men. Conversely, 34% of the men escape poverty at the split, whereas the figure is just 16% for women. Finally, poverty rates in the first year of divorce are 17% for men and 43% for women – 2.5 times greater.[10]

Facts like these provide the substance to the feminist analysis of the way that patriarchy has acted through the welfare state to protect the position of men and to confirm the dependent position of women.

Investment

The concept of investment has been used relatively infrequently to justify welfare transfers. It was used in some discussions of the problem of poverty in which the problem was defined as one of under-investment in the human resources of the people who are poor. Thus, in its *Fifth Annual Review*, the Economic Council of

Canada referred to "upgrading of human resources involved in combatting poverty."[11] The concept has also been used in a general way to support the relocation and retraining programs of the Department of Manpower and Immigration and the extensive subsidies provided to education programs.

There is now a renewed interest in these ideas spawned by the issue of Canada's competitiveness in the global economy. Courchene writes:

> My position is that we have no alternative but to remake Social Canada in a manner consistent with the emerging global economic order. Implicit in this is the assumption that, if we put in place an appropriate social and human capital infrastructure, then physical capital investment will be forthcoming. Moreover, the correct way to view the demand side is that the global demands for Canadian products are potentially infinite if we can meet the test of competitiveness.[12]

An investment ideology results in programs designed to concentrate resources on those who will benefit most. This diminishes the degree to which the programs are responsive to need and thereby decreases their effectiveness as welfare transfers. Indeed, it is questionable whether there is any welfare transfer effect in some social programs, such as higher education, where the primary approach to eligibility for benefits is based on a human resource investment ideology and a competitive process to determine who will be beneficiaries. Thus re-making "Social Canada" on the principles of social investment runs the risk of allocating welfare resources to those with the greatest ability rather than to those with the greatest need.

Economic Growth and Stability

Finally, arguments have been advanced for welfare expenditures on the grounds that such expenditures will themselves contribute to economic stability and growth. In the 1960s Samuelson[13] argued that welfare expenditures could be manipulated so as to increase total spending power in times of economic recession and thereby contribute to improved economic performance. A similar argument was advanced by Galbraith in *The Affluent Society*.[14] The post-war Family Allowance program was accepted partly because it was seen as a way of providing for greater stability of consumer demand and hence as an asset in avoiding the recurrence of the pre-war depression. These ideas were the products of Keynesian[15] economic thought, which was predominant until the 1970s when it was displaced by monetarism. Keynes advocated that government influence the economy through taxation and expenditure measures. Monetarism relies on control of the economy through money supply and interest rates (controlled by the Bank of Canada). Monetarism remains the current dominant school of macro-economic thought and government practice.

This review of the five approaches to justifying welfare transfers has treated them in the order in which they contradict market ideology. The greatest contradiction is present in the discussion of need; partial accommodations are made in the discussions of insurance and compensation; and full accommodation is obtainable in the discussion of investment and economic growth. The greater the degree of accommodation, the less the welfare transfer that is justified. These dynamics have additional effects on the choice of selective as opposed to universal transfer mechanisms; the extent to which the programs stigmatize their beneficiaries; the "workfare" debate; and the maintenance of public support for welfare transfers.

Selective vs. Universal Transfer Mechanisms

A *selective* transfer mechanism is one in which beneficiaries are determined by individual consideration of their circumstances. All means tests, needs tests, contribution records, and the like are instruments of selectivity. A *universal* transfer mechanism is one in which beneficiaries are determined on the basis of some recognized common factor and without consideration of their individual circumstances. Examples of selective transfers are social assistance and public housing. The one remaining example of a universal transfer is Old Age Security, which is now limited by the clawback provisions of the Income Tax Act whereby benefits above an income maximum are recaptured. Thus, for all practical purposes this once intense debate is over. The advantages of simplicity of administration, clarity of social rights, and lack of stigma that were the advantages of the universal transfer have lost to the need to target social welfare resources carefully and avoid providing Family Allowances or an Old Age Security to "The Wealthy Banker's Wife."[16]

Stigma

Stigma means the conferring of a negative repute or social status on the stigmatized individual and would appear to be endemic in social welfare programs. The degree of stigma generated by social welfare programs is much greater in needs-related programs than in those programs that compromise with market ideology by adopting a compensation, insurance, or human investment justification for their existence.

The effects of stigma are felt by the recipients of benefits through attitudes and stereotypes held by the public and reinforced by the media. Stigmatized persons are, unfortunately, second-class citizens. As such, they learn to expect that a variety of social conditions usually enjoyed by others, such as reasonably adequate income, will be denied. The recipients come to view their social situation as one that is deserved, if not personally, at least by other members of their class. Thus, it is typically found that stigmatized populations hold very negative stereotypes of one another. This, in turn, makes it difficult for them to work together politically to obtain change in the society around them.

Stigmatization has the effect of making recipients amenable to the idea that they should accept with gratitude whatever the society should offer them. Thus work, at whatever wages and under whatever conditions, should be accepted. The stigma of welfare assists in maintaining a considerable population in low-paid and unattractive occupations. As the 1971 Senate Committee on Poverty and every other study since has found, a majority of the poor are in the work force. The stigma of welfare assists in keeping them there.

Furthermore, the stigma has the effect of providing a justification for a series of erosions of normal social rights. At the less severe end of a continuum of such erosions, one has the effect of the classification "client," with its presumption that the client should be changed through rehabilitation or work opportunity programs. In the middle of the continuum of erosions of citizenship rights are various administrative incursions into the freedom people normally enjoy. Thus, in the past, welfare recipients have been denied full freedom to spend their welfare transfer income according to their own judgement. They have been prohibited from owning a car, renting a telephone, or visiting a beer parlour. If they offended these administrative policy guidelines, then the guidelines would be enforced by denying the recipient cash and by issuing vouchers to control spending patterns. In the severe part of the continuum are the extreme measures of depriving citizens of the right to vote; requiring that they live in designated places (poor houses, jails, mental hospitals); subjecting them to physical mutilations (sterilization); and breaking up families (neglect proceedings under child welfare legislation).

At different and recurrent points in the history of social welfare programs, these "social control" effects of stigma and the means to achieve them have been given explicit sanction in public policy. At other times, they have been concealed but remain as implicit contradictions of aspects of the welfare ideal. In the 1990s the increased emphasis on economic rationalism is being accompanied by measures that are increasing the stigma of receiving benefits.

Work Requirements and Workfare

In the history of social welfare provision there is no concern older or more persistent than the controversial requirement that the able-bodied poor be set to work. In 1349 in the reign of Edward III welfare to the able-bodied was denied in the following manner:

> Because that many valiant beggars, as long as they may live of begging, do refuse to labor, giving themselves to idleness and vice, and sometimes to theft and other abominations; none upon the said pain of imprisonment, shall under the color of pity or alms, give anything to such, which may labor, or presume to favor them towards their desires, so that thereby they may be compelled to labor for their necessary living.[17]

The historian Karl Deschweinitz, in *England's Road to Social Security*, cites the Elizabethan Poor Law provisions regarding the able-bodied and comments:

> In this first specification of a program of work, nearly four centuries ago, appears the same mixture of purpose that has characterised the use of work in relief ever since. The Elizabethan lawmaker proposes work as training for youth, as prevention of roguery, as a test of good intent, and as a means of employment for the needy. In the background is the House of Correction with its threat of punishment.[18]

In the current series of social policy studies by the C.D. Howe Institute the editors refer to a qualified case for workfare in the following manner.

A work requirement as a condition among employables for receipt of welfare serves to provide a kind of "social capital" – namely, the moral value of work. Erosion of the work ethic has potentially serious intergenerational effects by creating a culture of welfare dependency . . . in the end despite all the rhetoric, a work oriented welfare system has little to do with cost, especially in the short run. But it has everything to do with self-respect and the work ethic, and with the political legitimacy of our social programs.[19]

The case for and against workfare has its basis in the comparison between the situation of those who are working as opposed to those who are receiving social welfare assistance. Because social welfare programs recognize "need" and need is based on household measures, there are always some people who are better off on welfare than working. When people receiving social welfare benefits return to work, the social welfare benefit they receive is usually reduced on a dollar for dollar basis above some minimum of, say, $100. This means that there is no incentive to work above the $100 amount until the recipient's income can exceed the total amount of the social welfare payment for which he or she is eligible. The result is known as the "welfare wall," an incentive either not to work at all or to defraud the system by taking casual work that can be concealed. Many attempts have been made to solve this problem.

1. *Restricting benefits below the level of the lowest-paid independent worker.* This was the principle adopted in the British Poor Law reform of 1834. It survived as a central feature of social welfare administration until the twentieth century. It retains a work incentive for all. Modern attempts to operate on this principle have been linked to attempts to raise wages and family incomes to a sufficient level so that welfare rates at less than employment income do not cause extreme deprivation. However, raising wage levels by government regulation has had the perverse effect of decreasing the amount of work available, as employers have either substituted machines for workers, moved to lower-wage locations, or gone out of business. The problems of raising minimum wages to support minimum incomes have become more severe because of the changing nature of work in Canadian society and the relationship to the global economy. In the 1990s the increased prevalence of part-time and low-paid service jobs makes it impossible to see how this approach could be applied without causing severe hardship.

2. *Expanding work opportunities at reasonable wage levels.* This approach is a variation on the first one. If the private sector does not provide a sufficient number of jobs at decent wages, then, it is argued, this should become a responsibility of government working in co-operation with community groups. Cases for this approach have been made under such names as "social development" and "community economic development."[20] The problem with this approach is not so much with the concept but with the scale with which it would have to be applied and with the extent of the associated costs. These problems have become more severe with the increase in long-term unemployment that has occurred in the 1990s.

3. *Providing a financial incentive to all welfare recipients for any work that they do.* This approach has been the one most advocated in the social policy literature.

Examples are provided by the government of Ontario's *Transitions* report[21] and by proposals for social welfare provision based on a full integration with the tax system, often referred to as "negative taxation."[22] The problem of these proposals is that since some people will have to be dependent on the program for their total income, the lowest benefit paid has to ensure a minimum level of adequacy. In addition, the program has to be designed in such a way as to provide an incentive for any individual to work, usually set at 50 per cent of their earnings.

The problem is that this combination leads to programs that are excessively costly. Thus, if a poverty line of $20,000 per year is adopted for a family of four and if an earner is allowed to retain 50 per cent of his earnings, then income subsidies for families of four are extended up to the $40,000 per year income level (see Table 8).

TABLE 8: *Family of Four: $20,000 Poverty Line, 50 per cent Rate of Reduction*

Earned Income	Negative Tax Income Reduced by 50% of Earned Income	Total Income
0	$20,000	$20,000
$10,000	$15,000	$25,000
$20,000	$10,000	$30,000
$30,000	$5,000	$35,000
$40,000	0	$40,000

The dilemma posed by expanding the social welfare redistribution of income in this manner was judged irresolvable in the early 1970s within a level of public expenditure that was politically acceptable.[23] It has not become any easier since. However, a variation of this approach exists in the proposal (to be discussed in Chapter 4) to provide increased payments based on the number of children in the home.[24]

4. *Work incentive programs for those on welfare.* Some of the principles underlying the negative tax program, particularly the principle of a graduated approach to retaining earned income, have been incorporated into general welfare policy in the form of short-term incentive measures to ease the transition between welfare and work. During these transition periods the welfare recipient also retains such welfare benefits as support with child-care costs and full medical coverage. Welfare recipients are usually offered a right to choose for themselves whether or not they participate in such programs, although the right to choose not to participate is somewhat of an illusion, as welfare benefits can be terminated by a refusal to take available work.

5. *Workfare.* Workfare makes work for the able-bodied on welfare a program requirement. The argument for workfare is that as welfare payments should be kept at minimally adequate levels and as the economy does not provide, nor can it be expected to provide, a sufficient number of jobs above those levels to maintain an incentive to work, then there should be some work penalty to prevent those on welfare from choosing welfare over work. Without a workfare penalty, it is argued, there will be a continued incentive for people to switch from work to

welfare, a build-up of long-term welfare use, an increase in intergenerational welfare use, the development of a welfare underclass, and a continued erosion of public support for welfare measures.

The argument against workfare is that it offers no solution to the work incentive dilemma. A striking fact about the 400-year history of this subject is that workfare solutions have consistently failed to do what they were intended to. They have failed because it was impossible to organize and maintain a work program of sufficient scale without incurring two further problems: (1) a further increase in the costs of social welfare through the necessity of administering and supervising the work, providing materials, etc., and (2) to the extent that any useful work is done it displaces work that would have otherwise been done by independent workers and thereby further increases the number of people dependent on the social welfare system. However, despite the repeated failure of workfare type programs, our experience of the problems of long-term welfare abuse and of the development of an underclass and a culture of poverty suggest that such problems are less severe than anticipated. These concerns were expressed repeatedly during the depression of the 1930s, but the next generation of workers proved to be hard-working and productive – as soon as there was something useful to do. The argument against workfare also rests on the premise that if a program cannot be devised to improve a situation then it is better not to have one at all.[25]

The Effect on Public Support

The welfare transfer is an institutionalized form of gift. Thus, who gives and why are central to social policy. The most positive and, for welfare ideals, most supportive answers to these questions are based in the consciousness of sharing a common fate with one's fellow citizens. For this reason, positive approaches to the development of social welfare in modern society have sometimes occurred during or after times of war. The British and Canadian social welfare services were introduced following the experience of nations that had come to accept the principles of pooling and sharing during the emergency situations of the Second World War. In one of the most famous essays on the concept of the welfare state the British sociologist T.H. Marshall identified modern social security measures with the concept of citizenship.[26]

The paradox of social welfare transfers is that, *de facto*, they tend to destroy this sense of common cause. The effect of stigma on public support is to divide citizens into two separate social classes, the "givers" and the "receivers." The givers are identified with industry, self-support, and beneficence, while the receivers are identified with laziness, dependence, and self-interest. The welfare transfer thus creates alienation and undercuts the basis of its own public support. The transfer based on a shared citizenship is debased by the dynamic into a transfer based on the principle that those who are the givers are justified in expecting that the recipients conduct themselves on terms dictated to them. A transfer based on a gift thus becomes a transfer viewed as a means of social control.

The history of the development of social welfare programs has been marked by cycles in which high ideals are declared – the Welfare State, the War on Poverty – followed by periods in which the ideals erode. In such periods the social welfare transfer is viewed as a "burden" rather than as a desirable social expenditure. The form of this cycle in Canada is reflected in Appendix 2; for example, the 1940s were a period of substantial reform and review, which contrasted with the failure and chaos of the 1930s and the indifference of the 1950s;[27] likewise, the achievements of the 1960s and 1970s have in some measure led to the conservative reaction of the 1980s and 1990s.

Transfers and Taxation

Although taxes do not directly result in welfare transfers they do have an effect on the redistributive process as a whole because they determine how income is retained and, hence, what the final distribution of income is. Thus, the graduated income tax has an effect on the distribution of income, making the post-tax income distribution more egalitarian than the pre-tax income distribution. This result is not a welfare transfer in itself; there is no direct "gift" effect. However, the combined effect of the graduated tax and the welfare transfer changes the income distribution in a more egalitarian direction to a greater degree than would be achieved by the welfare transfer on its own.

A properly graduated taxation system (in which those with the highest incomes pay a higher percentage of their total income in taxes) is an important support to the goal of the redistribution of income in an egalitarian manner. Taken as a whole the Canadian tax system does not obtain this ideal. The effective total tax incidence is remarkably even so that all income classes part with approximately the same fraction of their total income in taxes. This is a result of the fact that the progressive graduations of the income tax system are almost completely counteracted by the regressive impact of sales taxes, housing taxes, social insurance premiums, import duties, etc. In all of these indirect taxes, the poor pay a higher proportion of their income than the better off.

In addition, the tax system has been used to distribute some social welfare benefits in the form of refundable tax credits, as in the case of the Child Tax Benefit, and to recapture social welfare benefits from those above a specific income threshold, as in the clawback provisions affecting higher income recipients of Old Age Security. In recent years, there has been a considerable amount of discussion of the advantages and disadvantages of expanding the transfer functions of the taxation system to such fields as child poverty and child-care costs. Finally, the income tax system also contains tax exemption provisions (tax expenditures), some of which have welfare purposes. The best known of these are the RRSP and registered pension plan deductions, which provide a financial incentive to taxpayers to make pension provisions for themselves.

Employment Equity Measures

A final approach to changing the income redistribution in order to provide for a greater degree of income equality and income equity has come in the form of government employment equity programs. Statistics Canada reported that for 1993, women working in full-time employment earned 72 per cent of what men earned, an average annual income of $28,932 as compared to $39,433. The gap between men's and women's earnings can be partly explained at one level by differences of employment type and differences in length and continuity of labour force attachment. But these arguments cut little weight when reviewed through a feminist analysis that equates difference in employment type to a combination of valuing men's work more than women's and discrimination against accepting women candidates in traditional "male" fields of employment. The argument about length and continuity of labour force attachment is also flawed because women have to leave the labour force for child-bearing and for most child and elder care. Thus the persistence of a gender wage gap is evidence of the operation of an economy that systemically discriminates against women.

The response to this analysis has taken the form of attempts to regulate employment practices to improve access for women to all occupations; provide proportionately higher increases in fields where women constitute the majority of workers; offer periods of leave for maternity and other caring roles under terms that permit women to maintain their jobs; expand day-care services; and introduce goals or quotas as a basis for affirmative action. A similar approach is also argued as needed for other groups, such as Aboriginals, visible minorities, and the disabled, who are not fully and equitably represented in the distribution of employment and income.

Employment equity measures are an attempt to deal with one problem of the income distribution – systemic discrimination – at its source. Patricia Evans writes:

> . . . there are several . . . lessons [that] grow in importance as the claims of social citizenship erode, along with public services and income support, while the pace of globalization and deficit cutting mount. First, it is essential to reassert the claims of women to paid employment, and to recognize that women's responsibility for caring for others will not be adequately compensated in the absence of labour force attachment. Second, that the claims to paid employment without a recognition of women's caring responsibilities are claims that only the most affluent of working women will benefit from, and claims that the most vulnerable, single mothers, are likely to be entrapped by. Third, that the full exercise of women's citizenship requires an equitable division of unpaid labour, and that this goal may be the most difficult to achieve through public policy initiatives.[28]

Employment equity measures, in the absence of full employment at adequate wage levels, represent only a partial solution to the redistributive objectives of social welfare policy. This partial solution can become a trap in that the existence of such policies can be used to expand the boundaries of women's employability[29] and thus reduce benefits from the social welfare system and/or make them subject to workfare or other employment conditions.

Changes, 1940-1990

The concepts behind the redistributive objectives of the post-war welfare state were clear. The objectives were framed in the context of the capitalist, industrial society and of a family unit with a male "breadwinner" and a female "home-maker." The system aimed to protect such a family unit from five major threats to its economic well-being:

1. *Unemployment.* To support income levels during periodic recessions and layoffs, there was Unemployment Insurance.
2. *Family dependencies.* As wage income did not recognize differences in family size, Family Allowances were paid for each child in the home.
3. *Old age and disability.* To provide for an income in old age or following disability there was a basic pension, Old Age Security, and a social insurance plan, the Canada/Quebec Pension Plan.
4. *Illness.* Through a combination of hospital insurance and medicare everybody was assured of the basic resources to provide for medical attention when needed.
5. *Industrial injury.* To protect the worker against the risk of industrial injury there was Workers' Compensation.

For risks that lay outside this social safety net there were the needs-based provincial social assistance programs. Although these ideas were all present in the literature in the 1940s, it was not until the 1960s that they were fully enacted.

The first attempt to move beyond this framework came in the late 1960s and early 1970s and was spurred by the realization that, despite these provisions, poverty persisted. The objective was to provide a single income program that would encompass all the risks, other than illness and industrial injury, and that would replace the social assistance programs. The attempt failed.

A second attempt to move beyond the original framework came with the first post-1975 wave of financial restructuring and the rise of a new conservatism. The objective here was to make the social welfare transfer system smaller and more focused on need, while encouraging individuals to make private provisions for themselves. A partial dismemberment of the 1960s social welfare system followed. Family Allowances were replaced by an income-tested Child Tax Benefit. Old Age Security was "clawed back" from higher-income earners through the tax system. On the other hand, RRSP and pension tax exemptions were raised to encourage private saving for old age.

A third attempt to move beyond the original framework, based in the feminist social movement, was occurring at the same time. Attention here was directed to the familial assumptions of the post-war welfare state and particularly the assumption that women would be "dependants." The objective was to add to, and modify, the redistributive system to provide equity of treatment to women. There have been some successes, for example, an increased attention to employment equity and a provision to divide pension assets equally between men and women on divorce or separation, but other major goals, such as a comprehensive child-care system and a commitment to equity throughout the redistributive system, have not been achieved. Other groups whose distinct relationship to Canadian society had not been recognized in the earlier formula, for example, Aboriginal peoples, refugees and recent immigrants, and gays and lesbians, also advanced claims for a more equitable redistributive system.

A fourth attempt is now taking place, spurred by a combination of changed industrial and financial conditions (the global economy) and internal fiscal constraints (the deficit). The objectives are similar to those of the second attempt but the pressures for change are economic as well as ideological. Thus, governments of all political persuasions are re-examining every aspect of the redistributive social welfare transfer. They differ more on the targets for change than on the necessity for change. The debate about the fourth (global economy) set of changes is overwhelming the debate about the third (equity-based) changes, just as the second (conservative) changes overwhelmed the first (poverty-based) ones.

Despite these four waves of change the original post-war framework has shown a remarkable persistence, with most of its structural features intact fifty years after they were formulated and thirty years after they were fully enacted.

Notes

1. The minority report of the British Poor Law commissioners of 1909-13, produced by Adrian and Beatrice Webb, foresaw that compulsion was essential to social security. For a full account, see Karl Deschweinitz, *England's Road to Social Security* (London: Oxford University Press, 1943).
2. C.B. Macpherson, "The Real World of Democracy," *Massey Lectures, 4th Series*, CBC, 1965, p. 48.
3. The welfare economics theory for determining the size and direction of the welfare function was outlined by Pareto, who based his consideration on the rule that "the test of a socially beneficial redistribution is that it should be voluntarily undertaken," contradicting one of the fundamental principles of welfare thought. For a full discussion, see Robert Pinker, *Social Theory and Social Policy* (London: Heinemann, 1971), p. 116.
4. Herbert Marcuse, *One Dimensional Man* (Boston: Beacon Press, 1966), p. 52.
5. Gary Teeple, *Globalization and the Decline of Social Reform* (Toronto: Garamond Press, 1995), p. 22.
6. Newman Land, Michael Prince, and James Cutt, *Reforming the Public Pension System in Canada* (Victoria: Centre for Public Sector Studies, 1993).
7. Carol Pateman, "The Patriarchal Welfare State," *Defining Women: Social Institutions and Gender Divisions* (Cambridge: Polity Press, 1992), pp. 223-45, as cited by Patricia Evans, "The Claims of Women: Gender, Income Security, and the Welfare State," in *7th Conference on Canadian Social Welfare Policy: Remaking Canadian Social Policy: Selected Proceedings* (Vancouver: Social Planning and Research Council of B.C., June 25-28, 1995).
8. See Thomas Courchene, *Social Canada in the Millennium* (Toronto: C.D. Howe Institute, 1994), pp. 45, 58ff.; also John Richards and William Watson, eds., *Unemployment Insurance: How To Make It Work* (Toronto: C.D. Howe Institute, 1994).
9. Terrance J. Boygo, "Workers' Compensation: Updating the Historic Compromise," *Chronic Stress: Workers' Compensation in the 1990s* (Toronto: C.D. Howe Institute, 1995), pp. 96ff.
10. Ross Finie, "The Economics of Divorce," in *Family Matters* (Toronto: C.D. Howe Institute, 1995), pp. 122-23.
11. Economic Council of Canada, *Fifth Annual Review*.
12. Courchene, *Social Canada*, p. 163.
13. Paul Samuelson, *Economics* (Toronto: McGraw-Hill, 1966).

14. J.K. Galbraith, *The Affluent Society* (London: Penguin Books, 1958), pp. 238-44.

15. John Maynard Keynes was the economic architect of the government response to the Great Depression of the 1930s. In *The Means to Prosperity* (New York: Harcourt Brace, 1933) and in *The General Theory* (New York: Macmillan, 1957) he developed the position that the role of government was to stabilize the market economy through a fiscal policy that combined deficits in times of depression with surpluses in boom times. While governments widely adopted the idea of deficits, none showed the ability to produce the balancing surpluses. For an account of Keynesian thought and its relationship to the Canadian welfare state, see Cy Gonick, *The Great Economic Debate: Failed economics and a future for Canada* (Toronto: James Lorimer, 1987).

16. The wealthy banker's wife was often referred to in the media to parody the provision of Family Allowances to all. For a postscript to this lost debate, see Linda McQuaig, *The Wealthy Banker's Wife: The assault on equality in Canada* (Toronto: Penguin Books, 1993).

17. England, Edward III, *The Statute of Laborers*, 1349.

18. Deschweinitz, *England's Road to Social Security*, p. 27.

19. John Richards and William Watson, eds., *Helping the Poor: A qualified case for workfare* (Toronto: C.D. Howe Institute, 1995), p. xxiii.

20. See Marilyn Callahan, Andrew Armitage, Michael Prince, and Brian Wharf, "Workfare in British Columbia: Social development alternatives," *Canadian Review of Social Policy*, 26 (1990).

21. Ontario Ministry of Community and Social Services, *Transitions: Report of the Social Assistance Review Committee* (Toronto, 1988), ch. 6.

22. For a full discussion, see Christopher Green, *Negative Taxes and the Poverty Problem* (Washington: The Brookings Institute, 1967); H.W. Watts, "Graduated Work Incentive: An Experiment in Negative Taxation," *American Economic Review*, LIX, 2 (May, 1964); Arnold Katz, "Income Maintenance Experiments: Progress Towards a New American National Policy," *Social and Economic Administration*, 7, 2 (May, 1973); John Richards and Aidan Vining, "Welfare Reform: What can we learn from the Americans," in *Helping the Poor* (Toronto: C.D. Howe Institute, 1995), pp. 1-36.

23. For example, see the Castonguay-Nepeuv proposals from Quebec in *Income Security*, Report on the Commission of Inquiry on Health and Welfare (Quebec City, 1971).

24. See proposals in Chapter 4 for benefits for families and children.

25. Ernie S. Lightman, "You can lead a horse to water, but . . . The case against workfare in Canada," in *Helping the Poor*, pp. 151-79, provides a clear statement of the arguments against workfare.

26. T.H. Marshall, *Class, Citizenship and Social Development* (Garden City, N.Y.: Anchor Books, 1965).

27. For an extended treatment of the cyclical nature of social welfare concerns in the United States and their relationships to the society, see F.F. Piven and R.A. Cloward, *Regulating the Poor: The Functions of Public Welfare* (New York: Vintage Books, 1971).

28. Evans, "The Claims of Women," p. 28.

29. Callahan *et al.*, "Workfare in British Columbia," show how this has happened in relation to workfare expectations of single mothers.

Chapter 3

REDISTRIBUTION:

SCOPE AND OBJECTIVES

The redistributive social welfare system, also known as the income security system, is a major fact of life for all Canadians. In 1993 approximately \$120 billion, 20 per cent of GDP, was redistributed, either as direct expenditures or as tax benefits for social welfare purposes. Every person received a portion of his or her income from the system and for many the system was the main source of income.

Definition of what constitutes income security may at first appear obvious because major, familiar, direct-benefit programs like Unemployment Insurance and Old Age Security are included. However, these programs must be viewed as only part of a still larger whole, which gives recognition to five added elements: (1) tax expenditures; (2) housing, health, education, and other service benefits; (3) employment goals and programs; (4) family care; and (5) charitable and voluntary activities.

1. *Tax expenditures.* Tax expenditures are decisions made by the government not to collect taxes. An individual's income is increased as effectively when the state waives a right to collect taxes as it is increased when the state decides to provide a specific grant. Thus the personal exemptions for a spouse or for the first child under the Income Tax Act increase the income enjoyed by single-earner households of two or more persons. The effect is similar to that of a program of direct grants for dependants, except that the benefits of tax expenditures are limited to those who have a taxable income. Another example is the Registered Retirement Savings Plan (RRSP) tax deduction, whereby middle and upper income earners can save, tax-free, for retirement.

2. *Housing, health, education, and other service benefits.* Income is valued for what it permits the recipient to purchase. The provision of income is thus a means to an end. The direct provision of goods or services to recipients short-circuits this chain of events.

The provision of social housing illustrates the importance of this relationship. Those recipients fortunate enough to live in social housing pay a reduced rent or co-operative charge, with the difference between this amount and the development and maintenance costs of the project being paid for by government. They also benefit by being less subject to some of the risks that renters face in the private sector, such as inadequate accommodation, eviction, discrimination, and rent increases. If social housing was available for all who wished to live in it (as in some European countries), the income needs of the poor would be reduced. In Canada, however, the social housing stock totals 6.5 per cent of all dwellings, only about half of which is available with rents geared to income. This is much less than is needed to house all poor individuals and families.

Health services are another example of a benefit that is in most cases provided directly to recipients. Physician and hospital services are universally available in Canada, and as a result Canadians do not have to make provision through their employers, private insurance, or savings as they do in the United States. However, the coverage of health services in Canada does not always include drug costs, dental services, and health appliances. Consequently, some people have to look to other ways of obtaining these services for themselves.

Education services are a third example. In Canada primary and secondary education is universally available at no direct cost to families. Higher education, on the other hand, is only partly funded by direct government payments to universities and colleges with the additional costs being covered by fees. Furthermore, the person pursuing higher education is, in most cases, not eligible for such programs as Unemployment Insurance and social assistance. As a result the government has developed a supplementary welfare (student loan) system for people seeking higher education who cannot afford to pay their education and living costs. These three examples demonstrate how the extent of the income security system is determined by the extent of the direct provision of services by government.

Debate as to whether need should be met by the provision of income or by the provision of goods and services has been dominated by concern, on the one hand, for the freedom of the recipient and, on the other, by concern for the general social interest and for the equity that accompanies the distribution. Where income is given directly the recipients are free to make their own choices about their welfare. This maximizes the recipients' choice, provided of course that the total income given is sufficient to purchase the required services. The provision of goods and services involves a decision by government as to what goods and services are needed – and as to their standard. This form of subsidy decreases the consumer's freedom. However, goods and services rather than cash have been considered to be in the general social interest in the fields of primary and secondary education and for most medical care. Providing goods or services rather than income is inherently more efficient in terms of ensuring the ultimate receipt of the intended goods or services, and where costs are high, unpredictable, or unevenly distributed over the population the provision of goods or services rather than income may be the only route to ensuring their ultimate receipt. A problem for recipients and for the design of other social welfare measures is created where, as in the case of social housing, only some people receive the service; or, as in the case of some medical services and higher education, the coverage of the universal service is only a partial one.

3. *Employment programs.* The employment policies and programs of government are a third influence on income security. These are broadly of three types:

(1) policies designed to affect the quantity and distribution of employment; (2) policies designed to set the terms of employment; and (3) policies designed to produce work incentives.

Until the 1970s full employment was a major objective of government policy. The goals of the 1973 income security review were to "maintain a high rate of employment, price stability, an equitable distribution of rising income, and a reduction of regional economic disparities."[1] These policy objectives did not prove to be compatible. In particular, economic growth and high levels of employment came to be seen as incompatible with price stability and an equitable distribution of rising income. In the 1960s, the commitment to full employment (variously defined as between 2 per cent and 6 per cent unemployment) was unambiguous. However, in the 1970s economic policies encountered difficulty in obtaining either full employment or price stability, and the commitment to full employment was weakened. In the 1980s, a 9 per cent national rate of unemployment and regional rates of 15 per cent were accepted, and the idea that government might itself be an employer of last resort was abandoned. In the 1990s we seem to be tolerating an 11 per cent national rate and regional rates as high as 25 per cent. Although politicians on the hustings retain the rhetoric of "jobs, jobs, jobs," there are no formal goals for full employment. High rates of unemployment make it impossible for some people who want to work to find work and have enormous implications for the size of the income security system.

The prohibition of child labour and the regulation of hours of work were some of the earliest examples of social legislation resulting from industrialism. The provisions for equity in employment practice and freedom from harassment at work are some of the latest. These measures have a relationship to income security as they establish rules of justice and fairness for the workplace and protect employees from exploitation. Minimum wages ensure that employers cannot exploit employees' need for work. In some countries, such as Australia and France, minimum wage policies have been a central feature of the design of income security. Although wage legislation, from an income security perspective, has the deficiency of not recognizing family dependencies, this deficiency can be remedied by a combination of wage legislation and family benefits.

Occupational benefits, which include such services provided to employees and their dependants as subsidized housing, dental plans, life insurance, sports clubs, and occupational health services, are also relevant. All serve to reduce the needs that must be met from income. Access to these benefits is limited to those who are employed by major companies and/or in employment covered by well-established union contracts.

Finally, the economists seem to be convinced that Canada's unemployment rate has been raised by several percentage points and the mobility of its labour force reduced by the availability of Unemployment Insurance and social assistance.[2] Thus, the fear is that the income security system is growing at the expense of the willingness to work. The antidote recommended is lower benefits for the unemployed and stricter conditions of receipt.

4. *Family care.* A fourth influence on income security is the extent of family care

and the mechanisms of enforcement. These used to be more extensive than they now are – during the 1930s, the extended family was viewed as a network to be used first by the unemployed. In the post-war social welfare programs, workers, who were then principally men, were relieved of the need to look to the family for support when they became unemployed, disabled, or old, but women and children were recognized in this system as the dependants of men. Exercise of their social rights was through enforcing men to be responsible, re-enforcing the dependency of women and children. These assumptions and associated program features remain in effect even though the social conditions that once supported them have changed. The result is a re-enforcement through the income security system of family inequities by gender and age of recipient.

5. *Charitable and voluntary activities.* There has always been some charitable and voluntary relief. Agencies like the Salvation Army and the St. Vincent de Paul Society have a long record of relieving destitution. To these long-standing efforts must be added the food banks that began in the 1980s recession. The growing prevalence of homelessness, the continuing process of tightening eligibility conditions for government programs, and the reduction in welfare benefits are all contributing to a new growth of charitable and voluntary activity as a last resort for those whose need is not otherwise met.

The Canadian Social Welfare Redistribution System

The total Canadian redistribution system is composed of the following cash programs:

Old Age Security
Old Age Security Guaranteed Income Supplement
Child Tax Benefit
Canada Pension Plan
Unemployment Insurance
Workers' Compensation
Veterans' pensions
Canada Assistance Plan (with provincial assistance plans)
On-reserve assistance for First Nations
Atlantic Fish Strategy
Farm income supports
Post-secondary student loans

the following fiscal measures:

Personal deductions
Tax credits
Retirement savings exemptions
Tuition fee deductions
Child-care expense deduction

Medical and charitable expense deductions
GST rebate

the following goods or service programs:

Hospital insurance
Medicare
National Housing Act – social housing provisions
Provincial shelter aid and rental subsidies
Home maintenance and renovation programs
Vocational training programs
Legal Aid
Education

the following employment-related measures:

Full employment policies
Regional economic expansion programs
Minimum wage legislation
Occupational benefits
Equity employment requirements

the following occupational welfare measures:

Sports and recreational facilities
Housing
Pension and insurance plans
Transport
Cars
Expense accounts
Tenured employment statuses (amounting to a guaranteed income)

the following family care and dependency measures:

Wives and children's maintenance acts
Unmarried mothers' acts
Elder and other homecare provisions

the following voluntary and charitable measures:

Food banks
Shelters
Soup kitchens.

The total amount of income provided through the redistributive system is enormous. Even if the costs of health care and education are excluded the total for major programs has more than doubled since 1984-85 to its present total exceeding $120 billion (see Table 9).

The Caledon Institute of Social Policy monograph, *Opening the Books on Social Spending*,[3] explores the background and reasons for the continuing growth of social spending. Going back to 1958-59, the earliest date when reliable and comprehensive data were available, and adjusting for inflation, the total increase is 800 per cent. Adjusting for the increase in the population reduces the increase to 500 per cent. As a percentage of the gross domestic product social spending has grown from 8 per cent to 20 per cent. New programs from the 1960s and 1970s – the Canada/Quebec Pension Plans, the Old Age Security Guaranteed Income Supplement, the Canada Assistance Plan, Medicare, Unemployment Insurance expansion, and the Child Tax Credit – account for much of the growth. In addition, benefits, particularly for the elderly, were improved as a partial but incomplete response to the War on Poverty.

However, the period of program expansion and benefit liberalization ended with the 1970s. Since then the pressure has been to restrict benefits and control costs, yet growth continues. The Caledon Institute concludes that:

> Social spending in the 1980s and 1990s is being driven primarily by powerful demographic and economic forces – chief among them the relentless aging of the population and the deadly combination of periodic recessions (which create mass, lingering unemployment) and a fundamental restructuring of the economy, the latter emanating largely from global changes whose ramifications we are just beginning to fathom.[4]

These powerful demographic and economic forces now meet the "wall" created by government deficits.

Objectives

The official view of the objectives of Canada's redistribution system is provided by the opening paragraph of the government of Canada's 1994 discussion paper on social security:

> Canada's social security system is a hallmark of our nation. Through it, we have defined ourselves as a country that aspires to give our children the best possible start to life, to enable all Canadians to meet their basic needs, and their families to live in dignity. It is a system dedicated to supporting the most vulnerable of our society, while creating opportunities for all Canadians to improve their lives. Social security embodies the values of justice, tolerance and compassion that mark our country.[5]

The ground-level view is provided by Kim Harvey, a twenty-four-year-old who has grown up with neglect, abuse, and poverty since her father left when she was a toddler:

TABLE 9: *Estimates of Government Social Security Programs in Canada, 1984-85 and 1994-95 ($billions)*

	1984-85		1994-95	
Target Group	Federal	Provincial	Federal	Provincial
Poor				
Canada Assistance Plan	4.1	4.1	7.3	9.3
Provincial tax credits*		1.6		3.0
Veterans' allowances	0.5		1.2	
On-reserve assistance	0.2		0.7	
GST rebate*			2.8	
Social housing	1.1		1.9	
Families				
Child-care deduction*	0.1			
Child Tax Credit/Benefit*	1.1		5.1**	
Family Allowances	2.4		**	
Child tax exemption*	0.9	0.5	**	0.5
Married exemption*	1.4	0.6	1.6	0.7
Employment Assistance				
Unemployment Insurance	11.6		15.6	
Workers' Compensation		1.6		3.8
Training programs	0.1	0.1	1.3	1.3
Student loans			0.5	
Atlantic Fish Strategy			0.3	
Farm income support			1.3	
Employment deduction*	0.8	0.4	**	
Elderly				
Quebec/Canada Pension	4.4	1.6(Q)	12.5	4.6(Q)
Old Age Security	8.3		15.8	
Guaranteed Income Sup.	3.1		4.4	
Age exemption*	0.3	0.2	1.5	0.7
Veterans' pensions	0.7		1.2	
RRSP/RPP/tax benefits*	4.7	2.3	14.9	7.4
Totals	45.8 61.5	13.0	121.7 90.1	31.6

*indicates benefits transferred through the tax system; total $40.2 billion.

**The Family Allowance, Child Tax Credit, child tax exemption, and employment deduction were replaced in 1993 by the Child Tax Benefit.

SOURCES: *Report of the Royal Commission on the Economic Union and Development Prospects for Canada*, 1985, p. 772; Department of Finance, *Creating a Healthy Fiscal Climate* (Ottawa, 1994).

"I have nothing. . . . I will never – ever – have children unless I'm in a position to make sure that they would not be on welfare – ever. I'd rather have an abortion first". . . . Seven years after striking out on her own, Harvey is back where she started – a short subway ride, yet a world away, from the glittering towers of downtown Toronto. It's a bleak and often boring existence, surviving on the $65 a month left after paying the rent on her two-room flat.[6]

The truth is that although government documents often applaud the redistributive system, the reality of the system and its achievements is far removed from the rhetoric.

Specific objectives for the system as a whole, or for its parts, are not to be found, perhaps because if they were available the lack of achievement would be more apparent. The 1973 social security review provided one of the better statements:

> First, the social security system must assure to people who cannot work, the aged, the blind and the disabled, a compassionate and equitable guaranteed income.
>
> Second, the social security system as it applies to people who can work must contain incentives to work and a greater emphasis on the need to get people who are on social aid back to work.
>
> Third, a fair and just relationship must be maintained between the incomes of people who are working at, or near, the minimum wage, the guaranteed incomes assured to people who cannot work, and the allowances paid to those who can work but are unemployed.[7]

It did not provide a definition of what was viewed as being "a compassionate and equitable guaranteed income" or "a fair and just relationship . . . between the incomes of people who are working . . . the guaranteed incomes, . . . and the allowances paid to those who . . . are unemployed." Nevertheless, these goals provide a basis from which the present redistributive system can be evaluated. Such an evaluation needs to take account of (1) poverty, (2) equity, and (3) employ-ability.

Poverty and Poverty Lines

The Senate Committee on Poverty (1971) was the first body to provide a definition of poverty. The Committee developed a series of poverty lines and then used them to establish objectives for the income security system. The poverty lines for 1969, 1985, and 1994 are shown in Table 10:

TABLE 10: *Senate Committee Poverty Line, 1969, 1985, and 1994*

Family Size	1969	1985	1994
1 person	2,140	8,850	13,300
2 person	3,570	14,750	22,190
3 person	4,290	17,700	26,620
4 person	5,000	20,650	31,050
5 person	5,710	23,600	35,490
6 person	6,430	26,550	39,920
7 person	7,140	29,500	44,350

SOURCES: Special Senate Committee on Poverty, "Poverty in Canada," Ottawa, 1973, p. 8; 1985 figures as published by Senate of Canada, "Poverty in Canada: Updated Poverty Lines 1985"; 1994 figures from Canadian Council on Social Development, "Fact Book on Poverty – 1994," p. 18.

Since the work of the Senate Committee a number of other government and private agencies have provided their own calculations of poverty lines or their equivalent. Methodologies vary and some lines vary, too, by size of community or province. Statistics Canada provides a series of "Low Income Cut-Offs" that vary by size of community. The Canadian Council on Social Development provides a series of "Lines of Income Equality." The methods used by the Senate Committee, Statistics Canada, and Canadian Council on Social Development differ, but they all approach the task by looking at the usual living standards of Canadians and then establishing a low-income minimum below which it would be difficult to live a normal life. The Montreal Diet Dispensary and the Fraser Institute, a conservative, Vancouver-based study group, use a more restricted approach that measures the cost of a basic "basket" of goods, including shelter, clothing, food, and transportation, that are essential to survival. The Fraser Institute provides figures for each province. The results of these different approaches are shown in Table 11.

TABLE 11: *Low-Income and Poverty Lines, 1994*

Low-Income or Poverty Line	Family Size			
	Single	2 person	3 person	4 person
Senate	13,300	22,190	26,620	31,050
Stats Canada: cities of 500,000+	16,609	20,782	25,821	31,256
CCSD	13,770	22,950	27,540	32,130
Montreal: basic needs	8,600	-	13,660	15,890
Fraser: Ontario	7,556	10,696	14,037	17,542

SOURCE: David Ross, Richard Shillington, and Clarence Lochhead, *The Canadian Fact Book on Poverty* (Ottawa: Canadian Council on Social Development, 1994), pp. 12-24.

Since 1973, Statistics Canada has maintained an annual count of the number of Canadians whose household income falls below the low-income cut-offs. Table 12 shows both the total number and the rate for people in poverty as a percentage of the total Canadian population.

TABLE 12: *Number of Persons in Poverty (Thousands) and Rate (%)*

	Singles		Families		Total	
Year	No.	Rate	No.	Rate	No.	Rate
1973	767	40.2	701	13.4	3,269	16.2
1981	940	37.5	721	11.3	3,339	14.0
1986	1,004	34.5	801	11.8	3,597	14.4
1991	1,259	36.6	949	13.0	4,230	15.9
1993	1,306	37.1	1,116	14.8	4,775	17.4

SOURCES: Ross et al., *Canadian Fact Book on Poverty*, p. 55; updated to 1993 with data from National Council of Welfare, *Poverty Profile 1993* (Ottawa: 1995), pp. 6-9.

The table shows that the total number of people in poverty has increased steadily, and although the percentage of Canadians in poverty fell from 1973 to 1981, since then it has increased and, for families, more than eliminated the gains made in earlier years. These figures are based on total family income, which includes both market income from employment and investments and redistributed income from social welfare programs. Most of those who are in poverty work. In 1993, 23 per cent of poor family heads and 15 per cent of poor individuals worked full time, while 37 per cent of poor heads of household and 48 per cent of individuals worked part time.[8] Despite this, Table 13 shows that market income for people in the lowest two income quintiles has been falling rapidly and has been increasingly replaced by redistributed income.

TABLE 13: *Family Income Shares and Sources, 1981-91*

Source of Income for Income Quintiles	Percentage Share		% Change
	1981	*1991*	*1981-91*
Market Income			
Lowest	4.8	2.9	-1.9
Second	13.4	11.4	-2.0
Middle	18.8	18.2	-0.6
Fourth	24.6	25.1	0.5
Highest	38.4	42.4	4.0
Total Income			
Lowest	6.9	6.2	-0.7
Second	13.9	12.7	-1.2
Middle	18.6	18.0	-0.6
Fourth	23.9	23.9	0.0
Highest	36.7	39.2	2.0

SOURCE: Ross et al., *Canadian Fact Book on Poverty*, p. 93.

The redistributive system has been working as it was intended to and has prevented what would otherwise have been a much more severe loss of family income. However, the replacement has not been complete, with the result that the number of people in poverty has continued to increase.

Equity

The figures for poverty and income are average figures for all Canadians. Although they give a good idea of overall trends they do not provide an understanding of the differences that occur due to gender, age, family type, origin, ability, and location.

GENDER

TABLE 14: *Poverty Rates by Age and Sex, 1993*

Sex	18-24	25-34	35-44	45-54	55-64	65-74	75-84	85+
Men	16.7	15.8	12.7	10.4	14.0	14.3	14.0	17.3
Women	23.6	19.9	13.8	12.1	18.5	20.2	31.3	35.6

SOURCE: National Council of Welfare, *Poverty Profile 1993*, p. 33.

In every age category women are more likely to be poor than men (Table 14). The gap is smallest between men and women in the prime working years of ages 35-54, rising for younger women and for older women. Overall the ratio of women to men in poverty was 1.33:1 in 1993, exactly the same as it was in 1982. If one looks at change in the ratio for different years there seems to be a pattern whereby the ratio rises during periods of prosperity and falls during periods of recession. In other words, men do better during the good times than women.

SENIORS

TABLE 15: *Poverty Rates for Seniors, 1980 and 1993*

Sex	1980	1993	Change
Men	27.3	14.4	-47%
Women	38.4	25.1	-35%

SOURCE: National Council of Welfare, *Poverty Profile 1993*, p. 73.

The rates of poverty among seniors have fallen dramatically, but 636,000 remain poor, including a disproportionate number of older women.

CHILDREN AND FAMILIES

The poverty of children is the poverty of the families to which they belong. Table 16 shows the slide of more and more children into poverty. The single-mother families are particularly vulnerable. For children in single-mother families, poverty is normal. Although two-parent families do better, there are still many of them in poverty, with more children in total than in the single-mother families. Poverty undermines the children's education, health, and expectations of living in a just and fair society.

TABLE 16: *Children under 18 Living in Poverty, 1980, 1986, and 1993*

Family Type	1980	1986	1993
Single Mother			
Rate	61.8	63.8	
Number	Not available	361,000	595,000
Two-parent			
Rate		12.2	13.4
Number	Not available	614,000	752,000
All Types			
Rate	15.0	17.6	20.8
Number	896,000	1,016,000	1,415,000

SOURCE: National Council of Welfare, *Poverty Profile*, 1980, 1986, 1993.

IMMIGRANTS AND ABORIGINAL PEOPLES

Data on the extent of poverty among recent immigrants and Aboriginal peoples are more difficult to obtain. The National Council of Welfare indicates that 65.5 per cent of single immigrants who came to Canada after 1979 are in poverty (compared to a national rate of 37.8 per cent) and 38.8 per cent of immigrant families are in poverty (compared to a national rate of 14.8 per cent).[9] Income data on Aboriginal peoples on reserve are not gathered by Statistics Canada as part of its annual incomes survey, leading to an understatement on the extent of poverty in Canada as a whole. The data on individual incomes available from special studies show that Aboriginal peoples in all groups have incomes much lower than the Canadian individual averages. As these data are not available for households, a poverty rate cannot be calculated.

TABLE 17: *Aboriginal Peoples, 15 and over, by Income Class, 1990*

| | Indians | | | | All | All |
Income Class ($)	On reserve	Off reserve	Metis	Inuit	Aboriginals	Canadians
<10,000	59.8	42.3	41.4	48.5	47.2	27.7
10-19,999	25.0	30.7	30.4	35.9	26.2	24.4
20-29,999	13.3	23.6	23.2	19.3	20.5	31.0
>30,000	1.9	7.7	7.5	8.3	6.1	16.9

SOURCE: Ross et al., *Canadian Fact Book on Poverty*, p. 40.

DISABILITY

Data on the incomes of people with disabilities are only available in a form similar to that for Aboriginal peoples. Although a poverty rate cannot be calculated, the disparity between persons with disabilities and all Canadians is apparent.

TABLE 18: *Persons with Disabilities, 15-64, by Income Class, 1993*

| | Persons with Disabilities, 15-64 | | | All Individuals, 15-64 | | |
Income Class ($)	Total	Men	Women	Total	Men	Women
<10,000	42.7	31.4	53.8	34.9	24.8	45.1
10-19,999	20.5	18.4	22.5	18.9	15.2	22.4
20-29,999	14.6	15.6	15.7	17.0	17.2	16.9
>30,000	22.2	34.6	10.0	29.1	42.6	15.7

SOURCE: Ross et al., *Canadian Fact Book on Poverty*, p. 42.

The figures also show that disabled women are much worse off than men, possibly because the incomes of disabled men are more likely to be supported by employers' disability plans or by Workers' Compensation.

LOCATION

Some differences exist in the extent of poverty between the different regions and provinces of Canada, although these have decreased during the last twenty years.

These variations by province are not as large as one might have expected, partly because of the success of redistribution programs in counteracting regional differences of income and of provincial government abilities to pay.

TABLE 19: *Poverty by Province*

| | Families | | Individuals | | All persons | |
	Number	Rate	Number	Rate	Number	Rate
Nfld.	25,000	16.1	16,000	41.4	100,000	17.5
P.E.I.	3,000	7.0	5,000	32.2	13,000	9.9
N.S.	36,000	14.5	34,000	32.4	147,000	16.5
N.B.	24,000	11.9	28,000	41.3	104,000	14.5
Quebec	338,000	17.6	422,000	45.0	1,431,000	20.7
Ontario	382,000	13.4	392,000	32.7	1,599,000	15.6
Manitoba	41,000	14.4	51,000	36.7	189,000	18.1
Sask.	36,000	13.8	37,000	31.2	160,000	17.0
Alberta	103,000	15.0	126,000	38.6	449,000	17.6
B.C.	128,000	14.0	194,000	34.4	584,000	17.3
Canada	1,116,000	14.8	1,306,000	37.1	4,775,000	17.4

SOURCE: National Council of Welfare, *Poverty Profile 1993*, p. 17.

Employability

In the discussion in this chapter on social policy objectives we have begun from the premise that Canada has, or should have, a commitment to a minimum standard of living for all its citizens. This minimum then becomes a floor income and one can only expect that people will work if they can take home a larger income after paying the costs of employment.

There are two problems with this approach. The first is that the wages that employers can afford to pay are determined by the market and are independent of poverty minimums. Thus, low-wage types of enterprise can only take place to the point where they can afford to pay more than the minimum. At lower rates they will either not take place at all or they will depend on unusual employees, for example, children or migrant workers, or unusual types of payment, as in the hidden economy. The second problem is that family needs are a function of family size. Thus, poverty minimums that are sufficient for family purposes are much higher than those for individuals. The result is that for family heads, the income they have to obtain before work is worthwhile is raised. In addition, families usually have added expenses, particularly for child care, that add to the cost of working.

In the 1960s and early 1970s Canada was confident that it could have a high rate of employment and a high-wage economy. In 1974 the minimum wage plus Family Allowances was sufficient to bring a family of three to the poverty line. By 1985 the minimum wage had fallen so far behind that the incomes of two wage-earners plus the Family Allowance and child tax credit were insufficient to bring the same family to the poverty line.[10] By 1993 the average minimum wage only reached 75 per cent of the poverty line for a single person, exceeding the average welfare rate for a single person by only $2,300/year.

In the context of the global economy (and the North American Free Trade Agreement) economists have become increasingly concerned that Canada is losing jobs to other countries, particularly the United States, that have lower social benefits and lower wage levels. A second and related concern is that the Unemployment Insurance program provides people with incentives to work only to the extent necessary to qualify for benefits. The evidence for these concerns is found in the fact that the unemployment experience of Canada and the United States diverged in the 1980s. The reasons given for this divergence include the provision by Canada of extended benefits in high unemployment areas, repeat use of UI by workers, particularly women,[11] and concerns that employers are providing more jobs on a part-year basis because they know that prospective employees can receive UI income the rest of the year.[12] The conclusion, many would argue, is that the current UI system is out of control – or, at the very least, being "used" by many participants on both sides of the labour market.[13]

Conclusion

The redistributive system has not achieved most of the objectives that have been expressed in statements of government policy. The successes are the reduction of poverty among seniors and the reduction of regional differences. These are offset by the increase in poverty in total, the presence of more and more child poverty, the failure to obtain equity, and the distorting effects of social programs on work incentives.

Notes

1. Canada, *Income Security for Canadians* (Ottawa: Queen's Printer, 1971), p. 11.
2. Christopher Green, Fred Lazar, Miles Corak, and Dominique Gross, *Unemployment Insurance* (Toronto: C.D. Howe Institute, 1994).
3. Ken Battle and Sherri Torjman, *Opening the Books on Social Spending* (Ottawa: Caledon Institute of Social Policy, 1993).
4. *Ibid.*, p. 13.
5. Human Resources Development Canada, *Improving Social Security in Canada* (Ottawa, 1994), p. 7.
6. Sandra Rubin, "If I have children, I'll raise them very differently," Victoria *Times Colonist*, April 17, 1994.
7. Canada, *Working Paper on Social Security in Canada* (Ottawa: Queen's Printer, 1973), p. 17.
8. National Council of Welfare, *Poverty Profile 1993* (Ottawa, 1995), p. 57.
9. *Ibid.*, p. 42.
10. Andrew Armitage, *Social Welfare in Canada*, 2nd edition (Toronto: McClelland and Stewart, 1988), p. 168.
11. Miles Corak, "UI Work Disincentives and the Canadian Labor Market," in John Richards and William Watson, eds., *Unemployment Insurance: How To Make It Work* (Toronto: C.D. Howe Institute, 1994), p. 147.
12. Christopher Green, "What Should We Do with the UI System," in Richards and Watson, eds., *Unemployment Insurance*, p. 2.
13. *Ibid.*, p. 32.

Chapter 4

REDISTRIBUTION:

PROGRAMS AND PROPOSALS

The problems of the redistribution system, along with proposals for change, require that the individual programs be reviewed. Major programs address the needs of Canadians in six social groups:

- Seniors
- Employable adults
- Disabled adults
- Children and families
- Students
- Poor.

The programs are organized in two tiers. The upper tier consists of programs directed to any of the first five groups and that are available as demogrants, social insurance, government compensation plans, loans, or tax benefits. The lower tier consists of the provincial and Indian Affairs social assistance and related programs, focused on the poor, that provide benefits on a discretionary basis following an individually administered needs test. Programs in the upper tier are *institutional* programs, as access to them is considered to be a normal response to private problems. Programs in the second tier are *residual*,[1] as access to them is based on need alone and presumes that the recipients have failed in some way to look after themselves. There is more stigma associated with the lower tier than the upper one.

Each of these levels has a different relationship to the major objectives of redistribution, i.e., poverty, equity, and employment, discussed in the last chapter, and each has its own issues of cost containment and relationship to Canada's public expenditure problems. A variety of reform proposals, presented by three major schools of thought and action, have been made to respond to these issues. The first are the agencies with a long-term concern for poverty. At the national level they include the Canadian Council on Social Development, the National Council of Welfare, and the Caledon Institute. The second are the feminist writers and organizations that have been at the forefront of seeking equity-based reforms. They include the National Action Committee on the Status of Women and academic writers and critics. The third are the agencies whose concerns and interests are dominated by the deficit, the global economy, and labour market considerations. They include the C.D. Howe Institute, the Business Council on National Issues, and the Fraser Institute, and, in a different way, the Canadian Labour Congress. Each of these agencies shares some interests in issues that the other agencies have identified, but which, for them, are not the primary ones.

Seniors

The needs of seniors are addressed by five programs:

- Old Age Security
- Old Age Security Guaranteed Income Supplement
- Canada and Quebec Pension Plans
- Provincial supplementary benefits
- Retirement savings provisions of the Income Tax Act.

1. *Old Age Security.* Old Age Security was introduced by the federal government in 1952. The elderly were defined initially as persons over seventy; subsequently, the age level for receipt of benefit was lowered to sixty-five. The program is administered by Human Resources Canada. The level of benefit is set at $392/month (August, 1995). The value of benefit is adjusted to inflation from a base figure of $100/month, established in 1973.

Old Age Security covers all Canadians. Immigrants require a minimum ten years' residence in Canada to qualify for any benefits and thirty-five years of residence to obtain a full Old Age Security payment. Old Age Security income is taxable and is "clawed back" from persons with annual income (1994) over $53,215.

The number of seniors eligible for Old Age Security was 700,000 in 1952 when the plan started. It rose to 1.5 million by 1970 and in 1995 exceeds 3 million. By the year 2005 it will be 5 million. Because of the growth in the number of recipients the amount paid has also increased from $2 billion (in constant 1993 dollars) in 1952, to $8 billion in 1974, to $16 billion in 1994.[2]

2. *Old Age Security Guaranteed Income Supplement and Spouse's Allowance.* The Guaranteed Income Supplement program was introduced by the federal government in 1966 as part of a comprehensive series of reforms affecting the income security of the elderly. The reforms included changes in the age of eligibility and the benefit of Old Age Security, and the introduction of the Canada Pension Plan. The total effect of these changes was intended to protect all elderly persons from poverty. A Spouse's Allowance was added in 1976 to provide support to persons between sixty and sixty-five who are married to people sixty-five and older.

Benefit levels under GIS vary with the recipient's income. The maximum benefit (August, 1995), paid to those with no income other than Old Age Security, is $466/month for single persons and $303/month for each member of a couple. The value of the benefits is adjusted automatically to offset inflation. Benefits are not subject to tax but additional income results in GIS payments being reduced by 50¢ for each $1 received. Assets are treated only to the extent that they produce income.

For the single person who is entirely dependent on Old Age Security and GIS the total annual benefit received is $10,296; for a couple the total benefit is $16,680. The value of these benefits in relation to poverty lines is shown in Table 20.

TABLE 20: *Federal Old Age Security and Guaranteed Income Supplement Benefits, Compared to Poverty Lines, 1974, 1985, and 1995*

		1974	1985	1995
Single Person	Poverty Line	2,780	8,850	13,300
	OAS/GIS	2,247	7,356	10,296
	% poverty line	81%	83%	77%
Couple	Poverty Line	4,620	14,750	22,190
	OAS/GIS	4,288	11,298	16,680
	% poverty line	92%	76%	75%

SOURCE: Senate Committee poverty lines, updated to 1994, have been used in this table for comparison purposes.

Because many seniors have other sources of income, including the Canada Pension Plan, the number of GIS beneficiaries (1.2 million) and the amount paid, in constant 1993 dollars ($1.3 billion), have increased only slightly since the program was introduced.

The number of beneficiaries of the Spouse's Allowance program (100,000) and payments ($400 million) have also remained constant in recent years because of improved private and CPP/QPP pensions. Gay and lesbian relationships are not recognized for benefits in the Spouse's Allowance program.

3. *The Canada Pension Plan and Quebec Pension Plan (CPP/QPP)*. The Canada Pension Plan and the associated Quebec Pension Plan were introduced in 1965. The two plans are compatible with respect to contributions and benefits. The Canada Pension Plan is administered by Human Resources Canada and the Quebec Pension Plan by the government of Quebec. Both are social insurance measures covering several types of long-term contingency. They are most widely known for their retirement pension provisions but also provide benefits at death, widowhood (including orphan's benefit), and severe, prolonged disability. Benefits are adjusted automatically to maintain a constant relationship to the average industrial wage. Full benefits are payable at age sixty-five with a reduced benefit available from age sixty.

Benefit levels under the CPP/QPP are based on contribution level (for all categories of benefit) and on the number of years in which contributions were paid (for disability and retirement benefits). Contributions are based on earnings. The contributor pays 2.5 per cent of annual earnings and the employer pays a similar amount. The ceiling (1994) on earnings for contribution purposes is $34,400. For the person who has made maximum contributions since the plan's introduction and who retired in 1995, the retirement pension was $713/month. Retirement pensions are subject to tax, with the first $1,000 being exempt. A single person receiving such a pension would have a total government income (assuming no private income) as follows:

Old Age Security	$4,704
Canada Pension Plan	8,556
GIS (5,592 less 50 per cent of 8,556)	1,314
Total	$14,574

The tax due on this amount would be approximately $1,000,[3] leaving the senior with $13,500, reaching the Senate Committee poverty line of $13,300.

CPP/QPP cover all employed (including self-employed) persons, but the unemployed and the unemployable are excluded from coverage. Women are covered equally with men, but the reality of the jobs they hold and the periods of absence from the labour force for caring mean that many more men qualify for full benefits than women. Since 1978 there has been provision to split pension credits on marriage dissolution. The marriage provisions have not been extended to gay and lesbian relationships.

Although the CPP/QPP are referred to as social insurance programs and operate through funds, the amounts accumulated in the funds are too low to cover the benefits to which the contributors are entitled. This was the result of a decision, at the time when the plans were introduced, to operate under a partial funding approach whereby full benefits became payable ten years after the plans were introduced, an insufficient time period to fund benefits by contributors, and as a result the contributions of current wage-earners are used to fund the benefits for the first years of the plan. The demography of the Canadian population meant that in the first twenty years of the program the total paid out each month was less than the total contributed. This period ended in 1995 with the result that the amount in the fund is now being drawn down. To maintain the value of payments and to prevent the fund going bankrupt, contributions would have to be increased from their present level of 5 per cent of payroll to between 13.7 per cent and 16 per cent by the year 2035.[4]

4. *Provincial supplementary benefits.* A number of provinces supplement these federal payments with a variety of programs. Some of these are based on need alone, some are tied to housing costs, while others cover some health care costs not covered by health insurance, such as drug prescriptions, on a universal basis for all seniors. The number and variation of these programs are such that the full detail cannot be provided here. However, the effect on the senior's income must be considered when an individual senior's entitlements are being established and the total public cost of pension provisions is being calculated.

5. *Retirement savings provisions of the Income Tax Act.* Total contributions and benefits under the Canada/Quebec Pension Plans have been kept low on the assumption that private and occupational plans will provide a third level of pension benefit for Canadians. Government support for the third level of pension benefits is provided by Registered Retirement Savings Plan (RRSP) deductions and Registered Pension Plan (RPP) deductions. The assumption is that this third level will close the gap between public plans that provide a "poverty-line" level of income and the level of retirement income necessary to maintain the standard of living enjoyed during working years.

The amounts that can be contributed as tax deductions to RRSPs and RPPs were raised substantially beginning in 1991 and are now 18 per cent of income to a maximum of $13,500. To make this full payment the taxpayer needs a taxable income of $75,000. Furthermore, interest on RRSP and RPP savings accumulates free of tax. Eventually, tax is payable on these funds, but not until they are withdrawn. It is difficult to know what level of pension would be payable on the basis of the contributions now being made as this will vary with years of contribution and level of income. However, the value of the deductions to taxpayers (the tax expenditure by federal and provincial governments) is estimated as exceeding $22 billion in 1994-95.

The tax deductions claimed rise with the taxpayer's income for three reasons. First, the amount that can be deducted rises with income; second, Registered Pension Plans are only available from major employers and governments, who also offer better wages; third, low-income earners do not have the cash to make even those contributions for which they are eligible. As a result, RRSPs and RPPs are a tax-supported benefit plan for upper-income earners.

Seniors: Proposals

Proposals for the seniors' income system are dominated by three considerations: the deficit, the problems of financing the Quebec and Canada Pension Plans, and the issues of equity. This is because poverty has largely been dealt with and seniors are considered to be past working age.

The costs of benefits and tax expenditures for seniors to the federal and provincial governments in 1994-95 are estimated at $63 billion, more than half the total of all government social security programs. Furthermore, this is the most rapidly growing part of the total due to the increasing proportion of seniors in the population. If total social security costs must be contained or reduced in order to reduce overall government expenditures, then programs for seniors have to participate. Consequently, a series of proposals have been made to reduce and restructure benefits. These include:

(1) Restructure OAS, OAS-GIS, and CPP/QPP into a single pay-as you-go income security plan focused on ensuring that seniors do not live in poverty. This proposal would respond to the concern that the present mix of these programs is complex and illogical. At present, as our examples above show, lower-income people who have contributed to CPP/QPP receive little benefit for their contributions as the benefits reduce their eligibility for OAS-GIS and for provincial supplements. Examples of proposals along these lines are made by the Caledon Institute, Courchene, and others.[5] Such a radical restructuring would also be the opportunity to recognize men and women and heterosexual and homosexual relationships on an equal basis, getting away from the existing program biases toward men, based on length of employment and contribution records, and heterosexual relationships, based on the lack of recognition of homosexual ties.

(2) Reduce the level at which benefits from Old Age Security are clawed back. This is a much milder form of the proposed restructuring of OAS that would not change the overall structure but would recapture OAS from higher-income earners

at a much lower level than at present, possibly based on household income rather than individual income.

(3) Raise the age of eligibility for benefits to seventy. This approach has already been taken in the United States where the age limit is being raised gradually to seventy. The effect is to extend the period of contribution (and employment) and reduce the period of benefit, reducing the overall cost of seniors' benefits.

(4) Reduce the tax benefits that support retirement incomes above the poverty line. At a time when Canada is facing major expenditure problems and an increasing number of people are living in poverty it is difficult to find an argument to justify the generosity of the RRSP/RPP provisions of the Income Tax Act. The result is a loss of tax revenue from those who are better off and a concentration of wealth in their hands. Proposals to reduce tax benefits are made by the Canadian Council on Social Development, Courchene, and others.[6] These proposals usually call for a lower tax benefit, through providing tax credits rather than tax deductions, or lower ceilings on the amounts that can be contributed. Few go as far as recommending the elimination of these provisions, fearing the reaction from an aging population that they need these provisions to finance their retirement.

The government of Canada has not yet taken a position on seniors' benefits, but the 1995 budget indicated that a review was under way and that using household rather than individual income as the basis for claw-back provisions was being considered.

Employable Adults

The needs of employable (but temporarily unemployed) workers are attended to by three programs:

- Unemployment Insurance (including training provisions)
- Resource industry adjustment programs
- Provincial programs for employable adults.

1. *Unemployment Insurance.* Unemployment Insurance was introduced in 1940 and has been revised several times. The major revision of the Act in 1970 expanded UI to all wage- and salary-earners, increased benefit levels, increased the period for which benefit could be obtained, decreased the minimum period of employment needed to qualify a wage-earner for benefit, and included maternity and sickness benefits for the first time.[7] UI is administered by Human Resources Canada. Payments to the unemployed are provided through the Unemployment Insurance Account, which receives revenue from the contributions of wage- and salary-earners and from employers. Prior to 1990 there was also a contribution from the federal treasury. This was then eliminated and the account is now expected to balance over the business cycle. As a result, contributions from employers and employees rose following the 1991-92 recession to pay for increased benefit payments.

Benefit levels from Unemployment Insurance are based on contributions. Employees contribute 3 per cent of earnings to an annual amount of $1,296 on

$780/week maximum insured earnings (1994). Employers provide 4.5 per cent of earnings through a payroll tax. Maximum benefits (as of August, 1995) are paid to a person whose income reaches or exceeds this ceiling for a specified number of weeks. This varies from twenty weeks, qualifying for seventeen weeks of benefit, where the unemployment rate is less than 6 per cent, to ten weeks qualifying for thirty-nine weeks of benefit where the unemployment rate is 16 per cent or higher. The maximum benefit payable is $448/week (August, 1995) and the maximum time that benefits can be received varies from thirty-five weeks in areas where the unemployment rate is less than 6 per cent to fifty weeks in areas where it exceeds 10 per cent. The benefit period for sickness and maternity coverage is fifteen weeks. The annual income at the maximum benefit rate of $23,296/year is sufficient to bring a wage-earner with one dependant to the poverty line. This annual income is proportionately lower than that available in 1974, when maximum benefits were adequate to bring a wage-earner with two dependants to the poverty line.

Unemployment Insurance was designed with the experience of the 1930s and 1940s and with the industrial business cycle in mind. It assumed that there would be periodic increases and decreases in employment and unemployment as the economy went from periods of expansion to periods of pause or contraction. It also assumed that the individual worker was powerless to do anything about these changes. As a consequence it was thought that the costs, in lost income to workers, should be shared among all workers and employers. This view of Unemployment Insurance did not take account of seasonal work, different unemployment patterns in different industries, structural problems, as when an industry disappears, or decisions by applicants to tailor their behaviour so as to maximize benefits. The result is a series of problems with Unemployment Insurance. These include:

Seasonal employment and UI use. In certain industries work has a seasonal character. The fishing industry is the best-known example but similar annual cyclical employment occurs in all farm-related work, the forest industry, and even in non-resource-based employment, for example, the employment of university sessional instructors and the summer shutdown periods for retooling in the auto industry. The result is that these industries have a predictable pattern of UI entitlement and use. In these circumstances the UI program is not working as an insurance program but as a type of guaranteed income program with workers receiving benefits on a regular basis as part of their normal annual income.

This is a problem for several reasons. First, it results in an income transfer from industries with stable employment patterns to those with cyclical patterns. Second, it makes it more attractive than it would otherwise be for employees to stay in seasonal employment. Third, it increases the rate of unemployment and drives up the cost of the Unemployment Insurance program as a whole.

Service employment and part-time work. The service industries in which women employees predominate are characterized by low wages and part-time work. Qualification for Unemployment Insurance from these industries is also high because of short employment periods. In some studies there is evidence that some of the mostly female workers who work in these industries tailor their work to UI eligibility. Corak reports:

females experience longer periods of benefit than males and the duration of their UI claims are strongly influenced by the replacement rate. . . . Female employment durations appear to be bunched along the minimum eligible weeks required to collect benefits, and the availability of UI may be part of the explanation. Patterns of repeat use also vary between genders. . . . over periods as long as five years females are more likely to be repeaters. . . .[8]

Although eligibility rules have also been tightened to disqualify workers who leave jobs voluntarily, enforcement remains a problem.

Contribution premiums and their impact on job formation. As with CPP/QPP premiums, the financing of Unemployment Insurance through a payroll tax is said to have had a negative impact on job formation. The concern is that in marginal situations all payroll taxes encourage employers to use machines rather than workers and in some situations such taxes make small business uneconomic.

Major structural adjustment problems. Some of the changes resulting from the global economy are major and affected industries are suffering irreversible losses of employment. To the employees of these industries, UI offers a year of benefits but it does not in any way address the problem as to where they will work later. As a result of this concern, since 1989, some UI funds have been used for worker training purposes ($2.6 billion in 1993-94).

The concern with structural adjustment and unemployment problems is not a new one. During the early 1960s, the view taken of what then seemed a relatively high unemployment rate (6 per cent) was that it was caused by "structural" unemployment, that is, workers were not suitably trained for the jobs that an increasingly automated and technical society provided. The Department of Manpower and Immigration was created in 1965 to respond to this perceived problem. The Department's brief to the Senate Committee on Poverty stated:

The primary goal of the Department is to contribute to the attainment of economic and social goals for Canada by optimizing the use, quality, and mobility of all manpower resources available to the country. Thus the policies and programs of the Department are essentially economic in character.[9]

The programs developed have served to screen the most qualified and educable workers, provide them with job opportunities and/or employment, and hence generally aid the operation of the labour market. These are not unimportant functions but they inevitably constitute an institutional creaming function that tends to leave unserved those who are least competitive. There is also evidence to the effect that even individuals who are singled out for employment (and/or training) are not necessarily the recipients of any increase in income. André Reynauld, chairman of the Economic Council of Canada, explained in 1973 why an increase in the supply of skilled workers does not lead to any change in the income distribution:

Put simply, the explanation is that wages and salaries are fixed for given tasks, and the best workers get the jobs. Workers thus compete for *jobs*, not wages.

From the point of view of the employer, the best workers are those who can be trained for the job at the minimum cost. If, for example, the supply of university graduates increases, they simply displace non-university graduates with no impact on the distribution of incomes.[10]

This view of the operation of the government training programs suggests that they provide a subsidy to employers and industry and often duplicate training functions that individuals or industry would perform for themselves. Opinion on the effectiveness of such expenditures and on the merit generally of a major government role in training remains divided. Courchene makes the argument for a major role: "Training and skills development is not a panacea, but it is surely a critical part . . . of making the transition from a resource-based mentality to a human-capital or knowledge-based mentality.[11]

The case against such a role is based on the reality that the people who are unemployed tend to be older or unskilled and the results of training have not been substantial enough to warrant the cost. Lazar, another labour economist, concludes his argument:

> Putting more money into training when the economy is operating with a high degree of slack will prove ineffective. . . . Bad jobs should be attacked directly, through full employment and industrial policies. Using UI funds to expand training programs will do little, if anything, to correct the structural defect of bad jobs. Moreover, training will do little to transform unstable workers into stable ones.[12]

The Canadian Labour Congress has also opposed the use of UI funds for training, seeing this as a diversion of dollars that should be available to support incomes through UI benefits.

Benefit-maximizing behaviours. We have discussed some of these earlier while looking at social insurance generally in Chapter 2. Generally, these problems can be said to make the other problems of UI worse. Employees and employers are not doing anything wrong when they structure their affairs to take full advantage of the benefits, including training periods, to which they are entitled. Nevertheless, from a policy point of view such behaviours have become costly distortions from the original program assumption, which was that such behaviour was not going to occur. It has been twenty-five years since UI was expanded to include seasonal employees and the self-employed and the UI benefits were liberalized. During that time a whole generation of workers has grown up with the program as a regular part of their working lives. It is perhaps not surprising that workers and their employers have organized their affairs to make the best use they could of UI benefits.

2. *Resource industry adjustment programs.* In addition to UI benefits, workers in devastated regions have received benefits where there are massive losses of employment. The payments to farmers who were not able to sell grain and the payments to Atlantic fishery workers when the ground fishery was closed in 1993 are

examples. These programs have faced the same problems that accompany the UI role in structural adjustment. It has been difficult or impossible to design a program that provides for an effective adjustment. A cushion can be provided that mitigates and delays the full income loss but this is far less than the programs have promised.

3. *Provincial programs for employable adults.* These programs form part of the second tier of redistributive programs and are discussed later in the chapter. They are mentioned here as a reminder that the full response to employment problems is fractured between the federal and provincial governments and between the UI and social assistance programs. Any change in one affects the other. Any reduction in benefits through UI increases the costs of provincial social assistance programs. Any training program that operates for the exclusive benefit of UI claimants does so at the expense of making it harder for those on social assistance to compete for the same jobs. Any work stimulation or workfare program that provides contributions to UI can increase UI benefit costs. One of the major problems of developing any coherent policy for the unemployed is the fracture line between the federal and provincial programs.

Employable Adults: Proposals

Proposals for employable adults are dominated by labour market considerations. The deficit is relevant only to the extent that proposals are expected to be self-financing and to improve the operation of the economy as a whole. The objective of providing some minimum level of income has not played any role in recent discussions, nor have issues of equity been prominent. There is a consensus that "something has to be done" but little agreement on what. Proposals that have been widely discussed include:

(1) Restrict the scope of Unemployment Insurance to people who experience temporary, infrequent unemployment. This could be accomplished by a system of industry and/or regional restrictions on access to the plan that would be intended to separate out the longer-term or more frequent use of UI found in declining and devastated industries and in regions with high and chronic rates of unemployment. The 1994 federal consultation paper *Improving Social Security in Canada* proposed a two-tier Unemployment Insurance system, with one tier comprising workers with good employment records and a lower tier, with income testing, training, and lower benefits, for workers who are in the frequent user group.[13]

(2) Restrict benefits through longer qualification periods and rules on the frequency of claims. One proposal of this type would do away with all regional variations and provide one uniform plan with a five-year cap to prevent frequent use;[14] another would have longer contribution periods;[15] and a third would scale benefits to the total number of weeks worked during the last year.[16]

(3) Make separate provision for major regional job losses. Commentators agree that problems of this type should be separated from Unemployment Insurance, but there is no agreement as to what should take its place beyond the proposal that any response should be time limited.[17]

(4) Integrate UI with social assistance in a revised program for all employable

people. This proposal takes an old form and a new form. The old form is the proposal for a negative tax program that has been discussed periodically since the 1970s. The Canadian Council on Social Development and the National Council of Welfare continue to remind us of the earlier proposals.[18] The newer form of this proposal takes the form of speculation about the restriction and perhaps eventual termination of UI. Social assistance, with some changes, would then have to undertake the whole of the task of responding to unemployment.[19]

Persons with Disabilities

Canada has no overall framework for social justice for persons with disabilities and, unlike for seniors or the unemployed, has never aspired to build one. Instead, four programs may, or may not, be available to persons with disabilities:

- Workers' Compensation
- Canada/Quebec Pension Plans
- Tax benefits for disabled persons
- Provincial social assistance programs for unemployable people.

1. *Workers' Compensation.* Programs of Workers' Compensation are typically administered by semi-independent commissions reporting to the provincial Minister of Labour. Levels of benefit under Workers' Compensation vary widely by province. A typical level of benefit is 75 per cent of pre-tax salary up to a maximum. The maximum level of benefit varies, with an average of $32,000/year (1995). This could bring a family of four to the poverty line, but many beneficiaries do not obtain maximum benefits. Benefits for widows and children are less adequate and, although these are now aided by the Canada Pension Plan, there are no provisions for integrating and co-ordinating the two. Unlike most other social benefits, Worker's Compensation payments are not taxed. As a result, in some cases, workers are better off receiving compensation than working.

Coverage under Workers' Compensation is required of all employers beyond a minimum size. But there are gaps in coverage. The self-employed are one such gap. In addition, there are gaps at the individual level. The worker who undertakes duties not usually in his or her line of work, for example, the office worker who assists with moving heavy equipment, may lose protection. The process of determining eligibility, particularly in cases where the results of injury are not immediately apparent, can be lengthy and contentious. Benefits can be refused to the recipient who rejects medical advice and, say, refuses to take treatment that could lead to a return to employment. Benefits are also lost, or reduced, when the person is considered to be fit for work of some sort, whether or not there is actual work available. Enforcement of these conditions has become much more difficult as unemployment has become more prevalent. It has also become more difficult as the process of establishing and maintaining eligibility has become the subject of litigation between claimants and Workers' Compensation authorities.

A basic problem of Workers' Compensation as a program for disabled persons is that it only recognizes disability that is the result of employment conditions. Most persons with disabilities are not covered.

2. *Canada/Quebec Pension Plan benefits.* CPP/QPP provide a maximum benefit of $855/month with an additional $161/month for each dependent child. To qualify for disability payments the recipient must satisfy contribution requirements and be permanently and completely disabled. Benefits are lost if the person returns to work. Benefits are taxable but can be stacked with Workers' Compensation payments.

As with Workers' Compensation, a basic problem of the CPP/QPP provisions for disability is the eligibility requirement. Persons without a labour force attachment have no means of establishing the contribution record necessary to obtain benefits. A further problem is the outdated notion of disability, which does not recognize the contribution that persons with disabilities can make. Receiving benefits requires a withdrawal from the labour force rather than integration into it.

3. *Tax benefits for disabled persons.* The Income Tax Act permits persons with disabilities to claim a tax credit of $4,233 (1984) and medical care, including attendant allowance costs, within prescribed limits. These allowances provide some recognition of the costs of disability for persons with taxable income.

4. *Provincial social assistance programs for unemployable people.* These programs form part of the second tier of redistributive income programs. All needs not met by Workers' Compensation and the disability provisions of CPP/QPP affect the need for and the costs of provincial social assistance.

Persons with Disabilities: Proposals

Proposals for persons with disabilities have not formed a prominent part of the debate on the future of redistributive social policy. This is partly because their relationship to issues of the global economy is slight and partly because of the way that issues of equity have been sidelined by economic issues. Proposals have been made from different groups, and these incorporate different and contradictory ideas. They include:

(1) The Council of Canadians with Disabilities has argued against programs that treat people differently because of the cause of disability, seeking:

> integrated systems, not separate systems. . . . If we are designing new programs in Canada, let's ensure within the design access for all people within the program, rather than design parallel streams, which have kept people with disabilities separate from their neighbours and the mainstream of Canadian society.[20]

(2) The C.D. Howe Institute's study of Workers' Compensation includes a proposal to lower the benefit level so that the replacement rate does not exceed 75 or 80 per cent of after-tax earnings in order to "reduce the length of temporary claims, discourage frivolous or even fraudulent claims, and encourage workers to assume greater responsibility in matters of safety."[21]

(3) Employers, particularly small businesses, have expressed mounting concern

at the cumulative effects of payroll taxes on jobs. When the payroll taxes from UI (4.2 per cent), CPP/QPP (2.5 per cent), and Workers' Compensation (2.6 per cent, average) are totalled, the result is a payroll tax of 9.3 per cent of payroll costs. In addition, some provinces also levy a health insurance payroll tax. As each of the programs could also increase the payroll taxes they charge as a response to the financing problems each faces, the cumulative effect has to be considered. In 1995, the Bank of Canada estimated that payroll taxes had reduced job formation by 130,000 jobs in the recovery since the 1991-92 recession.[22] It does not make sense, it is argued, to penalize the growth of small business or service employment, for these are important parts of the restructuring of the Canadian economy as it is integrated into the global economy.

Children and Families

Since the termination of Family Allowance payments (1992) the programs that provide a child or family benefit are all provided through the tax system. They are:

- the Child Tax Benefit and GST credit
- the child care allowance
- the child and married exemptions.

1. *The Child Tax Benefit and GST credit.* The Child Tax Benefit was introduced in 1992 following the ending of the Family Allowance and the child tax credit. In 1985 Family Allowances were $31/month/child. In addition, low-income families received the child tax credit of $384/year, for a total federal payment per child under eighteen of approximately $750/year. This total payment was 25 per cent of the Senate Committee poverty line for the cost of maintaining a child. The Child Tax Benefit is made up of two parts, a basic amount of $1,020/year/child (1993), clawed back at a rate of 5 per cent of family net income above $25,291; and an earned income supplement of up to $500/year/child clawed back at a rate of 10 per cent of net family income over $20,291, disappearing completely at $25,291.[23] The basic amount is now 23 per cent of the Senate Committee poverty line, rising to 34 per cent with the addition of the supplement. The Child Tax Benefit is non-taxable. It is paid following filing of an income tax return and is thus based on the previous year's income. It, along with the tax system as a whole, is only partially indexed to inflation, thus its value and the number of people qualifying erodes each year. The cost of the Child Tax Benefit is $5.1 billion/year.

The GST credit is available to low-income individuals and couples as well as to families with children. The value of the GST credit is $199/year for the first two members of a household and increases by $105/year for each additional child; the annual cost is $2.8 billion.

2. *The married and equivalent to spouse personal exemptions.* A federal tax credit of 17 per cent of $5,380 can be claimed for a non-working spouse or for the first child or other dependant living with a single person. The total value of this credit varies with the tax rate in each province but approximates $1,400/year. The exemption is not refundable; the cost is $1.6 billion/year.

3. *The child-care expense deduction.* This can be claimed on the basis of receipted child-care expenses up to $5,000/year for children under six and up to $3,000/year for children up to fourteen. Because this benefit takes the form of a deduction from taxable income it has most value to upper-income earners.

These three measures, of which only the first is a targeted benefit to the poor, constitute one of the weakest social policy responses to family need that can be found in Western developed countries (the United States has no program at all). In most countries, a family allowance or its equivalent is a cornerstone of the redistributive system, providing a major fraction of the total income of poorer families.[24]

Children and Families: Proposals

Proposals for children and families are dominated by poverty issues. One in five children live in families in poverty, and in single-parent mother families the ratio is two in three. In 1989 the House of Commons unanimously passed a resolution seeking "to achieve the goal of eliminating poverty among Canadian children by the year 2000."[25] Arguments for better support to poor families with children are made most strenuously by bodies like the Caledon Institute[26] and the National Council of Welfare but also receive support from labour market economists. The support from the economists is based on (1) a recognition that child poverty undercuts the education and labour force readiness of the next generation of workers,[27] and (2) the fact that a stronger program of child benefits, along with other measures, would reduce the disincentives to leave "the welfare trap."[28]

In response to the issue of child poverty, there is really only one proposal being made (although it takes different forms), that is, to expand the present Child Tax Benefit into an adequately funded national child benefit, integrating into the benefit the payments made for children as part of provincial social assistance programs.[29] The costs of such a proposal would not be negligible, but a substantial part of the costs would be funded by reducing the costs of provincial social assistance programs, leading some commentators to argue that Ottawa should concentrate its attention on providing families with sufficient income to keep children out of poverty and leave the issues of poor adults and work incentives to the provinces.

Students

Students in post-secondary education are supported in their studies by the Canada Student Loan (CSL) program and related provincial programs. Post-secondary education is a provincial responsibility but the history of federal support for university and college education is a long one, including direct grants to universities (1951), cost-sharing agreements with the provinces (1966), and, from 1977 to 1996, block funding to the provinces under the Established Programs Financing Act (EPF). Direct student aid began as early as the post-war veterans' programs; the current form of the student loan program was introduced in 1964. The CSL and related provincial programs share many features with other redistributive social welfare programs. Living allowances are similar to the poverty levels defined by the Senate Committee and considerably higher than the survival levels defined by the Fraser Institute (Table 21). In practice, because of payment caps and other limits within the student loan program, many students do not receive the full benefit of these allowances. Eligibility for the CSL program follows a test of income and assets.

TABLE 21: *Poverty Lines and Student Loan Living Allowances, Annual Rates, Child Tax and GST Benefits Added, British Columbia, 1995*

Household Size	Senate Committee	Fraser Institute	Student Loan Living Allowance		
			Amount	Senate	Fraser
Single	$13,300	$7,805	$13,499	101%	172%
Parent & child	$22,190	$10,817	$19,071	85%	176%
Couple & Child	$26,260	$14,443	$26,376	100%	182%
Parent & 2 children	$26,260	$14,443	$24,903	95%	172%

SOURCE: British Columbia Student Assistance Program Guide, 1995.

Student loans are distinguished by the admission and diligent study requirements of the program. They are also loans rather than outright grants. However, the loans are interest-free and require no repayment during periods of study. In addition, loan remission is provided above specific levels of indebtedness and on performance conditions, including evidence of "personal responsibility." These features make student loans an alternative means of personal support to other redistributive programs. The cost, in interest forgiveness, loan remission, and bankruptcy relief of the Canada student loan program is estimated at $500 million/year.

Students: Proposals

There is concern that rising fee levels for post-secondary education may result in the student loan program becoming less and less adequate to cover the costs of post-secondary education. In addition, repayment problems are becoming more severe as students have greater difficulty finding employment and total amounts of indebtedness rise. It is less clear how these concerns will be addressed. If Canada were to adopt some other features of the social policy proposals that are being discussed, for example, the child and family provisions, there would be an immediate and positive effect on the need for student loans and on the extent of indebtedness incurred by students with children.

The Poor

The programs for the poor form the second tier of the income security system. For many Canadians they are the true safety net. Programs at this level operate on a definition of need. Any person or family whose need is not met in any other way is eligible to receive a payment. Thus, for practical purposes, programs at this level define the conditions of poverty under which many Canadians live. There are five programs at this level:

- provincial programs of social assistance
- on-reserve assistance for Indians

- veterans' allowances
- enforced dependencies
- food banks and soup kitchens.

The provincial programs of social assistance establish a policy framework within which the other programs at this level operate. Veterans' allowances provide relatively generous support but receipt is restricted to an aging and declining number of people. On-reserve assistance for Indians has, since 1968, been administered under policies that parallel the policies in the province in which the reserve is situated. Thus, provincial policies indirectly determine the benefit rates and conditions of on-reserve assistance.

1. *Provincial and on-reserve social assistance.* Social assistance is the contemporary inheritor of the "poor law," "relief," "dole" tradition of income security. As such, it has a long history and no firm beginning point (unless we go back to the Elizabethan Poor Law of 1601). Monetary social assistance has no cultural roots in First Nations communities.

Canadian social assistance programming has been influenced since 1966 by cost-sharing agreements between federal and provincial governments through the Canada Assistance Plan (CAP). The CAP brought a uniformity of approach to social assistance, which before then had consisted of a series of different programs.[30] The CAP permitted the federal government to enter into agreements with provincial governments whereby the provinces were reimbursed for 50 per cent of their social assistance expenditures. This relationship began to change in 1991 when a 5 per cent limit was placed on the annual amount that CAP payments could be increased to the provinces of Alberta, British Columbia, and Ontario. The effect of the limit was particularly severe on Ontario, which by 1995 was receiving an estimated $1.8 billion less than it would have under the 50 per cent formula. In the 1995 budget the federal government gave a one-year notice that as of March 31, 1996, the CAP would be withdrawn and replaced by the Canada Health and Social Transfer (CHST) and the Human Resources Investment Fund (HRIF). The CHST provides for a federal financial transfer to the provinces for health, post-secondary education, and welfare costs. The amount to be transferred is established by a formula that includes tax points and fixed dollar amounts. However, the amount is reduced from that which would have been available under earlier federal-provincial cost-sharing arrangements by $2.5 billion in the first year and $4.5 billion in the second. The HRIF consolidates support for measures related to employment and, here again, the total is less than that earlier available.

Under the CAP, reimbursement was provided to the provinces on condition that they met national standards, including: benefits must be based on need; residence cannot be a condition of benefit; provision for appeal must exist. In addition, the federal government offered consultative services to the provinces and supported services to needy persons "having as their object the lessening, removal or prevention of the cause and effects of poverty, child neglect or dependence on public assistance."[31] Under the CHST the only condition affecting social assistance is that residence cannot be a condition of benefit. This opens the way to provinces having workfare or similar conditions of eligibility and to a much greater variation in assistance terms and benefit amounts.

Benefit levels from social assistance vary by province (Table 22). Gathering accurate comparative information on benefit levels between provinces is difficult because of major variations in categories within each plan and substantial administrative discretion in meeting beneficiary needs. However, it would appear that when the Child Tax Benefit is added, benefit levels have varied from a low of 50 per cent to a high of 80 per cent of poverty lines. The 80 per cent achieved by Ontario during Bob Rae's NDP government was a high point that has not been sustained. Among the first acts of Mike Harris's new Conservative government in 1995 was to reduce rates by 21.6 per cent, bringing them down to the figures typical of the other provinces. This supports the view that differentials in levels of payment by province are a product primarily of political choice rather than difference of living costs or ability to pay.

TABLE 22: *Minimum Social Security Payments and Poverty Lines, 1973, 1985, and 1993*

Province	1973			1985			1993		
	Amount ($)	Poverty Line ($)	%	Amount ($)	Poverty Line ($)	%	Amount ($)	Poverty Line ($)	%
B.C.	3,840	5,740	66.8	8,561	14,750	58.0	13,345	20,945	64.0
Alberta	3,736	5,740	65.0	9,560	14,750	66.0	11,281	20,945	54.0
Sask.	3,696	5,740	64.3	9,504	14,750	64.6	12,093	18,398	66.0
Man.	3,744	5,740	65.2	8,025	14,750	60.5	11,386	20,945	54.0
Ontario	3,896	5,740	67.8	9,949	14,750	67.4	16,790	20,945	80.0
Quebec	3,242	5,740	56.4	8,801	14,750	59.6	12,607	20,945	60.0
N.B.	3,260	5,740	56.8	7,611	14,750	51.6	10,150	18,398	55.0
N.S.	3,192	5,740	55.6	8,774	14,750	59.4	12,080	18,398	66.0
P.E.I.	3,153	5,740	53.2	9,439	14,750	63.9	12,773	17,973	71.0
Nfld.	2,880	5,740	50.1	9,239	14,750	62.6	12,986	18,398	71.0

SOURCES: Poverty lines: Senate Committee Report, adjusted for inflation to 1973 and updated in 1985; National Council of Welfare, 1993. Social assistance rates for 1973 from "Working Paper on Social Security," 1973; rates for 1984 from collected data; rates for 1993 from National Council of Welfare. Minimum social security payments consist of social assistance rates, plus Family Allowances, plus child tax credit or basic Child Tax Benefit. Poverty lines and rates for 1973 and 1993 are for a three-person unit; poverty lines and rates for 1985 are for a two-person unit.

Social assistance programs provide higher benefits for individuals who are considered unemployable. However, these benefits are limited to the individual affected and the amounts paid for other members of the household are calculated using the basic rates. For some groups of recipients it has also become more difficult to be considered unemployable. In particular, women with children at home have been increasingly defined as employable rather than unemployable,[32] reducing the benefits they receive and exerting pressure on them to join the labour force.

Social assistance programs often offer supplementary health benefits for recipients who are considered unemployable or who are in receipt of benefits for periods longer than a year. For the longer-term recipient there are also discretionary grants for such items as appliance replacement costs, school supplies, and unusual hardships. These supplementary benefits serve to ease the situation of those who have to use social assistance for long periods. On the other hand, they increase the contact with the social assistance system and tend to establish a dependent relationship on it.

Benefits from social assistance cannot usually be accumulated with any other form of income. If, for example, a beneficiary has a small disability pension, its value is simply deducted from the amount of social assistance for which the person is eligible. In addition, there are strict limits to the assets a person may have while obtaining social assistance. Employment income, too, is sharply limited, usually by a fixed amount which can be as low as $100. Beyond that amount social assistance income is reduced at rates that can be as high as 100 per cent and are never less than 50 per cent. The result is an income disincentive to leave social assistance for employment and an incentive to conceal income by working in the "hidden" economy. The disincentive to work along with the loss of supplementary benefits that follows taking work constitute what is known as "the welfare wall." In time, the low-level security behind the wall can come to be preferred to the uncertainties of the labour market.

Coverage of social assistance is broad but discretionary. It is broad in that there are no exclusions from coverage in the way that social insurance programs exclude persons who do not satisfy defined criteria. This leads to social assistance programs supporting all those persons whose need is not met by other income security programs (persons unemployed for more than one year, persons disabled but not severely disabled, elderly persons who are not yet sixty-five, etc.). Coverage is discretionary because no person is assured a right to a specific benefit level. Instead, his or her circumstances are examined and assessed by the administering agency, which then makes a judgement as to whether "need" exists. Subject to limited rights of appeal (which to this point have been guaranteed by the CAP but are not required under the CHST) the agency's judgement is final. This power is used to enforce a variety of types of dependency (e.g., on a separated or divorced spouse); to require specific types of training; and to require the beneficiary to take any available low-paid or unattractive work.

The stigma that accompanies receipt of social assistance is severe. The transfer is not concealed by universality, insurance, or compensation. Surveys of public opinion indicate uniformly negative attitudes toward social assistance recipients, often in the form of the "welfare bum" stereotype. The effects on recipients are seen in their adoption of alienated attitudes and lifestyles. For most, these take the form of shame, concealment, or chronic depression. For some, they take the form of petty crime and vulnerability to exploitation (prostitution, shoplifting, delinquency).

Social assistance programming is a *bête noire* to the advocates of a fairer and more just redistributive system because it visibly exhibits the failure to obtain the ideals of social welfare. Nevertheless, social assistance programming has proved very durable. Its durability is a product of its flexibility and of the lack of coverage by other programs for very common types of risk. The government of Canada recognized these problems in 1970:

. . . social assistance will probably remain the least acceptable type of income security payment. Because of this, income security policy should try to minimize the extent to which social assistance is used. Through the development of the guaranteed income, and social insurance programs, reliance on social assistance will be gradually reduced.[33]

This goal has never been fulfilled. As long-term unemployment has increased so has the number of Canadians who have no other choice but to use this last line of defence against lost income. In 1974 benefits were being received by approximately 1.2 million Canadians monthly; by 1985 approximately 1.9 million were in receipt; and by 1993 benefits were being provided to 2.4 million.

2. *Enforced dependency programs.* Enforced dependency income security programs operate in close relationship to the social assistance program. A person is considered not to be "in need" if he or she has an enforceable dependency. Such programming affects two principal groups, youth and women with dependent children.

Youth, meaning persons between fourteen and eighteen years of age, can be held ineligible for social assistance on the grounds that their parents can, or should, support them; in practice, a considerable degree of administrative discretion is exercised. Refusing benefits, of course, does not immediately lead to the young person living with his or her parents. Instead, young people may subsist, for example, as homeless street people by panhandling, shoplifting, or prostitution.

Women with dependent children can usually assert a claim against the children's father, on the basis of either legal status (e.g., Wives and Children's Maintenance Act) or presumed natural paternity (e.g., various acts with respect to putative fathers). In either case, the woman has to lay a charge in Family Court. The charge is then pursued by a variety of collection agencies. Collection procedures have been gradually improved through reciprocal, interprovincial enforcement procedures and through automatic deduction-at-source policies. Nevertheless, this part of the income security system continues to have major problems, which include:

- Amounts of court-ordered support payments are often inadequate, even to public assistance levels. As the woman is supported in part by public assistance, the payment reduces the payment to her from public assistance. The woman gains nothing for her effort in pursuing collection.
- Payments are only collectable where the man is in stable employment. Hence, stability is penalized and moving from job to job encouraged.

3. *Food banks, shelters, and soup kitchens.* The food banks occupy a distinct symbolic position in the income redistribution system as they developed as part of the response to the recession of the early 1980s and the first moves to downsize government. To conservatives they confirm the hypothesis that voluntarism is alive and can fill gaps in the welfare system; but to most social welfare advocates they are symbolic of the failure of the state to provide adequate income security policies. The primary users of the food banks are people on social assistance and Unemployment Insurance.[34]

The shelters and soup kitchens operated by voluntary charitable and religious organizations are the last line of the redistributive system. Although they originated outside the government system, most now contract their services to the provincial social assistance programs. These resources provide some respite for the increasing numbers of homeless people who do not qualify for social assistance as they lack an accepted identification document and/or a permanent address.

The Poor: Proposals

Proposals for the social assistance system are dominated by two issues, poverty and employment. A major problem for any proposal for social assistance reform is the relationship to programs in the first tier of the redistributive system, as change in these programs can have a direct affect on social assistance recipients and programs. Major proposals include the following.

(1) Raise benefit levels to poverty lines. The National Council of Welfare provides an annual estimate of the size of the "poverty gap." The poverty gap is the total amount of money necessary to bring all individuals and families below the poverty line to the poverty line. The estimate is a low one as First Nations, on reserve, are not included in the data from which the estimate is developed. The poverty gap in 1993 was $14.5 billion.[35]

(2) Establish a separate program for children in welfare families. This is the same proposal that was made for families and children. If such a program is not implemented at a national level then it could be implemented at a provincial level. Quebec made a beginning with the Parental Wage Assistance (PWA) program in 1988. The PWA consists of a supplement to employment income, the reimbursement of 55 per cent of day-care expenses, and a housing allowance, scaled to family size. The objective is to ensure that children are supported, without creating a situation in which their parents are better off on social assistance than at work. A similar proposal has been made for Ontario.[36]

(3) Introduce "workfare." Workfare is a coercive approach to the welfare wall issue. The theoretical case for and against workfare has already been discussed in Chapter 2. Despite the major reservations about workfare, several provinces are experimenting with programs that come close to it. With the establishment of the CHST, the barrier provided by the CAP prohibition to American-style workfare programs has been removed. It may not be long before social assistance recipients are collecting garbage along provincial highways as a condition of assistance.

Social Housing

Social housing occupies an anomalous position in relationship to all other redistributive programs. Program costs are substantial, in excess of $4 billion, but are committed to a fixed investment in buildings rather than to providing payments directly to people. Social housing became a major thrust of federal housing policy following the 1964 National Housing Act amendments. However, the program was operated under federal-provincial agreements that were conceived and managed in response to changes in housing conditions and costs, including concerns with affordability, housing quality, and housing management. Politics also played a significant role as housing projects served a symbolic role, providing visible evidence of government concern and action. The result is a varied group of projects linked to programs that seemed relevant in their time but that now seem less so. Fallis,[37] on whom I have drawn in this section, provides an overview of the origins and use of social housing (Table 23). In this housing stock only rent geared to income (RGI) units are relevant to the redistributive objectives of social policy. Tenants in these units typically pay 25-30 per cent of their income for rent. Other occupants in the same buildings pay rents or co-operative charges determined by market conditions or by building construction, mortgage, and operating costs.

TABLE 23: *Social Housing Stock, Canada, 1993*

Program	No. of units	RGI units	Ownership
Limited Dividend	40,000	none	private
Public Housing	206,000	all	public
Non-profit/co-op (pre-1978)	81,000	minority	non-profit and co-operatives
Non-profit/co-op (1978-85)	143,000	minority	public, non-profit, and co-operatives
Non-profit/co-op (post-1985)	65,000	majority	public, non-profit, and co-operatives

SOURCE: George Fallis, "The Social Policy Challenge and Social Housing," *Home Remedies: Rethinking Canadian Housing Policies* (Toronto: C.D. Howe Institute, 1995), p. 29.

Social housing forms about 6.5 per cent of all accommodation and 16.3 per cent of rental housing. RGI social housing forms about half of the total. The other half is occupied by modest- and upper-income earners, of whom half are seniors. Fallis comments:

> From a social policy perspective, I believe the most damning criticism of social housing is that about half of social housing units are occupied by middle- and upper-income households. These households most certainly would be living in decent housing accommodation without any assistance. In many cases the level of assistance is shallow; however, in other cases, . . . the level of assistance is large. . . . There are two answers. The first is that assistance to middle-income people is necessary to achieve income mix in social housing buildings. . . . The second is that the long term goal was to assist in providing housing for all modest-income households.[38]

Since 1994 no additional federally funded units have been added to the social housing stock. In the context of the deficit, construction of new RGI units, which at best only reaches a few of the people who in financial terms are eligible for assistance, is too costly. Furthermore, the broader objective of providing social housing on the scale needed to serve moderate-income households cannot be considered at all. This leaves social housing in the position of being an historically developed (and aging) fixed asset.

Social Housing: Proposals

The principal proposal being made about the future of social housing is that policy needs to be fully incorporated into social welfare policy and not continue as a separate policy field of its own.[39] In the short run, options for social housing that make better use of the stock are difficult to achieve because of the existing mix of tenancies, units, and finances. However, opportunities will occur as buildings age and require redevelopment, as mortgages mature and the costs of repayment decrease, and as tenancies and social conditions change. On the demand side are the problems of single-parent households and homelessness, which are major targets for any resources that become available.

Conclusion

It is difficult to come to any conclusion other than that the entire redistributive system is in severe difficulty. This is not to say that it is about to disappear. The $120 billion being redistributed is an enormous resource, equivalent to 20 per cent of GDP, and although some cuts are coming at the federal level, through the CHST, at this time they are less than 5 per cent of the total and will be shared with health and post-secondary education.

Seniors' programs are not in a sustainable form. The reasons for the growth of expenditures in this group are primarily demographic and long term. The demographic trends that are pressuring expenditures in the 1990s will not be completed until the third decade of the twenty-first century. As a result, the public programs that provide for retirement income have to be re-examined and reformulated. These include the RRSP/RPP programs, which, from a social justice perspective, are a misallocation of public resources. Thus, the issue for public policy is also one of redirecting existing resources to priority objectives.

The programs for the employed are caught in dilemmas that have arisen out of the changed relationship to the global economy and have also resulted from design problems of their own that have become more and more apparent with the passage of time. There is no reason to think that these changes will do anything but continue. As a result, the programs we have, particularly Unemployment Insurance, have to be rethought. They may even be abandoned altogether and integrated into the general social assistance program for the poor.

Programming for children and families remains a major hole in Canada's redistributive system, and that hole is growing larger as more children and mother-led families become poor. On the other hand, providing support to children and their families through an expanded redistribution system would solve many problems, not only for the women and children concerned but also for the community as a whole. An expanded program would support children and young people in preparation for their future roles in the economy and community; it would give substance to the commitment to combat childhood poverty; it would support single-mother families; it would provide for the support of working parents by reducing the size of the "welfare wall"; and it would contribute to the redesign of all other redistribution programs by dealing with childhood poverty. The basis for a national program already exists in the Child Tax Benefit. Expanding and redesigning the benefit to an adequate level of payment would not be cheap. It would require between $10-15 billion more to bring Child Tax Benefits to the poverty level. However, some of these funds could come from savings in other programs that would not have to be designed with families and children's needs in mind. In addition, once established, demographics would work for this program as the number of children is falling both in absolute numbers and as a proportion of the whole population.

The provincial social assistance systems remain the final definition of Canada's commitment to welfare. The replacement of the CAP by the CHST means there will be a much lower federal presence in decisions about the level of poverty and the terms of its relief. The provincial record has been very uneven, but, given the changes that have been made, advocates of adequate social assistance programs have no option now but to concentrate their attention and efforts on the provinces.

Notes

1. The terminology of institutional and residual forms of welfare was introduced in Chapter 1. It is based on the work of Wilensky and Lebeaux, *Industrial Society and Social Welfare* (New York: Free Press, 1965).
2. Ken Battle and Sherri Torjman, *Opening the Books on Social Spending* (Ottawa: Caledon Institute, 1993), p. 15.
3. The tax payable allows for the pension income deduction of $1,000, the age amount of $3,482, and the personal exemption of $6,456.
4. Thomas. J Courchene, *Social Canada in the Millennium* (Toronto: C.D. Howe Institute, 1994), pp. 69-70.
5. *Ibid.*, pp. 77ff.
6. Canadian Council on Social Development, *Social Policy Beyond the Budget* (Ottawa, 1995), p. 6; Courchene, *Social Canada*, p. 78.
7. Canadian Welfare Council, *Unemployment Insurance in the '70's* (Ottawa: Queen's Printer, 1970).
8. Miles Corak, "UI Work Disincentives and the Canadian Labor Market," in John Richards and William Watson, eds., *Unemployment Insurance: How To Make It Work* (Toronto: C.D. Howe Institute, 1994), p. 148.
9. Department of Manpower and Immigration, Brief to the Senate Committee on Poverty, 1968, First Session, No. 10, p. 372.
10. André Reynauld, "Income Distribution: Facts and Policies," speech to The Empire Club, Toronto, February 1, 1973.
11. Courchene, *Social Canada*, pp. 162-63.
12. Fred Lazar, "UI as a Redistributive Scheme and Financial Stabilizer," in John Richards and William Watson, eds., *Unemployment Insurance: How To Make It Work*, (Toronto: C.D. Howe Institute, 1994), p. 82.
13. Human Resources Development Canada, *Improving Social Security in Canada* (Ottawa: Ministry of Supply and Services, 1994), pp. 45-46.
14. Christopher Green, "What Should We Do with the UI System," in Richards and Watson, eds., *Unemployment Insurance*, p. 15.
15. Courchene, *Social Canada*, p. 278.
16. Canada, *Commission of Inquiry on Unemployment Insurance* (Ottawa: Ministry of Supply and Services, 1986), cited *ibid.*, p. 278.
17. *Ibid.*, p. 66.
18. David Ross, "Social policy reviews," *Perception*, 18, 3-4 (Ottawa: Canadian Council on Social

Development, 1995), p. 6; National Council of Welfare, *A Blueprint for Social Security Reform* (Ottawa, 1994), p. 49.

19. Courchene, *Social Canada*, pp. 32-34, 65, 311.

20. Council of Canadians with Disabilities, "Submission to the Standing Committee on Human Resource Development," Ottawa, March 9, 1994, as excerpted in *Canadian Review on Social Policy*, 34, p. 74.

21. William Watson, *Chronic Stress: Worker's Compensation in the 1990s* (Toronto: C.D. Howe Institute, 1995), p. 21.

22. Bank of Canada, press release, August 7, 1995.

23. There are also additional amounts of $75/year for the third and subsequent children and $213/year for children under seven for whom no child-care expense is claimed.

24. Shelley Phipps, "Taking Care of Our Children," *Family Matters* (Toronto: C.D. Howe Institute, 1995), pp. 203-11. In the U.K. family allowances account for 20 per cent of the income of poor families and in Sweden they account for 15 per cent, as compared to Canada at 4 per cent.

25. *Hansard*, House of Commons Resolution, 24 November 1989.

26. Ken Battle and Leon Muszynski, *One Way to Fight Child Poverty* (Ottawa: Caledon Institute, 1995).

27. W.G. Maynes "Child Poverty in Canada: Challenges for Educational Policy Makers," *Canadian Review of Social Policy*, 32 (1993).

28. Nancy Naylor, "A National Child Benefit Program," in Richards and Watson, eds., *Family Matters*, p. 227; Courchene, *Social Canada*, p. 324.

29. Sherri Torjman and Ken Battle, "Child Benefit Primer: A Response to the Government Proposals," *Canadian Review of Social Policy*, 29-30 (1992).

30. See Dennis Guest, *The Emergence of Social Security in Canada* (Vancouver: UBC Press, 1988), pp. 155-59, for an account of the evolution of the CAP.

31. Canada, *Canada Assistance Plan* (Ottawa: Queen's Printer, 1966), Sec. 2(m).

32. Andrew Armitage, Marilyn Callahan, Michael Prince, and Brian Wharf, "Workfare in British Columbia," *Canadian Review of Social Policy*, 26 (November, 1990).

33. Canada, *Income Security for Canadians* (Ottawa: Queen's Printer, 1970), p. 28.

34. For a fuller discussion of the role of food banks, see G. Riches, "Feeding Canada's Poor," in J. Ismael, ed., *The Canadian Welfare State* (Edmonton: University of Alberta Press, 1987); G. Riches, *Food Banks and the Welfare Crisis* (Ottawa: Canadian Council on Social Development, 1986).

35. National Council of Welfare, *A Blueprint for Social Security Reform*, p. 46.

36. Courchene, *Social Canada*, pp. 248ff.

37. George Fallis, "The Social Policy Challenge and Social Housing," in Fallis *et al.*, *Home Remedies: Rethinking Canadian Housing Policies* (Toronto: C.D. Howe Institute, 1995), pp. 1-50.

38. *Ibid.*, p. 37.

39. *Ibid.*, p. 38.

Chapter 5

COMMUNITY

Social welfare has a strong and continuing base in the expectations we have of our community. After redistribution, the concept of community is the second major component of social welfare. The importance of this concept is linked to the values of concern for the individual, diversity, faith in democracy, and community itself.

Boulding, writing in 1967, saw that part of the distinctive meaning of social policy is found in its concern for the integrity of life.

> If there is one common thread that unites all aspects of social policy and distinguishes it from merely economic policy, it is the thread of what has elsewhere been called the "integrative system." . . . The institutions with which social policy is especially concerned, such as the school, family, church, or, at the other end, the public assistance office, court, prison, or criminal gang all reflect degrees of integration and community. By and large, it is an objective of social policy to build the identity of a person around some community with which he or she is associated.[1]

The Roehr Institute indicated the continued commitment to the importance of community in its commentary on the concept of "well-being" in 1993.

> Individuals cannot obtain well-being by themselves. They do so in the context of the communities they belong to – geographic communities, as well as communities defined by common interest, language, culture, gender and other characteristics. Through institutions of education, government, media and culture, communities can transmit values and traditions to their members. They provide the language and ideas that people use to express what they want (Kymlicka, 1989) and the resources people need to participate and be included in society.[2]

The function of community in social welfare is to mitigate the anomie and alienation that result from the materialism of urban, capitalist society.

Urbanization, Capitalism, and Community

Population movements in Canada during the twentieth century have been dominated by migrations toward central Canada and toward the West, by a rural-to-urban migration, and by a continuing international migration to Canada's urban centres. First Nations, too, have increasingly participated in the rural-to-urban migration. The combination of these trends has made urban growth the dominant reality throughout Canada, but with the pace of growth varying between different metropolitan areas. The urban growth process is the product of Canada's economic development, initially as an exporter of commodities, then as a manufacturer, and now as a series of service centres. The by-products of this growth have been seen in the identification of a common set of problems, including poverty, housing, congestion, environmental decay, and social unrest.[3] Table 24 indicates the growth of selected Canadian cities.

TABLE 24: *Population and Percentage change in Population for Selected Metropolitan Areas, Canada 1941-1991 (population in thousands)*

	1941	1951	1961	1971	1981	1991
Halifax	99	134	183	222	277	321
Montreal	1,216	1,504	2,156	2,743	2,828	3,127
Toronto	1,002	1,264	1,942	2,628	2,998	3,893
Winnipeg	301	357	476	540	584	652
Calgary	112	156	290	403	592	754
Vancouver	394	562	790	1,028	1,268	1,602

Per Cent Change in Population Since Last Census						
Halifax	25.5	35.8	37.3	21.3	24.7	15.9
Montreal	12.1	23.6	43.3	27.2	3.1	10.5
Toronto	11.2	26.2	53.6	35.3	14.1	30.0
Winnipeg	2.4	18.1	33.4	13.5	8.1	11.6
Calgary	8.1	39.7	85.8	38.9	46.9	26.6
Vancouver	16.5	42.7	40.6	30.1	23.3	26.3

SOURCE: Leroy O. Stone, *Urban Development in Canada* (Ottawa: Dominion Bureau of Statistics, 1967), p. 278; *Census of Canada*, 1981, 1991.

The identification of these features of urban life as problems is testimony to the lack of congruence between the realities of urban living and the ideals that are held. Thus the reality of urban living is that the majority of contact between people is impersonal, either random in that strangers pass one another in a crowd or functional as where people meet at work. Neither form of contact is in accord with the ideal that people should know and understand each other. The reality of bringing large numbers of people together is that their competition for available space will result in the poverty of some and the gain of others. The reality of their diverse backgrounds and expectations is a disruption of their familiar patterns. The reality of asking that their young people learn to live in this new environment is conflict between groups and between generations.

Capitalism offers nothing that mitigates these tensions. Indeed, the emphasis on personal gain and materialism exacerbates them. All the great analysts of capitalism have been pessimistic about the social order it creates. Adam Smith foresaw the "moral decay" of the working class; Marx found optimism, not in capitalism, but in the working class liberating itself from capitalism; Keynes saw that capitalism could acquiesce to a world of injustice, inequalities, and unemployment, from which he saw it being rescued by government; and Schumpeter argued that the culture of capitalism corroded values as a by-product of the continuing process of creating "perennial gales of creative destruction."[4]

Community is the antidote to these pessimistic conclusions, for it is through community that a human response to social problems is conceived, organized, and provided. The American sociologist C.W. Mills saw the connection between "private troubles" and "public issues" occurring in the following way:

> Troubles occur within the character of the individual and within the range of his immediate relations with others: they have to do with the self and with those limited areas of social life of which he is directly and personally aware. . . . A trouble is a private matter: values cherished by an individual are felt by him to be threatened.
>
> Issues have to do with matters that transcend these local environments of the individual and the range of his inner life. They have to do with the organization of many such milieux into the institutions of an historical society as a whole. . . . An issue is a public matter: some value cherished by publics is felt to be threatened.[5]

Wharf, in his commentary on case studies of social movements and social change in Canada, recognizes the role of community in providing "a middle range location for aggregating personal troubles" and hence transforming personal troubles into public issues. The case studies that Wharf discusses – the women's movement, the First Nations movement, and the labour movement – show how this community dynamic works.[6]

Diversity

The conceptions of community that initially guided the development of the welfare ideal were developed in response to industrialism and urbanization. They had a pastoral, bucolic emphasis that suggested the welfare function was trying to fill a rural, small town void. Mills wrote:

> In approaching the notion of adjustment, one may analyze the specific illustrations of maladjustment that are given and from these instances infer a type of person who in this literature is evaluated as "adjusted." The ideally adjusted man of the social pathologists is "socialized." This term seems to operate ethically as the opposite of "selfish"; it implies that the adjusted man conforms to middle-class morality and motives and "participates" in the gradual progress of respectable institutions. If he is not a "joiner," he certainly gets around and into many community organizations. If he is socialized, the individual thinks

of others and is kindly towards them. He does not brood or mope about but is somewhat extrovert, eagerly participating in his community's institutions. His mother and father were not divorced, nor was his home ever broken. He is "successful" – at least in a modest way – since he is ambitious; but he does not speculate about matters too far beyond his means, lest he become a "fantasy thinker," and the little men don't scramble after the big money. The less abstract the traits and fulfilled "needs" of the "adjusted man" are, the more they gravitate toward the norm of independent middle-class persons verbally living out protestant ideals in the small towns of America.[7]

This 1941 conception was silent on women, ethnic origin, race, and ability, let alone sexual orientation. It allowed no place for diversity. It reflected a society in which dominance by patriarchy, European ethnic origins, able-bodied white people, protestantism, and heterosexuality was assumed. This once dominant view of the community ideal had a pervasive influence when the community institutions of the social welfare state were then in their formative period. The child welfare field provides many examples. McIntyre notes that:

> . . . women's private mothering, maintenance and caring for their own family members were transferred, through moral reform and rescue work, to "mothering on a national scale" (Ursel, 1992: 71) that included public caring for the poor, disadvantaged and the neglected. Protection of the family, however, included reproduction, the promotion of motherhood, and the defence of a patriarchal sexual code.[8]

The imposition of cultural and racial dominance was particularly severe on First Nations communities throughout Canada. The goals of Canadian Indian policy were, and some would say still are, "protection, civilization and assimilation."[9] For more than 100 years, first through the use of residential schools, then through the provincial child welfare systems, the mission was to remake the next generation of First Nations people in the image of the European settlers.[10]

The translation of these rural, patriarchal, racist, and culturally dominant expressions of the community "ideal" into public policy was directed toward the goal of integration – the establishment of one social community in which, nominally, differences would play no part in public policy but which was actually characterized by a suppression of differences. In Canada, Quebec was always regarded as an exception, but even in regard to Quebec there has been a continual and unsatisfying struggle to distinguish those matters in which Quebec should have its own institutions and policies and those in which it has to accept the institutions and policies of federal Canada. The 1995 referendum campaign provided many examples, with both Quebec and the federal government advancing competing claims to be in the better position to provide social programs.

The integration view of the role of community in social welfare policy seems out of place and time in the Canada of the 1990s, in which diversity is increasingly recognized and applauded. The social movements, as Wharf indicates,[11] are having, and have had, a major influence on our understanding of the community "ideal" and on its translation into social policy. Thus, the conception of community now most widely held is a *diverse* or "plural" one, in which the existence of many communities is recognized and in which the dominance of no single community ideal over others is accepted. Furthermore, the communities are seen in a dynamic relationship to each other, both producing changes in the whole and protecting those institutions and activities that are critical to their own presence and growth. First Nations are therefore acting as a collective community to obtain recognition of themselves as Aboriginal peoples with rights based in their presence on the land at the time of European settlement. Among those rights is the right to self-government, which also serves to strengthen and perpetuate a continued Aboriginal presence as a separate series of independent societies within Canada. The repatriation of the Canadian constitution and the proclamation of the Charter of Rights and Freedoms in 1982 confirmed the importance of the language rights, personal rights, and Aboriginal rights that are the foundations for recognizing diversity and establishing pluralism.

Despite these changes in the community ideal, which are being introduced gradually into social welfare policy, one should not underestimate the continued ideological and institutional presence and influence of earlier forms of the concept of the community.

Community Functions of Social Welfare

Warren provides a useful analysis of community functions that distinguishes the different ways in which the concept of community influences social welfare. The principal community functions are: production, distribution, consumption; socialization; social control; mutual support; and social participation.[12]

Production, Distribution, and Consumption

The economic functions of community used to be thought of as purely marketplace transactions outside the scope of social welfare. This was never entirely the case, In First Nations communities, for example, the economic functions of community were always integrated with the social functions. Justa Monk of the Carrier-Sekani people describes his life as a boy in the 1950s in British Columbia.

> Until the road was built the people of Portage and Tachie lived in almost complete isolation. Our survival depended on boats, sleighs, horses, fish nets, traps, guns and the medicine we found in the forest. If we had to make it to the outside world, my people knew that the trip would be long and that there would be much hardship and danger too.[13]

At the time, however, such a life was seen as primitive by the Canadian government and social welfare was seen as having a role, through the residential schools, of providing Indian youth with a way of leaving the reserve and integrating into the general economy.

In the 1990s, when the general economy has come to mean the global economy there is a growing realization that this economy may never provide the opportunities for work that a community needs. Nozick makes the case for "sustainable community development" in the following manner:

> I recently heard an economics professor being interviewed on TV say that we must accept the disappearance of "uneconomic communities" as a fact of modern life. Fishing villages, rural towns, are a thing of the past. . . . Community is not seen as having any inherent value worth preserving apart from economics. Furthermore there is no recognition that people have resources and means within their communities and regions to meet many or most of their needs. . . .
>
> What is needed is an approach which integrates economic, ecological, political, and cultural development as part of a strategy which has the revitalizing and reclaiming of community as its primary aim. I call this "sustainable community development". The goal is to: a) build communities that are more self supporting and that can sustain and regenerate themselves through economic self-reliance, community control and environmentally sound development; and b) build communities that will be worth preserving because they are grounded in the life experiences of people who live in them, and in the natural history of specific regions.[14]

Community is thus seen as a means through which people can organize their collective affairs to regain control of their lives from the capitalist global economy. Community economic development works within the market economy. It utilizes all the processes of capitalism except that the endeavours are owned by the community and are in a developmental and non-exploitative relationship to the community.

Socialization

Socialization has always been seen as a major community function and social welfare services help "individuals, through learning, [to] acquire the knowledge, values and behaviour patterns of their society and learn behaviour appropriate to their social roles."[15] This sphere of social welfare activity is not only a dominant focus of much work with children but is present in such fields of practice with adults as home support and homemaker services and counselling.

The original view of how these socialization functions were performed began with consideration of the role of such primary institutions as the family and the church and the ways they have traditionally provided the means for individuals to learn mutually acceptable patterns of behaviour. This view now requires substantial modification to recognize: (1) the role of culture and ethnicity in providing a variety of models of socialization, all of which need to be accorded an equal degree of legitimacy in our social policies; and (2) the role of social groups in providing alternate paths to adulthood that have often not been recognized by traditional systems. Examples are provided by gay and lesbian culture and by feminist models of social relationships.

Beyond these community institutions are the roles being played by such established formal organizations as schools, children's treatment institutions, and alcohol and drug abuse services. Here, too, one sees the influence of the social movements in establishing new organizations to provide, for example, services for the victims of rape and sexual assault, family violence services, transition houses, and AIDS prevention and counselling services. The First Nations movement offers support to persons through band and tribal council offices, friendship centres, and a growing network of specialized social agencies. The recent immigrant and refugee communities are served by a network of community and religious agencies that have the objective of assisting immigrants and refugees with the processes of arrival, establishing citizenship, and settlement.

Social welfare organizations performing these functions can be further distinguished by how they act as agents of socialization. The terminology of prevention developed by Kahn[16] assists in such a classification.

Primary prevention. At the primary preventative end of the continuum are the declared educational services, for example, family life education, sex education, drug information, language training, anti-racist workshops, and AIDS prevention. These services are distributed broadly to the community as a whole and the case is increasingly made that they should be established parts of the socialization all young people receive through their inclusion in the curricula of school systems.

Secondary prevention. At the secondary level of prevention are social utility services, such as day-care and homemaker services; recreational services such as those provided by Boys Clubs, which are intended to meet the needs of potential problem populations; mental health counselling services; services to the parents of handicapped children; support and advice to victims of sexual abuse; advocacy in dealing with immigration authorities; and advice, guidance, and support with substance abuse problems. The distinguishing feature of this secondary level of socialization services is that individuals or families seek the services on their own initiative.

The services at the primary and secondary levels of prevention may be provided for geographic communities by public or private agencies or may be provided by ethnic or interest group communities for their members. These changes cumulate in the trend toward the recognition of the diverse, plural nature of the community.

Tertiary prevention. Beyond these primary and secondary socialization services are the tertiary services where the law is used to make the receipt of service mandatory on specific populations, e.g., child protection services, correctional services, and the committal aspects of mental illness services. However, with the addition of these mandatory powers to force services on people, it would appear that the emphasis on social control is sharply increased. Thus, although these services also perform socialization functions, they are discussed under the heading of social control.

Social Control

Important social control functions are performed by social welfare, social control being defined as the "process through which a group influences the behaviour of its members towards conformity with its norms."[17] The means used to obtain social control may be classified with respect to the type of power they use: physical, material, or symbolic.

The use of a gun, a whip or a lock is physical since it affects the body; the threat to use physical sanctions is viewed as physical because the effect on the subject is similar in kind, if not . . . in intensity, to the actual use. Control based on application of physical means is ascribed as *coercive* power.

Material rewards consist of goods and services. The granting of symbols (e.g., money) which allow one to acquire goods and services is classified as material because the effect on the recipient is similar to that of material means. The use of material means for control purposes constitutes *utilitarian* power.

Pure symbols are those whose use does not constitute a physical threat or a claim on material rewards. They include normative symbols, those of prestige and esteem; and social symbols, those of love and acceptance. . . . The use of symbols for control purposes is referred to as *normative* or *social* power.[18]

Coercion. The most coercive social control agencies, the military and the police, are generally regarded as outside the orbit of social welfare (although some aspects of police work, for example, youth work, are similar in form and intent to the practice of social agencies). Throughout its history, however, social welfare has been associated with various total institutions – residential schools, jails, mental hospitals, work houses, and the like – that are testimony to the coercive social control functions of social welfare. In addition, social welfare has been the principal agent of social control dealing with relationships within the family, including the authority to remove children from their parents.

There is a high degree of ambivalence with respect to the use of coercive power for social welfare purposes. The record of the use of coercive power for social policy purposes shows that it is open to tremendous abuse. Nazi Germany referred to its policies of genocide toward Jewish people, gypsies, the mentally handicapped, and homosexuals as being social policies. Canada and other Western countries engaged in the sexual sterilization of handicapped people. Canada used the residential school system for 100 years in an attempt to eradicate First Nations culture by preventing the transmission of language and traditions between generations. More recently, children have been taken from First Nations communities and then placed for adoption without consent, often in the United States, as a way of changing the course of their lives.[19] Until 1975 gay men could be harassed and prosecuted because of their sexual orientation. The aftermath of these examples of the use of coercive power for social control purposes continues to affect all these populations in the form of increased rates of imprisonment, mental ill health, alcoholism, suicide, sexual abuse, and family violence. These effects linger long after the original policy and its purposes have been abandoned.

On the other hand, the right of individuals to protection from their fellows cannot be denied, nor can social welfare disassociate itself from the effects of social control measures on the populations singled out for sanctions. The sensitivity to authority that comes from perspectives other than the dominant patriarchal one increases the ambivalence with which the use of coercive authority is regarded.

Callahan develops a feminist view of the situation of women who have had their children apprehended because of neglect and concludes:

In any model, the so-called crime of neglect should simply disappear from the child welfare statutes. Instead, child welfare statutes could be reframed to define the caring services to be provided. . . . If chronic neglect is primarily a matter of poverty, frequently the poverty of disadvantaged women, then it should be dealt with as a resource issue rather than as a personal, individual problem. If situational neglect occurs, such as the abandonment of children, then such problems can be dealt with by providing care and resources to the children.[20]

Similarly the report by the Aboriginal panel that reviewed child welfare legislation in British Columbia decided to recommend community healing rather than imprisonment for those community members who committed sexual abuse.[21]

Utilitarian power. The use of utilitarian power for social control purposes also produces some ambivalence, but it is much more acceptable than coercive power. In the examples given above of recommended changes of practice from feminist and First Nations perspectives, services are substituted for coercion. Usually there is some negotiation with clients around such services and hence influence is exercised through the process of negotiating the terms and conditions under which support is given. A similar social control effect occurs in the behaviour of social agencies dealing with problems of substance abuse. For example, the use of medication programs, e.g., methadone treatment, places such agencies in the situation of seeking to obtain social control over people seeking services by utilitarian means. In children's institutions, mental health facilities, homes for the elderly, and other institutional settings rewards and sanctions often take the form of giving or withholding incidental items, privileges, and the like.

The institutions that use utilitarian power for social control are usually regarded as social welfare institutions and social workers frequently comprise a key component in their staff.

Normative power. Normative or social power would appear to be the most acceptable form of power to social welfare enterprises. The most pervasive use of such power is found in the way social welfare enterprises ascribe status to their service populations. The symbolic ascriptions used – "on welfare," debtor, addict, neurotic, etc. – all have stigmatizing consequences. Social welfare agencies obtain change in service populations partly by their power to ascribe such statuses and then symbolically to remove them when the process of rehabilitation is complete. This use of normative and social power for social control purposes represents the point at which social control functions blend with socialization functions.

The difference in the degree of acceptability to social welfare values of the three types of power is related to the alienating characteristics of the use of power for social control purposes.

The use of the coercive power is more alienating to those subject to it than is the use of utilitarian power, and the use of utilitarian power is more alienating than the use of normative power. Or, to put it the other way around, normative power tends . . . to generate more commitment than utilitarian, and utilitarian than coercive.[22]

Unfortunately, Canadian society exhibits social tensions and destructive behaviours we do not know how to control fully by normative or utilitarian means. Hence, coercive power remains essential. Nevertheless, the thrust of welfare values is toward the least possible use of coercive power for social control purposes. Part of the case for maintaining a stronger, and more costly, social welfare system in Canada than in the United States is that Canadians want to avoid the pervasive sense of violence and the attendant policing presence that characterize the cities to the south.

Mutual Support

It is to the mutual support function of community that social welfare must appeal for resources. The function is organized at three major levels: charitable gifts, taxation, and self-help. The charitable approach came first and still continues. It depends on an appeal directed at both the feelings of concern and of *noblesse oblige* that, it is hoped, people have for those who are less fortunate. The taxation approach came second and was necessitated by the scale of the community social provisions that were needed and by the advantages of providing services to recipients as social rights based in citizenship rather than as supplicants dependent on charity. The self-help approach was always present but has come increasingly to the fore in the development of new services in the period from the 1970s to the present. The self-help, mutual-aid approach is based in the application of community development principles by oppressed and under-served groups. The social movements of women, First Nations, gays and lesbians, the disabled, the visible minorities, social housing co-operatives, and other such groups are all examples of the power of self-help.

The self-help groups are also an important response to the inherently alienating and anomic nature of the urban community, the capitalist market, and bureaucracy. The major social agencies developed through the tax base have led to bureaucracies that are themselves alienating, thereby contributing to the problems they hoped to combat. The establishment of efficient but impersonal federated fund-raising mechanisms for charitable purposes have had a similar effect on some aspects of charity organization. The development of bureaucracy poses a threat to the mutual support function of social welfare by eroding the sense of common community identity necessary to mutual support. Bureaucracy also depends on hierarchical power relationships, leading to the disempowerment of both line staff and consumers. The self-help groups provide a strong response to all these problems.

Social Participation

Social participation as a systemic function of community receives considerable moral support from the social welfare ideals of diversity and democracy. People *should* exercise a right to be heard and to participate in decisions that affect them.

This thrust in social welfare thinking was endorsed in the American War on Poverty's Office of Economic Opportunity programs under the heading of "maximum feasible participation." A similar ideal was expressed in the social action goals of the Company of Young Canadians. The creation of the National Council of Welfare, with representatives of the poor forming half the Board, was additional evidence of the search for means to allow the participation of consumers in the design and operation of social welfare.

It has long been accepted that social welfare provides an opportunity for community participation to those of philanthropic means and high social status. Similarly, service groups provide a broad path to social participation to those community members willing to act personally for the collective good. There have been many attempts to extend this ethic further so that the consumers of social welfare services can also make a contribution to their own social development and welfare. In some communities strong grassroots organizations have provided consistent means for the least advantaged citizens to make their views known and to participate by serving on agency boards, government councils, and similar participatory structures. These grassroots organizations have been most successful where they have had control of the resources needed to ensure their continued existence. Where they depend on government funding, problems of a political nature have tended to obstruct the achievement of their goals. The following example from the early experiences of the Company of Young Canadians in the 1970s has features that many similar groups have experienced since.

> The desire of the Canadian government to encourage participation at the grassroots is matched by its apprehension about the people who are animating the neighbourhood population. The recent fervour over the Company of Young Canadians reflects this ambivalence, for the basic problem that emerged was not so much the adequacy of the CYC's performance as the uneasiness with which leaders in and out of government responded to the left-wing postures adopted by some of its members.[23]

The group that accepts government grants can find that the same grants become the means through which government control is obtained. As a result, considerable political and community development skill has been necessary to maintain effective and independent participation in policy and management processes.

The following cycle of events illustrates both the problem and the solutions. A self-help, mutual-aid group is formed on a voluntary, unsupported basis. The group would receive advice and support from a government agency and a development grant is provided so that it can rent an office, prepare a newsletter, and pay an organizer and its members' out-of-pocket expenses. The group, and particularly its newly appointed paid organizer, becomes more vocal and visible. They attract local media interest and organize pickets, sit-ins, confrontations, and the like to draw attention to their concerns. The authorities who are the objects of these demonstrations complain through both bureaucratic and political channels. The granting agency comes under considerable pressure to curb the protest group's militancy. The granting agency yields to pressure reluctantly, but conditions are attached to the grant, such as different organizers, co-operation with local authorities, and no disruptive tactics. The social action group is split into a moderate, funded group and a militant, unfunded faction. The subsequent internal quarrelling can destroy community respect and support for the group. On the other hand, the group may learn to negotiate this complex environment. It learns how it can, with the help of allies, hold on to both its sources of support and its militancy. It becomes the focus of a continuing social movement that changes the systems it threatened.

Some identities have proved to be better mandates for successful participation than others. In particular, the more successful organizations of oppressed or disadvantaged people appear to have been built on identities other than "poverty" or "welfare." It may be that these labels are too stigmatizing to be a basis for long-term community action. Thus, immigrants have always organized themselves around their ethnic origins, institutions, churches, and language – not their poverty. Similarly, First Nations are organized around their Aboriginal roots and culture, finding a heritage of pride and independence from which they can assert long-term goals for themselves as people. The feminist community is organized around common experiences of oppression and disadvantage that are part of the life experience of all women. Those who are not in poverty, as a result of the disadvantages intrinsic to women, readily recognize how easily the same forces of oppression and disadvantage could have led to them sharing the poverty of their sisters. These strengthened senses of identity and pride provide a basis for independent organization and hence the ability to participate in political action. The change processes that follow are contested and controversial. The struggle for equality rights by gay and lesbian groups in matters of social welfare benefits and adoption provide current examples of how contested the change process can be; but no doubt can exist concerning how essential such a process is to the achievement of the basic values of a society that is diverse in its culture and plural in its institutions.

Policy and Diversity

The recognition of diversity in social welfare policy has led to new issues for policy development and program administration. These issues include:

- the modification of policies and programs to remove disadvantages;
- the development and administration of different policies and programs for different peoples;
- the financing of different programs serving different people;
- the issues of separation;
- the problem of European racism.

1. *The modification of policies and programs to remove disadvantage and oppressive elements.* This is the most basic claim that any sectional group can make and is essential to the accommodation of social justice and minority rights. The claims of gay and lesbian people for equality of treatment in matters of benefit and adoption are of this type. Similar claims are made by immigrant groups whose cultural needs were not recognized at earlier stages of Canada's social evolution either

because they were not there or because they were once the subjects of racist and cultural oppression. First Nations also made such claims when they sought release from the oppressive sections of the Indian Act that banned the potlatch and the sun dance. The case for change in these instances is based in an argument for equality that recognizes that majority groups establish cultural organizations in their interest and it is only just to allow a similar right to minorities of all types. A supporting argument advanced by French Canadians, First Nations, Hutterites, and Doukhabors is that historic agreements were made at the time of settlement giving them a right to be recognized in matters affecting the continuity of their communities and culture. For all these examples the claim being made is for inclusion in Canadian society and for social welfare provisions on terms that are non-discriminatory.

2. *The development and administration of different policies for different peoples.* The development of different policies takes the subject of diversity a further step. Here the claim is not for inclusion but for separateness based on the recognition of difference. An example of such a claim is that made by First Nations for a separate justice system or for an independent mandate to organize and conduct their own child welfare programs. As Kymlicka points out, this is a more difficult claim for social policy because it requires the establishment of services that permit segregation and it raises questions regarding the rights of minorities within the groups seeking to establish separate policies. Should the protection of the Canadian Charter of Rights and Freedoms apply to the language rights of the English-speaking minority in Quebec? Should it apply to the gender rights of First Nations women? Should First Nations children be allowed to stay in non-Native foster homes rather than be repatriated to the care of their people if they so wish? If these and similar questions are answered positively then there are limits placed on the exercise of self-government and on the extent to which non-liberal expressions of diversity can be recognized. Kymlicka accepts these limits as a conclusion of his review of liberal values, citizenship, and diversity.

> These steps [to accommodating minorities] might include polyethnic and representation rights to accommodate ethnic and other disadvantaged groups within each national group and self-government rights to enable autonomy for national minorities alongside the majority nation. Without such measures, talk of "treating people as individuals" is itself just a cover for ethnic and national injustice.
>
> It is equally important to stress the limits of such rights. . . . minority rights should not allow one group to dominate other groups; and they should not enable a group to oppress its own members.[24]

3. *Different programs for different people.* The financing of different programs serving different peoples also poses some challenges. As long as programs are equally available to all, they can be financed from the common tax base in which all share. This breaks down when either programs are not available to all or all groups do not participate equally in paying taxes. In either case there is a tendency

to see the specialized services being provided as the exclusive responsibility of the group that has sought them. The arguments that have been made for the majority paying for such services are that they represent a payment in compensation for past disadvantage, or that they represent a payment based on equality of treatment, or that they represent a payment due under the terms that government to government relationships were established. The first two arguments, compensation and equality of treatment, both place the majority in control of deciding what is adequate compensation and what is equality of treatment. Only the last of these arguments, based on history and contract, is likely to provide a minority with independence of action.[25]

4. *Separation.* Separation is the final step in recognizing diversity. In many ways it is the most straightforward solution to the organization of different services for different people. Nor should it be seen as necessarily an extreme or hostile act. There is no reason to think that the example of Norway and Sweden, which separated in 1905 and have flourished since, should not be the example to which we should look. However, for many groups a territorial separation may not be possible. For those situations where separation is adopted as the way to recognize diversity, it will be important to attend carefully to minority community rights during the process of transition in order that each separate national state will recognize the minorities within its borders.

5. *The problem of European racism.* The problems posed by European racism appear to be the most serious of all the issues faced in the development of plural social policies that recognize diversity. In most if not all of the countries of Western Europe and in the United States racism undermines a common sense of community. In each case people of African or Asian origin can find that their opportunities are restricted because of the colour of their skin or the shape of their facial features. In Canada there have been numerous incidents of police violence against members of the black community, racist political parties begin to operate, and the social discourse is full of euphemisms for "race," such as "non-traditional immigrants" and "visible minorities." While the number of incidents of racism was small they seemed unusual and were often regarded as the results of personal bias. However, with rising numbers of vulnerable people and the increasing numbers of incidents, they can be seen to be based in European attitudes of racial superiority that are embedded in European culture. We cannot expect that these attitudes will be changed by a general policy of multiculturalism. Instead, clear anti-racist policies will increasingly be needed.

Community Governance

Community participation implies that there should be established and continuing means whereby communities can participate in the policy and management of the social welfare services they receive. The earlier charitable forms of organization achieved this goal for an elite comprised principally of community leaders who could assist in raising funds. The self-help groups obtain this objective through their own memberships. However, achieving this objective for government services has been difficult. Wharf, speaking of child welfare, summarizes the advantages of community governance.

> The first advantage of community governance is that it provides an opportunity for social learning – for citizens to gain some understanding of the complexities of child neglect and abuse and some appreciation of the impact of factors such as poverty and the lack of affordable housing. Second, community governance requires that communities *own* child welfare. Rather than being seen as the exclusive responsibility of a provincial bureaucracy that is supposed to solve all problems and is subject to severe criticism when it fails to do so, child welfare becomes a community concern and challenge. Third, community governance allows for the possibility of tuning services to meet local needs, for experimenting with local innovations, and for involving citizens in a variety of voluntary activities. Fourth, community governance spells the end of large and cumbersome provincial bureaucracies.[26]

Despite these advantages, one can find as many examples of centralized, non-community-based systems of governance as one can find examples of systems that allow for local community input. Furthermore, there are many examples of local community governance structures that have been introduced and then discontinued. The reasons for this failure to follow the community government values appear to be connected to the problems of bureaucratic organization and political control of the larger social service organizations.

Healthy Communities

Public health has always been a major goal of public policy. Initially, establishing healthy communities was identified with issues of water quality, sanitation, and protection against the transmission of communicable disease. When these goals had been largely achieved, maintaining health was identified with public access to doctors, drugs, and hospitals. This was achieved through the introduction of hospital insurance, medicare, and provincial pharmacare or similar programs in the 1960s. This achievement resulted in a new attention to the meaning of "health" as representing more than the absence of disease. Some of the health problems that remained, for example, substance abuse, eating disorders, violence, sexually transmitted diseases, road accidents, and environmental health conditions, had a social origin. Others were a product of unhealthy living conditions – e.g., the continuation of respiratory illness among people who were homeless or poorly housed, and the effects of chronic poverty – that required social rather medical intervention. Finally, community planning and services, rather than treatment, provide the most effective response to a series of medical problems. These include homecare services for the elderly, a recognition of the effects of disabilities, de-institutional ways of providing for the needs of both the mentally handicapped and the mentally ill, and campaigns to reduce smoking.

As a result of these issues the concept of health as an objective of public policy has been expanded and health has been identified more and more with conditions of healthy living, a lifestyle that contributes to the maintenance of health, and communities that are healthy places to live.

The consequence is a convergence between the concepts of community welfare and health. The convergence is marked by overlapping interests of health and social agencies in all the examples provided above. The overlap raises new questions for community governance, too. Should communities have a health council and a welfare council or should they have one body that provides a community government forum for both? Should budgets for health and social agencies be separate or should there be a way of recognizing that funding social services may be a more effective response to community problems than funding casualty departments? The overlap raises new questions, too, for the professions. Nursing and social work once seemed to have clear and distinct roles. These clear boundaries no longer exist as community care replaces hospital care and as conditions once defined as medical problems are redefined as social ones.

Changes, 1940-1990

The application of the concept of community in the development of post-war social welfare services is, in retrospect, clear. In the 1940s Canada, along with other Western nations, was confident that a new and better society could be created and that community social services had a significant role to play. The new society would recognize the problems of industrialism, capitalism, and urbanization by developing an array of social services that would provide a means of social integration to deal with the anomie and alienation that was apparent. Services that had been provided on a charitable basis were established as government services, first on a residual basis to deal with immediate problems (during the 1940-50 period), but increasingly on an institutional basis as fundamental citizenship rights (1960-70). Toward the end of the 1970s an attempt was made by the federal government to consolidate this pattern through the establishment of an overall framework for the financing of social services throughout Canada as part of the social security review. If it had succeeded it would have established an institutional commitment to community social services as a Canadian citizenship right. It failed, however, partly for financial reasons (the first wave of financial restructuring) but also because of provincial opposition to the further extension of federal authority. It is also possible that these government social services were beginning to be affected by the lack of informed community participation and by the alienation that their size and bureaucratization were causing.

At the same time as this consolidation of the federal framework was being planned there was the assertion of diversity claims that had been ignored. The 1970 Royal Commission on the Status of Women in Canada, the 1971 multicultural policy recommendation of the Royal Commission on Bilingualism and Biculturalism, and the rejection by First Nations of the 1969 White Paper on the Indian Act all indicated that diversity was the emerging issue for Canada's social discourse and hence for community social services. The assumptions of an earlier period concerning patriarchy, English-speaking dominance over other ethnic groups, and assimilation of First Nations had to be set aside. Community economic development also had its origins in this period in the 1973 Local Employment Assistance Program and the 1975 Community Employment Strategy.[27]

In the 1980s the claims of other groups to separate recognition became more apparent as visible minorities, the handicapped and disabled, gay and lesbian members of the community, and immigrants and refugees asked to be heard. The 1982 Canadian Charter of Rights and Freedoms provided important legal support to their claims. The changes begun in the 1970s also led to the development of new forms of community social service as the social movements went beyond criticizing the existing services' insensitivity by establishing services of their own. The development by feminists of sexual assault services and transition houses, the establishment by First Nations of child welfare services, and the establishment by the gay and lesbian community of AIDS-related services all indicate the strength of this trend. The 1980s were also the time when community social welfare activists began to take a serious interest in alternative forms of economic institution that offered the promise of development opportunities more under community control and less vulnerable to global economic influence. The concept of health was also broadened to a concern with community living conditions and social issues that defied medical intervention and required a community service response.

The changes that have now begun are working deeper and deeper into the social affairs of our communities. There is no way back to a simpler society based on principles of integration into a single dominant Canadian society. Instead, the society is itself changing and must now deal with the conflict between the earlier sense of community dominated by established interests and the new plural and diverse community. The community economic development movement offers an alternative approach for economic viability to that offered by the global economy. The healthy community movement offers an alternative to medical intervention as a means of ensuring personal well-being.

The discussion of community in this chapter has endeavoured to keep redistributive considerations separate from community ones. Conceptually and analytically, this has its uses. However, the reality of the development of social programs necessarily involves both sets of considerations. Thus, a typical day-care program has both community and redistributive objectives. The socialization objectives include the provision of an enriched social environment for the child. The redistributive objectives include the provision of a financial subsidy to day care to permit the attendance of children from families that need, but cannot afford, the service. In the analysis of any social program, the effects of both community and economic objectives require consideration.

Notes

1. Kenneth Boulding, "The Boundaries of Social Policy," *Social Work*, 5, 12 (January, 1967).
2. Roehr Institute, *Social Well Being: A paradigm for reform* (Toronto: Roehr Institute, 1993), p. 41, citing Will Kymlicka, *Liberalism, Community and Culture* (Oxford: Clarendon Press, 1989).

3. See N.H. Lithwick, *Urban Canada: Problems and Prospects* (Ottawa: Central Mortgage and Housing Corporation, 1970).

4. Robert Heilbronner, *Capitalism in the Twenty-First Century* (Concord, Ont.: Anansi Press, 1992), pp. 95-100.

5. C. Wright Mills, *The Sociological Imagination* (New York: Oxford University Press, 1959), as cited by Brian Wharf, *Social Work and Social Change in Canada* (Toronto: McClelland & Stewart, 1990), p. 9.

6. Wharf, *Social Work and Social Change*, p. 12.

7. C. Wright Mills, "The Professional Ideology of Social Pathologists," *American Journal of Sociology*, XLIX (September, 1942), pp. 175-76.

8. Ewan McIntyre, "The Historical Context," in Brian Wharf, ed., *Rethinking Child Welfare in Canada* (Toronto: McClelland & Stewart, 1993), p. 19, citing Jane Ursel, *Private Lives, Public Policy: 100 years of state intervention in the family* (Toronto: Women's Press, 1992).

9. John L. Tobias, "Protection, Civilization, Assimilation: An Outline of the History of Canada's Indian Policy," *Western Canadian Journal of Anthropology*, 6, 2 (1976), pp. 13-29.

10. For a full account of a policy that had its origins in British imperial objectives, see Andrew Armitage, *Comparing the Policy of Assimilation: Australia, Canada and New Zealand* (Vancouver: UBC Press, 1995).

11. Wharf, *Social Work and Social Change*, pp. 144ff.

12. Roland Warren, *The Community in America* (New York: Rand McNally, 1963).

13. Bridget Moran, *Justa: A First Nations Leader* (Vancouver: Arsenal Press, 1994), p. 13.

14. Marcia Nozick, "Five Principles of Sustainable Community Development," in Eric Shragge, ed., *Community Economic Development* (Montreal: Black Rose Books, 1993), pp. 18-20.

15. Warren, *Community in America*, p. 174.

16. Alfred J. Kahn, *Social Policy and Social Services* (New York: Random House, 1973), pp. 139-42.

17. Warren, *Community in America*, p. 177.

18. Amitai Etzioni, *Modern Organizations* (Englewood Cliffs, N.J.: Prentice-Hall, 1964), p. 59.

19. Armitage, *Comparing the Policy of Assimilation*, p. 116.

20. Marilyn Callahan, "Feminist Approaches to Child Welfare," in Wharf, ed., *Rethinking Child Welfare*, p. 204.

21. British Columbia, *Liberating Our Children: Liberating Our Nations* (Victoria: Ministry of Social Services, 1992), p. 107; see recommendations, pp. 96-99.

22. Etzioni, *Modern Organizations*, p. 60.

23. Ben Lappin, *The Community Workers and the Social Work Tradition* (Toronto: School of Social Work, University of Toronto, 1970), p. 167.

24. Will Kymlicka, *Multicultural Citizenship: A liberal theory of minority rights* (Oxford: Clarendon Press, 1995), p. 194.

25. See Armitage, *Comparing the Policy of Assimilation*, pp. 239-40.

26. Wharf, ed., *Rethinking Child Welfare*, p. 224.

27. Ken Watson, "A Review of Four Evaluations of CED Programs: What have we learned in two decades?" in Burt Galloway and Joe Hudson, eds., *Community Economic Development* (Toronto: Thompson Educational Publishing, 1994), p. 134.

Chapter 6

COMMUNITY:

THE WORKING LEVEL

Social and community services surround us everywhere. While some are offered directly by governments, others are provided by non-profit organizations, both with and without government support, and still others are offered by private organizations working under contract for government agencies. These services are organizationally separate from the redistributive functions of social welfare but are directly related in two ways. First, changes in the extent and effectiveness of redistribution, and particularly increase in poverty, affect all their objectives and achievements. Second, funding for these services comes, in whole or part, from government and is under the same deficit-driven constraints as are the redistributive programs.

The current auspices of these services include organizations with:

(1) an original philanthropic and charitable mandate
   – family services agencies, neighbourhood houses, Big Brothers/Sisters;
(2) a government mandate
   – provincial departments of social welfare or social development: e.g., social assistance social services, child welfare services, child-care services, and children's institutions;
   – provincial departments of health: mental health, family planning, substance abuse, etc.;
   – school boards and provincial government departments of education: special education, alternative schools, etc.;
   – federal and provincial justice departments: family court, probation, juvenile correctional institutions, etc.;
   – local government or non-profit social planning departments and health councils;
(3) a mandate from an active social movement
   – non-profit organizations of women: transition houses, rape crisis centres, abortion clinics;
   – Aboriginal peoples' organizations: friendship centres, band and tribal council social service organizations, child welfare and substance abuse agencies;

– organizations for services to mentally handicapped;
– organizations of persons with disabilities of all types;
– ethnic organizations and organizations of and for refugees and immigrants;
– labour organizations;
– seniors' organizations;
– non-profit community economic development organizations;
(4) a personal service or entrepreneurial organizations
  – marriage counselling, and some forms of day care, child care, foster and group homes, home services, etc.

In this complex of auspices and agencies, governments provide a core set of services that have become established as essential to community functioning, usually on the basis of the socialization and social control functions of community. The services in this group include those that perform a *residual* function, such as child protection, and those that perform an *institutional* function, such as child care. Sometimes the role of government agencies is the direct one of providing service to clients; sometimes it is an indirect one, as when a government agency contracts for service with a community-based social service agency. Regardless of these differences in the ways that services at the community level are provided, the government-funded services constitute a "mainstream" of community provision in which clients with recognized problems receive services. The services are managed by bureaucracies operating under legislative mandates, sometimes guided by some form of community governance, such as an appointed or elected board.

The services based in the social movements are the second major stream of community service provision. These services are newer and have been developed from the mutual support and social participation functions of community. Often inherent to these is an analysis of social conditions based on a common experience of oppression, disadvantage, and disempowerment as in the feminist, First Nations, and gay and lesbian social movements. The services that result are consumer-driven and designed so that service providers work with and for consumers rather than by applying government policies and programs to clients. The analysis of social conditions provided by the social movements and the services that have been developed are evidence of community change. The change is away from an approach that assumed a process of social control and assimilation and toward approaches and communities in which diversity is a principal characteristic. The influence of the social movements is found not only in policy fields and services they have developed but also in changes being made in the mainstream government agencies.

Mainstream Government Services

The mainstream government community services were not designed as a total system. As a consequence they are characterized by a series of independent service enterprises. Some of the major ones include:

• social assistance social services

- child welfare services
- child-care services
- youth corrections services
- family and youth mental health services
- substance abuse services
- social planning and community development services.

Social Assistance Social Services

Social assistance social services have been developed around the social assistance income security program and are administered by either municipal or provincial government departments. Expansion of such services was one of the major objectives of the Canada Assistance Plan, which, in contrast to earlier cost-sharing arrangements with the provinces, included provision for the federal government to provide 50 per cent of the costs of "welfare services." Welfare services included casework, homemaker, day-care, and community development.[1] The objectives of these services through the CAP was broadly stated as being "the lessening, removal or prevention of the causes and effects of poverty, child neglect or dependence on public assistance." Coverage of social assistance social services has been limited to people on the social assistance income security program and those whose income falls below poverty lines. In some provinces, for example, Alberta, these services are organized as separate preventative services while in others they are provided alongside the social assistance payment program.

Evaluation of the effect of social services on the poor has not encouraged the idea that such services offer an effective strategy to deal with poverty. However, this is not to say that such services are not important in themselves as community supports for those who need and qualify for them. In particular, they have been the means through which community services for persons with disabilities, including the mentally handicapped, have been developed. As a result of the value that these services have in themselves as social supports, there has been considerable interest in separating the social assistance service and income programs and developing the services in their own right. The Senate Committee on Poverty advocated such a separation by removing all responsibility for income security to the federal level of government while leaving the provinces to provide social services, supported by a revised and expanded CAP. The federal income security review of the 1970s considered a similar proposal. In neither case was any change made. Now, in 1995, with the conclusion of the CAP and its replacement by CHST, there is the opportunity to re-examine how these services should best be organized. There is also the risk that they will be substantially reduced as the provinces absorb the effects of both reduced funding under the CHST and the absence of a cost-sharing formula.

Child Welfare Services

Child welfare services were developed initially in urban centres by Children's Aid Societies, supported by organized philanthropy.[2] In most provinces, this pattern was replaced by government services in the sixties and seventies when government support to Children's Aid Societies reached up to 95 per cent of their budgets. Government child welfare services are now usually provided by provincial departments of social welfare and operate alongside, but separate from, the same department's social assistance programs. Child welfare services have also been included under the cost-sharing provisions of the Canada Assistance Plan.

The objectives of child welfare services are to ameliorate or correct a series of specific problems, including child abuse, child neglect, and other parenting problems. To provide resources for these purposes, child welfare authorities also operate foster homes, group homes, and more specialized institutional-type treatment homes. Child welfare agencies also provide adoption services. This residual, problem-oriented group of services can in no way be identified with any comprehensive view of the welfare of children. The position taken is that the welfare of children will be looked after by the family. However, if, in unusual circumstances, the family fails to perform expected functions, child welfare authorities can intervene to make alternative arrangements for the children. This view of the role of child welfare has been challenged in three different ways.

One challenge came from looking at child welfare services from an institutional perspective. This approach recognized the difficulty experienced by *all* families in fulfilling their child-care functions in society. An institutional response to child welfare problems takes the form of a broad array of family supportive services – family life education, day care, homemaker services, family counselling services – that would be made available to parents as social rights.

A second challenge comes from the experience of First Nations with the child welfare system. Following the closing of the residential schools in the 1960s, provincial child welfare services were extended to Indian reserves. The experience was particularly harsh. By the late 1970s, 40 per cent of all children in care in the western provinces and in northern Canada were from First Nations, yet First Nations children comprised only 5 per cent of children.[3] First Nations resisted and challenged the loss of their children, and began to organize child welfare systems for themselves based in their own experience and culture.

The third challenge has come from the feminist social movement and has centred on the experience of mothers who have had their children apprehended because of neglect. Callahan writes:

> The more disadvantaged the mother or caregiver, the more disadvantaged is the child. This is the crux of the argument. The unequal status of women has two principal consequences for children: they are more likely to live in poverty and suffer the results because their mothers cannot earn sufficient wages and they are at greater risk of violence and sexual abuse because their mothers cannot protect them from likely offenders.[4]

By looking at the experience of women as caregivers and service providers, Callahan comes to the conclusion that the problem of neglect should be framed as a problem of poverty and dealt with by supporting women with practical services, not framed as a problem of inadequate parenting to be dealt with by taking children away as a form of punishment.

Recent child welfare legislation has been influenced to some extent by these challenges. Durie,[5] reviewing the 1994 British Columbia Community, Family and Child Service Act, finds evidence of the impact of the institutional point of view on the emphasis and provisions for family support, as well as some recognition of the need for separate provisions for First Nations, but less evidence is apparent of the impact of feminist thought. The Act, along with other Canadian child welfare statutes, provides primarily a mandate to receive, investigate, and act on reports of child abuse and neglect. The call from the feminist community to rework fundamentally the approach to child welfare and discard the concept of neglect is not present. The broader institutional service and preventative objectives of child welfare acts that have been introduced during the past decade are also vulnerable to funding constraints as the CAP is replaced by the CHST.

Child-care Services

Up to the 1960s the proportion of women with children in the labour force was under 20 per cent and the prevailing view was that women with small children should be at home. The need for government-supported child care was placed on the social agenda by the 1970 Royal Commission on the Status of Women, which identified the increasing number of women who were entering the work force. In 1984 the *Report of the Royal Commission on Equality in Employment* said unambiguously:

> Child care is not a luxury, it is a necessity. Unless government policy responds to this urgency, we put women, children and the economy of the future at risk. Considering that more than half of all Canadian children spend much of their time in the care of people other than their parents, and that more than half of all parents need child care services for their children, social policy should not be permitted to remain so greatly behind the times.[6]

The need for expanded child care continued to increase. In 1986, the federal Task Force on Child Care[7] recommended a comprehensive child-care and parental leave system that would be implemented through new federal-provincial cost-sharing agreements. In 1988, the child-care deduction was introduced as part of the budget, providing some income tax relief for the child-care costs of middle- and upper-income parents. In the same year the Canada Child Care Act was introduced. By this time, 65 per cent of mothers with children worked outside the home, including 57 per cent of mothers with children under three.[8] The Canada Child Care Act was never passed. The bill was not adopted by the time Parliament was dissolved for the 1988 federal election, and neither it nor any alternative was introduced after the election. The objective at the time was to support an additional 200,000 subsidized child-care spaces. This would have led to a doubling of the existing subsidized spaces, then numbering 243,545 and serving 13 per cent of the children needing care. Since 1988, thought of federal legislation and action waned with each passing year. In 1995 the passage of the Canada Health and Social Transfer Act, along with the decrease in federal funding, appeared to bring the pursuit of a national child-care strategy to a dead end. However, at the end of 1995 the federal minister, Lloyd Axworthy, announced that the government was again offering the provinces cost-sharing provided that all participated.

Any further action can only be at the provincial level, where progress has been mixed. Some provinces, particularly those with stronger financial bases, have developed strategies of their own; but others have lacked the resources to do so. The child-care debate, and the failure to act, demonstrated the problems of the social services in the 1980-90 period. The federal government failed to act on a central issue of equity affecting primarily women and children.

Youth Corrections Services

The development of correctional services for youth can be dated from the Juvenile Delinquents Act of 1908. The Act was revised several times and then in 1984 was replaced by the Young Offenders Act, which abolished the general status of "delinquency" in favour of the more precise status of "offender," defined by the Criminal Code. The Young Offenders Act is a federal statute, part of the Criminal Code of Canada, and provides, in effect, for a series of court procedures and court dispositions for persons between the ages of twelve and eighteen that are different from those applicable to adults. The Act also decriminalized behaviour for children under twelve by withdrawing authority for criminal proceedings.

All aspects of the administration of the Young Offenders Act are provincial. Family courts, probation services, and institutional facilities are all operated by the provinces. These services tend to fall across major established lines of provincial departmental bureaucracy, causing the development of a variety of administrative patterns. The Juvenile Court is usually administratively responsible to the provincial Attorney General. On the other hand, some of the resources needed by a service to juveniles are obviously child welfare services (foster homes and children's institutions). The result is that while in some provinces the probation service is established within the Attorney General's department, in other provinces it is established within the provincial Department of Social Welfare and in still others it works directly for the Juvenile Court.

The objectives of juvenile correction services are even more clearly focused social control than is the case with child welfare services. The central function of juvenile corrections has been to control and rehabilitate adolescents adjudged "offenders" by the courts. The implicit theory behind this function has the following features: the community cannot overlook (or tolerate) any form of criminal behaviour; if the offender can be caught, he should be punished and reformed; however, the punishments contained in the Criminal Code are too severe and overlook the importance of growth and change in young people's lives. Thus, flexibility is needed in the measures that can be taken, which include discharging offenders to parents, probation, and children's institutions. In addition, correctional authorities have increasingly recognized an obligation to work with families and communities to build both support and control at the community level.

At the core of the problem of youth crime are a small number of brutal acts that endanger the life or health of other persons. These, indeed, cannot be overlooked, and most eventually appear before the court. They are surrounded by a much larger number of offences involving property (shoplifting, joy-riding in a "borrowed" car, etc.), disturbance of the peace (noise late at night), and the use of alcohol or drugs. This second group of offences merges into an array of normal adolescent behaviours. In fact, to have committed some, if not all, of the offences at some time or other can be considered sociologically normal behaviour.

To this view of the scope of youth correction services must be added the view derived from "labelling" theory, which suggests that the effects of any "label" are not neutral but tend to convey an identity that is subsequently acted out. Naming youth "offenders" is thus viewed as an act that, in and of itself, has the effect of increasing the chance of their becoming confirmed criminals in adult life. Thus, far from wanting to see youth correction services expanded to full coverage of all offences, it is desirable that the use of labels be as restricted as possible. That is not to say that the community should simply tolerate property damage or disturbance. It suggests that the point of intervention is not offences, but the structure of community facilities and services that makes community life worthwhile to adolescents, together with support to parents as a child welfare provision.

Public concern with the Young Offenders Act and with youth correction generally in the 1990s has centred on the fact that children under the age of twelve cannot be prosecuted and on the maximum sentence of three years that can be imposed under the Act. Both concerns reflect a "law and order" orientation to youth and to social problems, which does not reflect an informed understanding of how the community can best be protected.

Mental Health Services

Mental health services include a variety of major independent programs brought into association with each other in the 1960s and 1970s. They included the operation of the large mental hospitals that are the inheritors of the asylum tradition of mental illness segregation; the work of independent medical practitioners, psychiatrists, working in office-based practice and seeking to modify behaviour by counselling and drugs; the community-based mental health clinics that had been developed from the earlier child guidance clinics; the psychiatric wards within acute-care general hospitals; and the independent and largely volunteer-operated services provided by such organizations as the Canadian Mental Health Association. This trend was a result of the combined influence of the availability of new forms of drugs that allow behaviours to be controlled in the community; the demands of parents and support groups for accessible services; professional preference for treatment in the community rather than institutionalization; concern for the civil rights of persons institutionalized on the basis of a medical diagnosis; and cost considerations. In the past two decades cost considerations, particularly the high per capita costs of institutional care, have been a driving consideration in a continued trend to community care.

Mental health services have been organized under a number of governmental auspices, including departments of health, departments of mental health, and departments of health and social welfare. These services were not covered by the Canada Assistance Plan, which tended to separate them administratively from child welfare and social services. The objectives of this complex of services are not easily stated. As with the residual child welfare and juvenile correction services, a core phenomenon, severe mental illness, requires a specific form of intervention. Beyond that core phenomenon, there is a much more diffuse arena in which behaviour can be labelled by using the terminology of mental illness (depression, anxiety, or character disorder), or it can be viewed as a by-product of the societal condition. If someone is destitute and alone it is not surprising to find that person also anxious and depressed. For the core phenomenon, the objectives of mental illness services are clear enough. For the more diffuse surrounding phenomena, the mental health objectives are not at all clear. The 1991 B.C. Royal Commission on Health Care and Costs noted that:

> while some mental illness may not be preventable, countering the effects of poverty, poor housing, physical and sexual abuse, the lack of meaningful employment and the abuse of drugs and alcohol is as important as medical treatment in the management and social integration of the mentally ill.[9]

As the definition of mental health is broadened to include all efforts to improve social life and deal with social problems, the name becomes increasingly inappropriate. Mental health, with its implications of a known or knowable set of ideal behaviours, is not an appropriate way of addressing the problems of political alignment, power, and change. Mental health services addressed to helping the poor cope with inequality can serve to sustain an unjust social order in which the mental illnesses of the rich (greed, avarice, and delusions of wisdom) are untreated. Mental health, with its inevitable connection to the prestige and status of the medical profession, tends to lead to the devaluing of the contributions of lay persons and of other professions. Finally, mental health, with its tendency to organize reality on a health-to-illness continuum, has particular problems when used as a planning or developmental base.[10]

The trend toward community care has meant that considerable numbers of people who might have been hospitalized, or indeed who are hospitalized for short periods, are present in the community. Community mental health clinics with specialized nursing and social work programs have been developed to provide some community support to the mentally ill. The "Lifeline" programs of the Canadian Mental Health Association serve a similar function. These services have expanded and continue to expand as community rather than institutional care objectives are pursued.

The people who receive these services in the community are more than often also in receipt of social assistance or are homeless and receive limited support from shelters, food banks, and soup kitchens. Others receive help from child welfare or correctional services. Thus, these community social services frequently overlap with each other, raising questions as to whether they should not be organized and managed in a way that recognizes their relationship. As matters stand, inadequate services tend to struggle with one another over how to share the responsibility of providing service or distributing the blame of failure.

Substance Abuse Services

Substance (alcohol, drug, tobacco) abuse services are usually organized and supported by ministries of health. Substance abuse is not only a major health problem but also a major social problem both to personal relationships and at work. Estimates of the financial consequences of substance abuse vary widely, but the costs of alcohol abuse alone are placed in the range of $10-20 billion a year. The RCMP estimates that the retail value of illicit drugs sold in Canada in 1985 was over $10 billion, while public revenues from the sale of alcohol and tobacco are of a similar order.

The prevention of substance abuse has increasingly been seen as being first and foremost a public health social problem rather than a medical treatment or law enforcement problem, although both these latter strategies have a role to play. The substance abuse services through ministries of health deal principally with public education and treatment, but they also have a policy and advisory role in the regulation of consumption and law enforcement. At the community level public education takes several forms, including general public education, school programs, and programs aimed at specific populations, such as the elderly, employee groups, and ethnic groups including First Nations, in each of which substance abuse has unique characteristics. Treatment, too, has increasingly been developed so as to work closely with community groups and other social supports both in the workplace and outside it.

Community Development and Social Planning Agencies

To this point, the agencies considered have been primarily case-and problem-oriented. Even the occasional reference to supportive services has basically been within a vision of stable social institutions that need outside resources, for example, day care, to perform their function. Community development and social planning agencies are directed to intervention at a different point in the symbiotic relationship between a community and its members – community governance. The community as a whole, not the members as individuals, is the target for intervention.

Community development had its origins in the processes through which economic development was introduced in post-colonial (so-called underdeveloped) societies in the post-war period. However, the first applications of community development in Canada were during the 1960s and focused on issues of social policy, particularly issues related to the War on Poverty. Initial use was by organizations such as the Company of Young Canadians, and target groups were First Nations, other Aboriginal peoples, and the poor. Community development work was largely initiated by government, although in some centres voluntary social agencies employed community development workers. The initial enthusiasm for community development was substantially dampened by a cyclical effect in which successful community work led to organized groups who expressed their own ideas as to what services they needed and who were critical of the services they were getting. Threatened by such challenges to existing services, the funds for community development work were sometimes cut back or withdrawn. Nevertheless, it had been demonstrated that communities were able to take an interest in the services they were receiving. The democratic ethic of social welfare supported the idea that they should be heard and that services should be responsive. The 1990s equivalent to these early beginnings is found in both the social movements and community economic development, which are discussed later in this chapter.

The first social planning councils were organized in the 1960s, usually within the voluntary sector of social service activity. Their initial role was to identify need and suggest ways in which need might be served by voluntary social agencies. These activities were seen as helpful to the fund-raising and allocating activities of Community Chests. In that the voluntary agencies were but part of a larger whole, it was inevitable that the studies of social planning councils also had to deal with the government sector of social service, if for no other purpose than to establish a frame of reference for the voluntary sector. The role of social planning councils was thus broadened. In recognition of the contribution to planning that was being made, some cities (Vancouver and Halifax) established their own social planning departments. These early beginnings established the methodology and value of social planning as a support to community governance.

The 1980s and 1990s have seen a multitude of community studies, to the point that many communities have been exhausted by the study process and have become pessimistic as to whether the studies are worthwhile. Many workers in this field have concluded that community development and planning studies should not be undertaken unless there is a commitment to follow through on their results. Pulkingham comments on her own experience of a community development project in British Columbia:

> While the point of departure for community development is an explicit value-based perspective committed to the extension of "democratic dialogue. . . . community based strategies nevertheless remain highly susceptible to manipulation which encourages a form of conservatism and protection of vested interests that equals the more blatant social pathological approaches which individualize social problems.[11]

Despite these reservations, the need for a forum for community governance is beyond dispute. The social (and health) community-based social services cannot do their work in isolation from the communities they serve. Without the reality of continuing contact they become internally oriented and focused on their own bureaucratic problems. They can easily become part of the problem of alienation and anomie that characterizes capitalist society, rather than part of the solution.

Contracted Services

Since the 1980s there has been a strong trend by government agencies toward contracting for services rather than providing service directly. Many factors have contributed to this trend, including financial and organizational factors. Services can be obtained at lower costs on a contract basis from community agencies than by employing staff under government collective agreements. If services have to be reduced it can be done more readily by the non-renewal of a contract than by laying off or relocating government staff. However, there are also more positive reasons for this trend. Contracting for services with local community agencies ensures a degree of contact with the community that is rarely achieved in direct government service. The services provided tend to be less bureaucratized and more accessible, and for the community agencies the government contracts are an important source of revenue.

In nearly all communities agencies that were once thought of as voluntary, for example, family service agencies and neighbourhood houses, have now become partially or largely dependent on contracted work for government agencies. With the increase in the number and value of contracts there has also been a trend toward competitive tendering practices. Initially, the approach to government-community agency relationships was often in the form of a partnership. The contract terms were loosely drawn with the expectation that flexibility and accommodation on both sides of the relationship would provide best for the development of services to clients. However, the logic of contracting has tended to take over: service specifications have been clarified; cost savings have been sought; and contracting has come increasingly to mean competitive practices. Contracting has many consequences for community social agencies and for their work. Entrepreneurial, negotiating, and management skills in obtaining contracts have become essential. The agency community has come to take on some of the features of an industry. The willingness to criticize government and government social agencies in public has been diminished.[12]

Although the initial contracted agencies were usually community-based non-profit corporations, entrepreneurial, profit-based companies have increasingly entered the field. Such companies have often come into being as a direct result of government staffing cuts. Indeed, the effect of such cuts has often been softened by offering the staff being severed the opportunity to contract for services with government. On the positive side, competitive contracting practices lead to increased clarity as to what service is being sought and a desirable search for economy in providing the service. Achieving these objectives without sacrificing service quality requires that attention be given to the credentials and experience of those providing direct service to clients. Clear minimums must be stated in the tender documents. Attention must also be given in residential facilities to the expense parts of budgets necessary to provide for a healthful diet, recreation, and so on.

Despite the mixture of advantages and disadvantages in delivering services through contract, the trend toward more contracting seems irreversible. Already, service contracts would appear to comprise half or more of all service expenditures, and the financial and management advantages to cost-conscious governments in pursuing contracting for service is limited only, in the end, by the need to retain legislative, financial, and some systems functions in government hands.

Issues of Social Service Organization

The existing complex of major social services delivery systems is not without substantial merits, the foremost of which is the developed ability of some of the separate parts to provide good services to their clients. In addition, the separate identities have provided clients with some choice of service; the client who did not like the services received from the child welfare agency might do better with the services received from a family service or mental health agency, and so on. The separate services have provided independent foci for growth and political support; hence, the resources they have in total may be greater than could have been obtained by a unified approach. Finally, the independent services have provided the context for the development of specialized professional expertise.

Nevertheless, the existing array of major delivery systems has two major defects. The first is that none of the individual delivery systems provides the basis for the comprehensive service that is needed. Each is built around particular sectional interest and most share a social problem/residual services approach to service design. The second type of defect is that the existence of a series of independent systems, serving overlapping populations, produces enormous inter-system boundary problems. These include such major problems as service interconnection, gaps, and co-ordination; they also include inter-system competition for resources, professional rivalry, and excessive administrative costs. In response, there has been a history of reorganization of the personal social services with the intent to find simpler and more economic means of service delivery.

Signs of dissatisfaction with social service delivery were widely evident during the early 1960s. One major indicator was the continuous concern with the co-ordination of social services. Another was the design of experimental programs in which services from a number of agencies were integrated through one worker. These experiments were directed toward change in the "multi-problem family." Nevertheless, they also served to demonstrate the possibility of service integration in other areas.

In Britain these same issues were reviewed by the Seebohm Committee, which published its report in 1968.[13] Britain had already tried to operate a series of co-ordinating committees in order to relate its social services to each other. In effect, this approach was pronounced a failure. In addition, the whole idea of developing social services around such foci as problems, other institutions (hospitals and schools), age groups, or social units (the family) was also viewed as having failed. In the place of these service delivery patterns, local social service departments were proposed. These departments include all the services previously given and are organized geographically rather than functionally. The front-line staff are defined primarily by the population for whose social services they are responsible. Whether a family member is in hospital, in school, in the juvenile court, or suffering mental distress, the social service department and the social work team would be the same. The local social service departments were made responsible to local county governments, which have social service committees to provide a focus for policy development. The Seebohm recommendations were legislated in the Social Services Act of 1970, which came into effect in July, 1971. The finer details of the British reorganization[14] are less relevant to Canada than the demonstration that comprehensive reorganization of social service delivery is possible.

Two major approaches to the reorganization of social services in Canada have been pursued: co-ordination and integration.

Co-ordination

In a number of communities, local initiatives have produced combinations of services at the point of delivery. The extent of combination has varied from the type of "centre" created by a series of independent agencies sharing physical facilities to integration of such common elements between all agencies as reception, filing, community liaison, and development. The services themselves, and their staffing, remain under the control of the existing major service systems. The detail of relationships has increasingly been specified in protocol documents designed to ensure that reciprocal responsibilities are clearly defined and fulfilled.

Approaches based on co-ordination do not overcome the fundamental design problems of the existing major systems. In addition, they are vulnerable to one system or another being unco-operative. However, co-ordination appears to be one of the few strategies that can be applied at the local level and with the co-operation of existing organizations. As it offers some improvements in social service delivery to the consumer, it should not be neglected. Co-ordination is essential, too, as there will always be some services that are necessarily managed separately but that have a contribution to make to the overall enterprise. Alternative schools provide a good example of an important social service that should be operated by one service – the school system, reflecting the primary objectives – but still needs to be managed in co-ordination with other social services to be effective.

The weaknesses of co-ordination are illustrated by the existence of service gaps, a problem that has become more severe as restraint in government expenditures has forced each agency to examine priorities closely and, where possible, to narrow its mandate. Common examples include:

- *Offences of children under age twelve.* The Young Offenders Act did not provide any route to prosecute a child under twelve for a criminal offence; implicit is the assumption that such children will be assisted as a child welfare matter. However, the child welfare agencies do not necessarily share this view and provide services only where the child was being neglected, abused, or abandoned.
- *Youth in need of financial assistance.* Social assistance programs provide for aid to persons nineteen years of age or older. Implicitly, assistance to those under nineteen is a child welfare matter, but the young person under nineteen may not be in any "need of protection" – hence, no child welfare service was given.
- *Homemaker service.* Needed homemaker services may not be given if they fall between the services provided by ministries of health for the long-term care of adults and the services provided by ministries of social services as family support measures for those families where the alternative is protection action.

This list could be extended, but the examples indicate how gaps between related services occur, and these gaps cannot readily be closed by co-ordination.

A second serious problem of co-ordination is the extent to which professional, financial, and systems resources are duplicated and consumed in providing for effective co-ordination. Instead of a social worker and supervisor being able to decide the direction to be followed in a case, they are rendered incapable of decision until they have consulted and co-ordinated with related services. Decisions, or non-decisions, are made in committee and require the attendance of large numbers of professionals. This is all professional service time that is not available for direct client contact. In addition, each social service maintains separate intake functions for its own work: assessment, rather than helping, becomes the primary enterprise. From the perspective of the client, he or she has to repeat a personal story time after time . . . only to find that the result is a further referral and request to repeat it again.

The *B.C. Inter-Ministry Child Abuse Handbook* (107 pages) is a model of both the strengths and weaknesses of co-ordination. Four ministries – social services, health, education, and justice – were involved in writing the *Handbook*. The strength is in the specific and detailed attention the *Handbook* gives to clarifying relationships between the four ministries whose roles all bear on child abuse. The weaknesses are (a) that detailed attention is necessitated in the first place by having four ministries involved rather than one; (b) that the detailed interfaces are costly to maintain, each requiring at least two professionals to discuss the situation before acting; and (c) that observing the detail becomes the test of good service rather than the exercise of professional judgement.

Integration

Quebec's Bill 65, passed in 1972, was a major and enduring attempt in Canada to create a Seebohm-type comprehensive reorganization of social service. The reformed pattern of social service delivery was based on the following types of delivery and governing units.

The local community service centre (LCSC) was the first level of service delivery. Its emphasis was on prevention and support related to both health and social needs. For intensive services, the personnel in the LCSC made referrals to the other service units of the system – the hospital centre, the social service centre, and the reception centre. Each LCSC was seen as serving a designated geographic area. The intention was that services should be readily accessible; hence, an upper limit of a thirty-minute travel time to an LCSC was sought. In population terms, urban LCSCs served a minimum population of 30,000, while rural LCSCs served a minimum population of 10,000. The LCSC was governed by a board made up of: five persons, residents of the area, elected at an annual meeting; two persons, residents of the area, appointed by the Lieutenant-Governor (a measure to ensure that socio-economic minorities were represented on the board); one person elected by the professionals practising in the centre; one person elected by the non-professional staff of the centre; one person from the associated hospital centre; one person from the associated service centre; and the general manager of the centre (advisory capacity only). The function of the board was to identify needs, oversee services, and serve as a focus for community action.

After the opening of approximately forty LCSCs in 1975, this march toward community control and service integration was halted because of professional and bureaucratic opposition – and the conflict and disruption such opposition occasioned. Control and direction were reasserted centrally through a budget and administrative process that distributed services to centrally defined target groups. The service philosophy changed to that of "complementarity" between the LCSCs and other existing services. Quebec has continued to build on this service base. The result is a comprehensive approach to community social services that is not replicated anywhere else in Canada.

Attempts to produce a similar pattern in other provinces either have been less comprehensive, as with Alberta's municipally organized preventative social service departments, or have been rejected following political change, as in the case of British Columbia's Community Resource Boards. The issues of service integration have not been resolved and further attempts to organize services in a more comprehensive way, linked to attempts to strengthen their community governance, can be expected. As the funding restrictions of the CAP no longer require that social assistance services be distinct, it is possible that these services will disappear and their functions will be assumed by other agencies. At the same time, community health and social services could come together under a common form of community governance.

Social Services and First Nations

Social services for First Nations on reserve have been developed independently of other government services and have characteristics of their own. Until the 1940s social services for First Nations were entirely under the control and management of the federal Department of Indian Affairs. For the most part social services were non-existent. There was one exception, the residential school, which was much more than an educational institution. Initially it was intended to prepare young Indians for assimilation and Christian citizenship, but by the 1960s it had also become a general welfare resource for the care of children who in the view of local Indian agents were not being competently cared for by their parents.

The separate nature of welfare institutions for status Indians attracted attention during the 1946-48 hearings of the Special Joint Committee of the Senate and House of Commons Appointed to Consider the Indian Act. In a joint presentation to the Committee by the Canadian Welfare Council and the Canadian Association of Social Workers the argument was developed that Indian people should enjoy the same services that were available to other Canadians. This included the family and child welfare services provided by the provinces. Patrick Johnston[15] summarized the argument of the brief:

> the brief said that "the practice of adopting Indian children is loosely conceived and executed and is usually devoid of the careful legal and social protections available to white children," and as wards of the federal government, "Indian children who are neglected lack the protection afforded under social legislation available to white children in the community."[16] The practice of placing children in residential schools was also condemned. . . . The brief concluded that the best way to improve the situation was to extend the services of the provincial departments of health, welfare and education to the residents of reserves.

The argument presented in the submission was accepted by the Joint Committee and led to changes in the Indian Act. In 1951 the Act was amended and provision was made for the operation of provincial health, welfare, and educational services on reserves, under the terms of agreements to be negotiated with the provinces. The negotiations did not result in a single pattern of services across Canada. The stance of each province toward extending services to Indian families and children differed and each sought financial arrangements that in the view of the province were beneficial. The result is referred to by Johnston as:

> an incredible disparity in the quantity and quality of child welfare programs available to status Indians from one province to another. In some instances there are disparities within a province. This myriad of differing policy approaches results in unequal treatment of Indian children across Canada.[17]

Consider the services referred to in this chapter.

(1) Social assistance social services are not generally available on reserve as they have been provided under the terms of the Canada Assistance Plan, requiring a 50 per cent provincial contribution. As the federal government has a constitutional responsibility for all services to Indians, the provinces have not been prepared to contribute 50 per cent of the cost and provide such services under the CAP.

(2) Child welfare services are available on reserve as the federal government has been willing to pay 100 per cent of the cost of a limited number of child welfare services, principally, child protection, foster care, and adoption costs. However, the full range of child welfare services developed by provinces, particularly the preventive and home support services, have not been available, with the result that, until recently, apprehension of children has been the principal form that on-reserve child welfare service has taken.

(3) Child-care services provided by the provinces have not been available on reserve.

(4) Youth correctional services have been available on reserve under similar terms to child welfare service. The result is that there was, until recently, an emphasis on incarceration rather than on community diversion.

(5) Provincial community mental health services have not been available on reserve.

(6) Substance abuse services provided by provincial governments have not been available on reserve.

(7) School-based social services provided by provincial governments have not been available on reserve.

(8) Community development and social planning services by provincial or local governments have not been available on reserve.

Where provincial services have not been available the Department of Indian Affairs has funded some social services of its own. These services have usually been provided through contracts with bands and tribal councils. Nevertheless, the range of services available to First Nations on reserve has always been more limited than that available to other Canadians, the quality of service has often been lower, and for substantial periods some services have not been available at all.

The Social Movements and Community Services

The development of a series of autonomous social movements, each of which has developed community social services of its own, is the most significant development since the 1960s. Major contributors to this trend include the feminist movement, First Nations organizations, ethnic and immigrant organizations, the associations for the mentally handicapped and other persons with disabilities, and the gay and lesbian communities. Each of these movements has approached the task of developing social services from the perspective of mutual support. The services developed are not for others' benefit; they have been developed for the benefit of the members of the social movement. Such services are usually characterized by such features as: a clear statement of who is being served and why; an approach to staffing and working relationships that is egalitarian and expresses values important to the movement; a political mission to demonstrate to the community that the movement can and will act; a unifying ideology anchored in a structural analysis of the origins of the movement. The following examples from the feminist, First Nations, and gay/lesbian movements show the nature of these newer forms of community social agency.

The Feminist Movement

There is, of course, no single feminist movement, but there is a central feminist experience of gendered differences, prejudices, disadvantage, and oppression. Beginning in the 1970s women took their analysis of the feminist experience a step beyond a critical review of social structures and institutions when they banded together to act on the basis of their experience and analysis. Major policy fields in which the feminist movement has established services include:

- spousal abuse, where transition houses for women and children have been developed as a means of obtaining shelter and protection from abuse and as a way to leave abusive relationships;
- rape relief and sexual assault centres, where the victims of rape and sexual assault can receive immediate advice and assistance and longer-term support and counselling;
- abortion clinics, where women's right to make reproductive choices is protected;
- sexual harassment services, where women subject to discrimination and oppression in employment relationships can receive support and counsel in dealing with their situation and in seeking redress;
- social housing co-operatives sponsored by women's groups, where the first considerations in housing are security of tenure, support with child care, and a welcome to women and children.

Callahan indicates four particular ways in which women's services have "come out on the side of the clients":

First, individual organizations have focused on one specific aspect of women's oppression: violence toward women or sexual assault or reproductive rights. . . .

Second, organizations have written their commitment to social change into their mission statements and have attracted those with devotion to this mission.... Third, most feminist organizations include a structural analysis in their day-to-day service with their clients.... Finally, some feminist organizations have developed umbrella organizations without service responsibilities but with a clear social change focus.[18]

The development of services by feminist organizations has involved struggle and contradictions, particularly with regard to fund-raising and organizational form. Although some funds have been raised by voluntary donations, establishing continuing services has required support from established funding agencies, both private and government. The result is that the operation of the transition house, say, takes precedence over confronting the funding body on other issues of women's oppression that are within its mandate. Taking money involves compromise. In a similar way, establishing services that require continuity of staffing leads to a gradual professionalization of helping relationships and a reduction of early emphases on mutual support. Joan Gilroy expresses this concern in her discussion of the women's movement:

> Within the women's movement it is fairly often observed that transition houses are becoming more like traditional social agencies and that this is a consequence of their government funding. Feminists who work in these houses or who serve on their boards and committees are faced with difficult choices. On the one hand, the service is needed and providing it requires government funds. On the other, seeking and obtaining government money means emphasizing the personal rather than the social and political nature of the problem.[19]

First Nations

The view of First Nations is that the right to self-government is inherent in Aboriginal status. Taking control of social services is thus the taking back of rights that have been appropriated in the past as acts of cultural racism and colonialism. The remarks of two First Nations leaders before a nation-wide Aboriginal child-care inquiry eloquently express this view.

CHIEF GORDON ANTOINE
COLDWATER INDIAN BAND
MERRITT, BRITISH COLUMBIA

The Coldwater Band has been able to take control of its own child welfare programs, but Chief Gordon Antoine explained that formal authority has yet to catch up with the community's informal decision to take action.

While the Coldwater band has no children in the care of the provincial agencies, it does have eleven living with relatives in a total of ten homes. "These placements have only the authority of the Band Council," Antoine said, "and our staff are subject to attack and undermining by both the Province of British Columbia's legislation and the funding the band accesses from the Department of Indian Affairs." The discretionary nature of the funding means that services available to children are extremely limited.

"We would like the force of the national Constitution to acknowledge this process," he said. The Constitution should also ensure sufficient funding "to provide our children the necessary services for their sound development as future citizens."

Antoine made a strong plea for "ourselves as Indian people, and more particularly from people such as ourselves in leadership positions from within Indian country, to eradicate the abuse – sexual, physical, and mental – we tend to foist on our children." He said that this process would call for clear and honest recognition of the extent of the problem itself, as well as an acknowledgement that "the support systems, either in place or being proposed by senior levels of government, are not readily accessible by our members, or [are] designed not to be accessible to our on-reserve population."

"Appreciate that the judiciary systems of this country are punitive in nature and not designed to assist the healing process required by victims, nor [are they] of a nature that is rehabilitative to abusers." Communities must take responsibility for initiating the action needed "in order for our citizens to enjoy a safe and caring environment within which to grow up."

Antoine said investigations into the extent of sexual abuse in his community revealed 497 cases of physical and sexual abuse and forty-nine cases of incest. He talked about the lifelong scars the abuse had left on both the abusers and victims, noting that "we have to acknowledge and own the damn problem".

Since Health and Welfare Canada has failed to fund programs to help heal the situation, he added, "we have to look inside our own resources to equip our front-line workers with the skills and information they need to cope with the problem". "We have to heal the abusers and the victims," he said.

Myrtle Bush thanked him for coming forward on this issue as a chief. It was becoming apparent in the course of the inquiry that abuse is a key child care issue. "We're going to make a very strong reference to all the things you and others have been telling us on this issue," she said, adding that Health and Welfare will have to allocate resources toward solving the abuse problem if child care is to be more than a band-aid solution to a larger problem. She congratulated the Coldwater Band for putting resources into sexual abuse education.

Antoine made it clear that he supports child care and recognizes it as an important need, "but there are unresolved issues that must be addressed. . . . My children need a warm and loving and safe place to grow up in". He again emphasized the importance of treating abusers, as they themselves had been victims. It was impossible for him as a chief "to tell these people they're not welcome in the community. There has to be a rehabilitative process".

Linda Jordan echoed Bush's appreciation of Antoine's remarks and asked whether Coldwater was using any traditional models for dealing with the problem, such as women's and men's circles. A community member appearing with Antoine explained that a new circle had recently been started by two families, and a separate one had been started for young boys. There are plans to start new circles for women, men, and children, based on ongoing discussions with elders.

On the issue of child apprehension, Antoine clarified his view that the law should get the children out of the home, then find them a place within the community that is safe.

ELDER LAVINA WHITE
COUNCIL OF HAIDA NATION
VANCOUVER, BRITISH COLUMBIA

"I stand before you and our Creator to speak on behalf of those who cannot speak for themselves," said White. "I speak on behalf of the forgotten children in the urban areas." White talked about the need to repatriate adopted children in urban centres back to their home communities, even though the whole concept of reservations was destructive. "We have to think as nations," she said. "We have to think of things holistically."

She talked about the importance of going back to terms such as "village" or "community", and she said that people must begin to name their homelands again. "I am a Haida," she said. "I am from the Haida Nation." "The problem really begins at the cradle," said White. "If we don't have our identity in our home community, we have no identity."

White called for a national First Nations declaration that "we're going to take care of our own children". But she cautioned against taking information and statistics to government or the media, who end up using that information against First Nation people. For the media, she said, the approach must be that "we're dealing with the problems we have, and they are alien to us." White also talked about the need for self-government and the prophecies of a time when First Nations will govern themselves: "If we move toward governing ourselves, we can look after our children".

She emphasized that First Nations leaders must be instructed to go forward and "not be submissive" in their efforts to redress the impact of a residential school system that did not nurture native children. These children, she said, are now parents who lack the necessary teaching to know how to nurture their own children. White called for a healing process to deal with "the boarding school syndrome" and urged First Nations to set up "our own systems of education and justice".

Aboriginal children are neglected for many reasons, White said, and the underlying problems must be dealt with first at the family level and then within the Nation as a whole. But she cautioned against using white systems unless absolutely necessary.[20]

Two levels of action have followed. The first is the return of powers that have been taken away. This has often taken the form of agreements whereby First Nation organizations have acted with the authorization of provincial ones, as in the establishment of agreements for child welfare services. The scale of these changes can be seen in Table 25.

TABLE 25: *First Nations Agencies Administering Child Welfare Programs*

Year	B.C.	Alta.	Man.	Ont.	Que.	Atl.*	Yukon
1981-82	1(1)	1(1)	2(9)				
1982-83	1(1)	1(1)	5(34)				
1983-84	1(1)	2(10)	6(59)		1(1)	3(3)	
1984-85	1(1)	2(10)	6(59)		3(5)	6(6)	
1985-86	.1(1)	2(10)	6(59)		5(7)	9(21)	
1986-87	2(14)	3(15)	6(59)	1(14)	5(13)	11(23)	1(1)
1987-88	2(14)	3(15)	6(59)	4(56)	7(15)	11(23)	1(1)
1990-91	2(19)	3(15)	7(60)	7(84)	7(15)	11(20)	1(1)

*Atl. refers to the Department of Indian Affairs Atlantic region, including the provinces of New Brunswick, Nova Scotia, Newfoundland and Prince Edward Island.

SOURCE: Department of Indian and Northern Affairs, Ottawa.

First Nations organizations view this form of organization with some ambivalence. It provides for some autonomy of operation and provides for financial support, but it does so at the price of acknowledging the continued role of provincial authorities established under colonialism. The second approach is where First Nations act independently, under their own authority, and establish mechanisms as Chief Antoine describes for the exercise of their own role in the welfare of their people. This second approach goes beyond the form of self-government recognized by the Canadian government and can lead to confrontation with police and other authorities.

Gay and Lesbian community

The AIDS epidemic and the ambivalent response of government to it had a major impact on the gay and lesbian community. In the early stages of the epidemic, homophobic reactions to the plight of victims were common. They were defined as having "deserved" their fate. Government action to develop strategies to provide accurate information was slowed by resistance to the idea that homosexual relationships should be recognized in public policies. Even access to drugs and treatment was slowed by resistance to the public being asked, through hospital and drug costs, to "pay for" victims' costs. Proposals to isolate victims from the community in quarantine and to require blood tests also showed how close public policy came to asserting a coercive response.

The gay and lesbian community responded with services of its own.

As early as February 1983, AIDS Vancouver was formed, and a month later the AIDS Committee of Toronto was set up. These groups were rooted in the gay and lesbian communities. They were also the first to organize education and prevention campaigns, as well as being the source of social support for people living with AIDS. . . . These community groups formed a national association in 1985 – the Canadian AIDS Society; by 1990, 31 ASOs (AIDS Service Organizations) belonged to the society. . . . Early in the crisis, ASOs in Canada resembled their US counterparts – they were volunteer organizations, financed mostly from private sources. Over time, however, several Canadian ASOs secured funding from municipal, provincial, and federal governments.[21]

Critical comment on all of these services in the feminist, First Nations, and gay/lesbian communities has been concerned with the way they are used by government in its quest to download program responsibilities to community groups while asserting control over social change.[22] However, the other side of this argument is the value of the services that have been provided and the way that sevices also serve to strengthen the communities that offer them. These developments can also been seen as part of the movement toward a more diverse, plural, and decentralized society. The established government services and the resources they command appear locked in dilemmas of their own. A point comes when pragmatism takes over from criticism and new community services are established – services that preserve their roots and become part of the means of gathering support for further change, including change in the established community social services.

Community Economic Development

Community economic development (CED) is the establishment by communities of self-sustaining economic enterprises that provide employment and operate in the market, but which are owned and managed collectively (rather than by capitalists) and seek community welfare values rather than purely economic ones. CED is expanding rapidly and the boundaries of what constitutes CED are not yet defined. Nozick names five major principles of this approach to welfare as:

- Gaining economic self-reliance: reclaiming ownership of our communities.
- Becoming ecologically sustainable: developing green, clean, and safe environments.
- Attaining community control: empowering members of a community to make decisions affecting their community, workplace, and daily lives.
- Meeting the needs of individuals: looking after our material and non-material needs.
- Building a community culture: getting to know who we are.[23]

Gaining self-reliance for the local community is the antithesis of the community's existence being subject to the economics of the integrated global economy. It does not mean economic isolation from other communities. All communities interact with others, and the objective of CED is not a separate self-sustaining commune but a community that can work together and grow with social and economic objectives of its own, a community that is not rendered powerless by the anonymous and distant operations of banks and large corporations.

Becoming ecologically sustainable is another objective. Looking for ways to do business that are environmentally responsible is pursued as a moral objective, not merely as a response to government regulation. Nature is not seen as an infinite resource to be exploited and dominated. Instead, oneness with nature is recognized. The objective is to preserve the diversity of nature and of relationships with it, while conducting continuing economic enterprises.

Attaining community control includes ensuring that communities operate their own enterprises but also includes the development of co-operative and consensual models of ownership and management. In such models all community members – men, women, children, young, old – participate. Community economic development aims not to be hierarchical or patriarchal, with power and control in the hands of a few and all others being alienated and dependent.

Meeting the needs of individuals means recognizing that individuals constitute the community. Each person has unique needs to be met and unique contributions to make. This value is the antithesis of the way that urban communities dissolve the bonds between individuals. Instead of dissolved bonds, new ones are forged and individuals are not abandoned. Such communities also attend to welfare and redistributive objectives through direct relationships between people rather than through the indirect and bureaucratic ones that constitute the formal organization of social welfare.

Building a community culture indicates a commitment to develop and sustain the ways of life that form our communities. Nozick refers to this objective as developing a "community of communities" in which different groups, "ethnic, religious, but also women's groups, arts groups, gay and lesbian groups," have their uniqueness respected and celebrated.[24]

Determining the extent of CED is not easy in such a rapidly developing field. The National Welfare grants program of Human Resources Canada has sponsored a series of studies of CED, the latest of which lists twenty-five studies with publication dates between April, 1993, and September, 1995.[25] Lewis[26] distinguishes four CED models. (1) A "growth equity" model focuses on building wealth-generating assets. Most of the examples of this model are in Aboriginal communities, which have 180 development corporations. Other examples are the non-profit housing development organizations that have been formed to develop and sometimes manage social housing. (2) A "loan/technical assistance model" provides debt financing to individuals and to worker co-operatives, together with business development advice. Aboriginal communities own thirty-three Aboriginal development corporations with loans of $100 million and additional capital commitments of $70 million. There are also thirteen First Nations-controlled business development centres (BDCs). Outside First Nations communities there are 215 BDCs in communities under 60,000 population. One study analyses forty-four urban-based CEDs with budgets from $40,000 to $6.5 million.[27] (3) A "human resources and employment development" model focuses on job readiness and skills, supported by outreach to communities to build opportunities. (4) A "planning and advisory" model provides planning and technical assistance to a defined membership or geographic area. Examples include the services provided through First Nations tribal councils, community futures committees, and economic development commissions.

Community economic development is sustained in small communities by the federal Community Futures program and by the work of provincial and municipal ministries and departments of economic development. In Aboriginal communities CED is supported by Indian and Northern Affairs Canada. Because these programs lie outside the traditional social program boundaries, they may be less vulnerable to deficit-related cuts.

Conclusion

Community-based social welfare programs are not immune from the issues of reduced public expenditure arising from the deficit, but they are less vulnerable than the redistributive programs. The most vulnerable are the major established government service programs and related service contractors. The government organizations also have problems of their own arising from the scale of organization and the alienation that this produces. Purchase of service contracting is also being used to scale back expenditures in the major service organizations. As well, these organizations can enshrine a concept of community integration and of single uniform standards of service that are outdated, in that they do not respond to diverse and plural communities. The future of these major organizations would seem to be a reduced one, although in total size they remain dominant.

The programs based in the social movements have their origins and strength in community mutual support and social action. As the scale of their work has grown, government funding has become more significant in their affairs. However, the structural model of analysis used by the social movements supports their independence by encouraging a distrust of government control. Their continued growth would seem to be assured, regardless of government funding and deficit issues. The community economic development programs provide a new response to the issues of the global economy that is in keeping with the principles of social justice and economic needs. They, too, would seem to have an important future. The social service programs of the social movements and the community economic development enterprises are also expressions of a much more diverse and plural community. The First Nations communities have been prominent in both the social service and CED fields and the feminist community has been a leader in the development of new fields of social policy and service. All of these developments reject the community integration model that dominated community social service development until the 1980s.

Notes

1. Canada, *Canada Assistance Plan* (Ottawa: Queen's Printer, 1965), Sec. 2(m).
2. For an account of the development of child welfare in Canada, see Ewan McIntyre, "The Historical Context of Child Welfare in Canada," in Brian Wharf, ed., *Rethinking Child Welfare in Canada* (Toronto: McClelland & Stewart, 1993).
3. Andrew Armitage, "Family and Child Welfare in First Nations Communities," in Wharf, ed., *Rethinking Child Welfare*, pp. 147ff.
4. Marilyn Callahan, "Feminist Approaches: Women Recreate Child Welfare," in Wharf, ed., *Rethinking Child Welfare*, p. 182.
5. Helen Durie and Andrew Armitage, *Legislative Change: The Development of B.C.'s Child Family and Community Service Act, and Child, Youth and Family Advocacy Act* (Victoria: School of Social Work, 1995).

6. Canada, *Report of the Royal Commission on Equality in Employment* (Ottawa: Ministry of Supply and Services, 1984), p. 192.

7. Status of Women Canada, *Report of the Task Force on Child Care* (Ottawa: Ministry of Supply and Services, 1986).

8. National Council of Welfare, *Child Care: A better alternative* (Ottawa, 1988), p. 3.

9. British Columbia, *Closer to Home: The Report of the British Columbia Royal Commission on Health Care and Costs* (Victoria, 1991), Vol. 2, C-73.

10. See, for example, Canadian Council on Social Development, *Case Studies in Social Planning*, ch. 2; *Field Unit, McMaster University: A demonstration project in community health* (Ottawa, 1971); Michael Boyle, "Children's Mental Health Issues," in Laura Johnston and Dick Barnhorst, eds., *Children, Families and Public Policy* (Toronto: Thompson Educational Publishing, 1991).

11. Jane Pulkingham, "Community Development in Action: Reality of Rhetoric," *Canadian Review of Social Policy*, 32 (1993).

12. Josephine Rekart, *Social Services and the Market Place* (Vancouver: Social Planning and Research Council of British Columbia, 1995).

13. United Kingdom, *Report of the Committee on Local Authority and Allied Personal Social Services* (London: H.M.S.O., 1968).

14. For an introduction to the issues, see Kathleen Jones, *The Year Book of Social Policy in Britain 1971* (London: Routledge and Kegan Paul, 1972).

15. Patrick Johnston, *Native Children and the Child Welfare System* (Toronto: James Lorimer, 1983), p. 3.

16. Canadian Welfare Council and Canadian Association of Social Workers, *Joint Submission to the Special Joint Committee of the Senate and House of Commons Appointed to Examine and Consider the Indian Act* (Ottawa: Canadian Welfare Council, 1947), p. 3.

17. Johnston, *Native Children*, p. 20.

18. Callahan, "Feminist Approaches," p. 192.

19. Joan Gilroy, "Social Work and the Women's Movement," in Brian Wharf, ed., *Social Work and Social Change in Canada* (Toronto: McClelland & Stewart, 1990), p. 78, note 28.

20. Assembly of First Nations, *National Inquiry into Child Care* (Ottawa, 1989).

21. Guy Poirier, "Neo-conservatism and Social Policy Responses to the AIDS Crisis," in Andrew Johnson, Stephen McBride, and Patrick J. Smith, eds., *Continuities and Discontinuities: The Political-Economy of Social Welfare and Labour Market Policy in Canada* (Toronto: University of Toronto Press, 1994), p. 139.

22. Jean Panet-Raymond, "The Future of Community Groups in Quebec: The Difficult Balance Between Autonomy and Partnership with the State," *Canadian Social Work Review*, 6, 1 (1989).

23. Marcia Nozick, "Five Principles of Sustainable Community Development," in Eric Shragge, ed., *Community Economic Development* (Montreal: Black Rose Books, 1993), p. 20.

24. The similarity of these values to the liberal social welfare values introduced in Chapter 1 is apparent.

25. National Welfare Grants, *Community Economic Development Products* (Ottawa: Human Resources Development Canada, 1995).

26. Mike Lewis, "The Scope and Characteristics of Community Economic Development in Canada," in Burt Galloway and Joe Hudson, eds., *Community Economic Development* (Toronto: Thompson Educational Publishing, 1993), pp. 48-58.

27. Michael Lewis, Stewart Perry, and Jean-Marc Fontan, *Revitalizing Canada's Neighbourhoods* (Vancouver: Westcoast, 1995).

Chapter 7

POWER, POLITICS,

AND ORGANIZATIONS

Provision for social welfare, that is, the translation of welfare values into welfare programs, requires the exercise of power. The $120 billion redistributed annually and the expenditures on community social services evidence power in operation. Hundreds of thousands of civil servants, administrators, contractors, social workers, child-care workers, homemakers, and others are employed in social administration. They are a large industry and lobby group by any standards. There are the millions of Canadians who depend on the social welfare system to pay their bills in whole or part. They, too, are a substantial vested interest and voting block. There are the social movements of feminists, First Nations, multicultural and refugee organizations, gays and lesbians. They, too, are not without political voice. This concentration of money and interests attracts the attention of all other major interests. Corporations, banks, the media, the courts, wealthy individuals, international economic and political organizations, organized labour, and politicians of all persuasions have interests of their own in the conduct of such a large enterprise because its affairs affect theirs. Power is the essence of social welfare and this chapter will deal with principal features of the way the organization of power in Canadian society affects social welfare. As such, it will deal principally with the operation of the Canadian state.

In the following discussion the concept of the Canadian state should be distinguished from the concept of a Canadian government. Canada possesses not one government able to exercise power over welfare but a multiplicity of governments – federal, provincial, and municipal. Furthermore, important powers are held by the courts and by the administrative bureaucracies created to oversee social provision. All of these are parts of the Canadian state. Only the state can organize resources on the scale needed for social welfare, and so the state and its politics determine the scope of social welfare and the direction of public policy. The dominance of the state in social welfare matters is also desirable. Social welfare involves the exercise of considerable coercive, utilitarian, and normative powers. It is a mark of civilized society that coercive power is unified – which, in a democratic capitalist society, implies a state function. Further, establishment of social policy involves decisions and moral choices. It is desirable that these decisions and choices at policy, program, and administrative levels are accountable to the society. This is achieved through the state exercising major authority over social welfare.

The interested parties in social welfare and their interaction with the state are shown in Figure 1.

FIGURE 1: *Social Welfare in Canada: the Political Map*

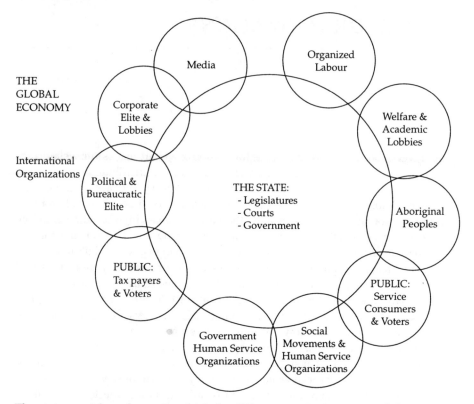

The state provides a forum in which the different parties interact and the means whereby decisions are made. For these reasons, all students of social welfare have to concern themselves with the way the Canadian state works.

The Constitutional Context

The Canadian state is a federal state, the constitution of which provides formal sanction for the existence of a federal government and ten provincial governments. Power for social welfare functions is divided between the federal government and provinces. In specific terms the British North America Act, now incorporated into the Canadian constitution, states:

91. It shall be lawful for the Queen, by and with the Advice and Consent of the Senate and the House of Commons, to make Laws for the Peace, Order and good

Government of Canada, in relation to all matters not coming within the Classes of Subjects by this Act assigned exclusively to the Legislatures of the Provinces; and for greater Certainty, but not so as to restrict the Generality of the foregoing Terms of this Section, it is hereby declared that (notwithstanding anything in this Act) the exclusive Legislative Authority of the Parliament of Canada extends to . . .

2. The Regulation of Trade and Commerce

2A. Unemployment Insurance

7. Militia, Military and Naval Service and Defence

11. Quarantine and the Establishment and Maintenance of Marine Hospitals

24. Indians, and Lands reserved for Indians

25. Naturalization and Aliens

27. The Criminal Law, . . .

28. The Establishment, Maintenance, and Management of Penitentiaries . . .

92. In each Province the Legislature may exclusively make Laws in relation to Matters coming within the Classes of Subject next hereinafter enumerated; that is to say,

6. The Establishment, Maintenance, and Management of Public Reformatory Prisons, in and for the Province

7. The Establishment, Maintenance, and Management of Hospitals, Asylums, Charities and Eleemosynary institutions, in and for the Province, other than Marine Hospitals

16. Generally all Matters of a merely local or Private Nature in the Province

94A. The Parliament of Canada may make laws in relation to old age pensions and supplementary benefits, including survivor's and disability benefits unrespective of age, but no law shall affect the operation of any law present or future of a provincial legislature in relation to any such matter.

This formal division of powers has been interpreted as providing to the provinces primary jurisdiction over social welfare. The combined effect of sections 91 and 92 resulted in the provinces having all the general powers in the field of social welfare that are not included in the specific list of federal powers included under sections 91 and 94A. This interpretation has been established as a result of the federal government seeking increased powers, certain of the provinces opposing such powers, and the issues of division of powers ultimately reaching the courts.

The role of the courts, and specifically of the Privy Council, was seen when, in 1937, the federal Employment and Social Insurance Act was deemed *ultra vires*. In that instance the Attorney General for Ontario brought action against the Attorney General for Canada. The Supreme Court of Canada ruled 4 to 2 in favour of Ontario. Canada appealed to the Privy Council and the judgement of the Supreme Court was upheld. In 1940, the legislative authority for unemployment insurance was obtained by the federal government through the adoption of a constitutional amendment specifying parliamentary jurisdiction (section 91, subsection [2A]).

Forewarned by this sequence of events, the federal government sought and obtained a constitutional amendment in 1951 giving it authority to make laws in relation to old age pensions (Section 94A). This authority was extended in 1964 to cover survivors, disability, and supplementary benefits, allowing the introduction of the Canada Pension Plan. The power of the Parliament of Canada to make laws affecting social welfare has thus been limited by the constitution and the courts.

There is one exception. The federal government has the exclusive power with respect to Indians and land reserved for Indians (section 91(24)). However, in 1951 the federal government introduced an amendment to the Indian Act (section 88) that has the effect of incorporating into the Indian Act all provincial law that is not contrary to federal law. Thus in matters of child welfare, where the Indian Act is silent, provincial child welfare laws govern Indians. Nevertheless, the situation of First Nations remains different from that of all other Canadians. The federal government remains the only government with financial responsibility and retains the authority to legislate in any way that it chooses.

The principal reasons for federal powers over social welfare were stated by the government of Canada as part of the background preparation for the 1968 constitutional conference.[1] Dealing with income security measures, the reasons given were:

1. *Income redistribution.* The federal government asserted a role in redistributing income nationally, benefiting the populations of poorer provinces at the expense of the wealthier. Only the Parliament of Canada could provide for such a redistribution, hence the need for federal powers.

2. *The sense of community.* The range of social welfare income security measures, such as Family Allowances (now the Child Tax Benefit), Old Age Security, and Unemployment Insurance, has been viewed by the federal government as contributing to a sense of national unity. Receipt of cash by persons is seen as one of the most tangible benefits conferred by a government. The federal government wishes to exercise this power.

3. *Portability.* The Canadian people move frequently between provinces. It is undesirable that benefits vary sharply between provinces. Such variations would tend to deprive some people of benefits they might have expected and hence would tend to impede the movements of people.

4. *Economic policy.* Because income payments made by the federal government affect the total demand for goods and services, they are a part of the means used by the government of Canada to stabilize the economy. Thus, the federal power over economic policy requires the exercise of welfare powers.

5. *Service equality.* In the field of social services, the federal government was prepared to concede a primary role to the provinces. However, a national interest was asserted in social services, that of ensuring a reasonable measure of service equality between provinces.

These goals reflected one of the central objectives of federal social policy, first asserted by the Royal Commission on Dominion-Provincial Relations (1940). The Royal Commission wrote its report in response to the economic chaos and misery that had resulted from the economic depression of the 1930s. It was particularly concerned by the regional impact of the depression, which had been most severe in the Maritime provinces and on the Prairies:

Not only national duty and decency, if Canada is to be a nation at all, but equity and national self-interest demand that the residents of these areas be given average services and equal opportunities, – equity because these areas may have been impoverished by the national economic policies which enriched other areas, and which were adopted in the general interest.[2]

To these earlier reasons for a strong federal role in social welfare, an additional one can be added. As a result of the establishment of a Charter of Rights within the Canadian constitution, Canadians have been given constitutional assurances that require Canadian – implicitly federal – interpretation and administration. Language rights and provisions for freedom of movement are two such examples, the latter having the effect of rendering *ultra vires* a variety of provincial residency conditions that formerly restricted welfare rights.

These reasons for the assertion of a federal power with respect to social welfare are in no way peculiar to Canada. Indeed, the history of the development of social welfare programs throughout the Western industrialized world suggested, until the last decade, a general tendency toward the extension of the welfare powers of national governments. In the 1990s these classical arguments for a major national role are heard less often in Canada and other countries. The reasons for this include the federal deficit and the problems it is creating for the federal government to be able to perform the role it has sought. They include, too, a measure of disillusionment with the effectiveness of social policy in achieving its stated objectives, or disillusionment with the unexpected consequences of the achievements, for example, the apparent development of regional and personal forms of "transfer dependency." In addition, it seems that governments have been influenced by the conservative critics of all social policy who consistently argue for a larger role for the capitalist market and for a smaller role for the state.

Distinctive to the Canadian experience has been the opposition of certain provinces to federal authority and the effects of that opposition. The principal reasons given by certain provinces for seeking to ensure their control over social welfare include the following:

1. *Quebec.* The Quebec government is the leader of a "distinct society" of French culture and language that is a minority society within Canada. The provincial government has thus sought to represent and develop French-Canadian society within the province of Quebec. Social policy has been viewed as playing a central role in the maintenance of French language and culture and has been referred to in each referendum campaign. Quebec therefore wants full powers over social policy for exactly the same national reasons that the federal government does. The separatist Parti Québécois would go further and assert that the history of federalism shows that this has not and cannot be achieved within federalism. They point to the Meech Lake Accord and the Charlottetown Accord as failed attempts to obtain the necessary powers. The Quebec federalists have used the same line of argument to oppose extensions of federal powers and to retain in as full a form as possible the provincial social policy powers that exist in the Canadian constitution.

2. *Ontario, Alberta, and British Columbia.* The effect of the redistributive welfare

function is that the wealthier provinces, specifically Ontario, British Columbia, and Alberta, lose money to the poorer provinces and to the people who live in them. Sometimes the governments of these provinces have accepted the federal argument that this transfer is a national necessity. On other occasions they have opposed the transfer and have sought to keep jurisdictional and financial responsibility for social welfare at the provincial level. This argument is being reasserted as the federal government cuts back its contribution to social welfare spending while seeking to maintain national standards. If the federal government is not paying half the cost of programs its control of policy is questioned.

3. *Provincial diversity and politics.* Canada is the second largest country, geographically, in the world. The distinct regions and their distinct peoples have differing welfare needs and governments of differing political persuasions. At different times, different provinces have established precedents in programming, for example, the introduction of medicare in Saskatchewan in 1962, which would not have been possible if the provinces lacked jurisdictional power. On other occasions some provinces have wanted to offer more restricted services and expand the role of the private market. These initiatives can and have conflicted with federal policies, resulting in contradictory programs and policies. Within the administration of joint programs these political contradictions result in major conflicts and competitiveness between federal and provincial bureaucracies. The net result for both governments is usually a largely wasted effort, with public resources consumed in purely political competition.

4. *Administrative efficiency and accountability.* The effect of federal actions – in combination with provincial action – has been to produce major administrative burdens on both levels of government. Furthermore, the existing divisions of power obstruct the proper accountability of governments for the services they render by diffusing political accountability and transferring the forum for decisions from publicly elected legislatures to closed-door meetings between federal and provincial officials and politicians.

The leaders of First Nations are also seeking to obtain recognition of social policy as an inherent Aboriginal jurisdiction. Like the Quebec government, they want to be able to use social policy as a means of developing and protecting their distinct identities. In the 1990s these arguments by provinces and First Nations work in support of the federal government's own reasons for a diminished role in social welfare. The result is movement toward a smaller federal role, as seen in the Canada Health and Social Transfer Act (1995). As a consequence, however, federal standard setting is increasingly questioned.

The Federal Role

The existing federal role in social welfare has been built using five different policy and administrative mechanisms.

1. *Use of existing federal powers.* The federal government has made extensive use of those welfare powers it has been able to develop on the basis of the existing constitution. Thus, a wide array of employment services and training subsidies has been developed on the basis of the powers of the federal government with respect

to the economy and on the basis of the Unemployment Insurance amendment. The federal responsibility for the militia and for military service has been the basis for the organization of extensive welfare services for veterans. Similarly, the federal responsibility for Indians has been used, somewhat less comprehensively, in the development of welfare services for Native peoples. The federal responsibility for naturalization and aliens has been used to develop services for immigrants and also to provide support to multicultural activities under the general heading of "citizenship" services. The federal responsibility for the criminal law and for penitentiaries has been used in the development of national parole services.

2. *Taxing and spending powers.* As a result of federal-provincial income tax agreements the federal government has exclusive income tax authority in all provinces except Quebec. Even in Quebec, where there is a separate provincial income tax, the federal government has its own income tax authority. Thus the federal government can make a tax expenditure or provide a refundable tax benefit.

The government of Canada has also asserted the right to make payments directly to individuals. Thus, Family Allowances were introduced in 1945 without constitutional amendment. However, while asserting this right, the government has introduced little legislation of this nature and has now withdrawn Family Allowances. Instead, constitutional amendments have been sought. This could be the result of apprehensions that, if challenged in the courts, such powers would not be upheld.

3. *Equalization payments.*[3] Equalization is enshrined in the Canadian constitution. The purpose of equalization is to ensure "that provincial governments have sufficient revenues to provide reasonably comparable levels of public services at reasonably comparable levels of taxation."[4] Equalization is the key federal-provincial program for social welfare, as it is designed to ensure that the revenue base for social welfare (and other government services) is similar in all provinces. The wealthy provinces, Ontario, Alberta, and British Columbia, receive no funds from equalization while Newfoundland, for example, received $1,524/capita and Quebec received $500/capita in 1992-93.[5]

4. *Established Programs Financing.* Established Programs Financing was introduced in 1977 to replace cost-sharing in the fields of hospital insurance, medicare, and post-secondary education. Through EPF, tax points and cash were made available to the provinces in place of cost-sharing. (A tax point is the amount of money yielded by 1 per cent of income tax revenue in the province; no money changed hands with tax points; the province simply keeps a larger share of income tax revenues.) Originally, the tax points and cash were similar in amount, but with the imposition in 1982 of an overall ceiling on EPF transfers, the proportion of the payment in tax points is rising and the amount paid in cash is falling. This is important because of the relationship between EPF and the Canada Health Act. The Canada Health Act is the cornerstone of national medicare standards (universal access, no user fees, no provincial residency restrictions, and comprehensive coverage). If a province fails to adhere to these standards the amount it receives in EPF payments is reduced by the amount it has reduced its medicare costs. However, as the EPF cash transfer to a province falls toward zero, the Canada Health Act penalty to a province going its own way on medicare becomes more questionable

as a province is already paying most of the costs of health from its own revenues. At the point when it falls to zero, penalties would no longer apply and medicare as we know it would no longer be guaranteed by the federal government. The CHST was designed, in part, to delay the point at which the cash portion of EPF payments drop to zero. It does this by adding the former Canada Assistance Plan shared-cost payment to the EPF transfer, albeit at a reduced level.

5. *Shared-cost programs.* Historically, shared-cost programs were the most important means used by the government of Canada to extend its influence over social welfare. A shared-cost program was one in which the federal Parliament approved legislation permitting the payment of federal funds to provinces in support of provincial welfare programs. Such programs are also referred to as "conditional grant" programs. Shared-cost programs had a significant effect on the use of provincial powers. To be eligible for cost-sharing, the province had to design a program that met federal requirements; elsewise, it would have to forgo the available program funds. As their electorates were already contributing to program costs in Canada as a whole through the federal taxes they were paying, the provinces were obliged to enter such agreements. To influence provincial priorities and programs, the federal government used cost-sharing extensively in this way throughout the post-war period until the 1980s. The Canada Assistance Plan, hospital insurance, medicare, support for post-secondary education, and the public housing provisions of the National Housing Act were all introduced as shared-cost programs. The result is seen in the development of a similar array of basic social welfare provisions throughout Canada.

The use of conditional grants did have problems, however. (1) The less wealthy regions and their provincial governments benefited less from such programming than the more wealthy regions whose provincial governments could better afford the provincial contribution to program costs.[6] (2) Conditional grants had the generally undesirable effect of diffusing government accountability for social welfare programs. Instead of clear responsibility residing at either the federal or provincial level, it rested with both. (3) In addition, administrative, legal, and fiscal complexity compounded with each passing year. Governments at the provincial level use their resources to seek the widest possible cost-sharing, while at the federal level the definition of eligible expenditures was narrowed to restrain costs.

Despite these problems the CAP remained a shared-cost program as cost-sharing provided an assurance of federal participation in the unpredictable changes in welfare costs that accompany the business cycle and its differential impact regionally. The withdrawal of the CAP as a shared-cost program was done to allow the federal government to limit its exposure to these risks. With the conclusion of the CAP and the introduction of the CHST the use of cost-sharing is limited to social housing and some other minor activities. It would seem probable that cost-sharing for these programs, too, will eventually be ended.

The Influence of Electoral Politics

The influence of electoral politics on Canadian social welfare policies and programs is exercised within the context of the divided jurisdiction over social welfare between the federal and provincial governments. This division of jurisdiction affects the power of any government, federal or provincial, to pursue its policy aims. Thus, electoral politics does not have the same direct impact on policies and programs that can be expected in a unitary state.

The election in 1963 of a Liberal government, headed by Prime Minister Pearson and committed in its electoral platform to the establishment of the Canada Pension Plan, led to extensive federal-provincial negotiation. The federal government needed to secure a constitutional amendment to introduce the plan. To obtain this concession, changes in the original thrust of the government's intention were negotiated. These included the establishment of a separate parallel plan by the province of Quebec (the Quebec Pension Plan) and provision for the establishment of a pension fund that would be invested in provincial government bonds, providing the provinces with a dependable source of capital. The federal situation is basically the same in the 1990s. The election of a Liberal government, headed by Jean Chrétien, seeking to contain and reduce federal expenditures has again led to extensive federal-provincial negotiations.

The situation of a provincial government elected with a clear mandate for social reform is constitutionally clearer. However, the provincial freedom to act has been constrained by national program standards, as in the Canada Health Act, and by the detailed cost-sharing agreements under the CAP. The result has been that provincial governments seek to obtain federal permission and financial support through negotiation. While such negotiations are being conducted, the introduction of new programs and policies is delayed, and failure in negotiation may lead to their abandonment. This is not to suggest that electoral politics are without influence on social welfare. It does imply that political compromise between governments of different political persuasions has been the characteristic route to change.

Further, it has not been possible to distinguish one political party, federally or provincially, as being exclusively the proponent of social welfare ideals while another is characterized exclusively by opposition. Instead, each party can rightfully claim to have made some contribution to building social welfare in the 1960s and 1970s, while in the 1980s and 1990s each has participated in dismantling and restraining costs. During the 1960s and 1970s, the concluding stages of debate at both provincial and federal levels have been more frequently characterized by multi-party support for social welfare.

Despite these modifying influences on the expression of a clear welfare ideology within the field of electoral politics, significant differences exist between the major political parties.

The New Democratic Party has been the most consistent advocate of social welfare in the Canadian political spectrum. The party's political statements, more clearly than those of other parties, have committed it to the welfare ideal of the redistribution of income, wealth, and power. When elected to office (in British Columbia, Saskatchewan, Manitoba, and Ontario), New Democratic governments have shown a willingness to introduce social welfare programs not legislated anywhere else in Canada or, indeed, in North America. An example of an initiative of this type was the enactment by Saskatchewan of a provincial medicare program in 1962. The effects of these initiatives have extended beyond the provinces in which they were enacted. The federal government has been co-opted to their support and other provinces have tended to establish similar provisions at later dates.

In the federal Parliament, in which the New Democratic Party has consistently held a minority of seats, the party's spokespeople have been the advocates of social welfare programs. Long before Liberal or Progressive Conservative governments have introduced social welfare legislation, members of Parliament from the New Democratic Party and its predecessor, the Co-operative Commonwealth Federation, have brought the need of Canadians for such programs as pensions, medicare, housing, and income guarantees before the House of Commons.

These consistent long-term objectives have been challenged in the 1980s and the NDP has found itself in the position of an opposition party defending the status quo from government-initiated dismantling and restraint policies. When elected as a government the NDP has had to face the same revenue and expenditure problems that confront all Canadian governments. The result for NDP leadership has been difficulty in acting as they would wish in such areas as welfare rates and reform. Ralph writes:

> We asked anti-poverty activists in British Columbia, Saskatchewan and Ontario to comment on how the poor are faring under their respective NDP governments. While acknowledging small improvements, all three are disappointed by the failure of the NDP to make good on their commitment to challenge inequality and poverty and by their capitulation to the "corporate agenda."[7]

The Liberal Party can rightfully claim to have comprised the federal government when nearly all significant social welfare legislation has been passed by Parliament. They also formed the federal government for most of the post-war period: 1945-57, 1963-79, 1980-84, 1993- . Furthermore, committed Liberals are proud of their party's record in the welfare field. Judy LaMarsh wrote of the Department of National Health and Welfare and of her being asked to be minister (1963-65):

> It is a department to a Liberal that is cherished indeed. Such greats in their time as Paul Martin and Brooke Claxton had served in that portfolio. To any Liberal, the subject matter dealt with in National Health and Welfare are "gut" issues – basic to their whole philosophy of the role of Government in modern society.[8]

Although very significant social welfare programs were legislated by Liberal governments in the 1960s, the record of the federal governments led by Pierre Trudeau generally was one of rhetorical support for welfare ideals accompanied by increasing bureaucratization of welfare functions. Sometimes it seemed that the true beneficiaries were increasingly the service staffs rather than the needy groups within the society. The recent record of the Chrétien government has been one of managing the process of containing costs and reducing the federal presence in social policy.

At the provincial level, Liberal governments have shown various attitudes toward social welfare legislation. Some Liberal governments, such as the Saskatchewan Liberals under Ross Thatcher, have run against the welfare proposals of their New Democratic Party opponents. Other Liberal governments have established positions of leadership in the introduction of social welfare programs in their own provinces and in the influence they have brought to bear on the federal government. Liberal governments in Quebec have shared this emphasis. The comprehensive and substantial social reforms resulting from the Commission of Inquiry into Health and Welfare (the Castonguay-Nepeuv Report, 1971) are a good example.

During the years when the Progressive Conservative Party formed the federal government (1957-63, 1979-80, 1984-93), no major welfare programs were ever enacted. During the Mulroney government there was a general failure to match the early rhetoric proclaiming that "social programs are a sacred trust" with action. The work of the Task Force on Child Care led to the introduction of legislation that was never enacted. Family Allowances were replaced by the Child Tax Benefit. A process of partial de-indexation was put in place that means that inflation will continue to erode the value of federal social program benefits. Yet the Mulroney government also failed to deal with the mounting problems of public expenditure and the deficit, allowing these long-term threats to social programs to grow unchecked. Given the neo-conservative emphasis of the 1980s and the enthusiasm with which Mulroney was a fellow traveller of the right with U.S. President Ronald Reagan and Britain's Margaret Thatcher, it is in fact surprising that there was not stronger federal leadership aimed at restraint and simplification. However, the Canadian federal Conservatives exercised great caution in the welfare field, leaving it to the provincial parties to articulate and apply restraint. The years from 1984 to 1993 were largely wasted in incremental bureaucratic "tinkering" with social programs by a government that did not appear to treat matters of social policy as priority issues.

Those provinces that have had Progressive Conservative governments for extended periods, such as Ontario, have shown cautious or negative attitudes toward social welfare programs. Thus, the original opposition of Ontario to the federal medicare program was not only based in the province's desire to protect a field it viewed to be part of provincial jurisdiction. It was also an expression of conservative political philosophy. Despite the fact that at the provincial level Conservative parties have held office more frequently than Liberal parties, it is not possible to find examples of provincial Conservative parties that have shown a strong commitment to welfare. On the other hand, it is not difficult to find examples of Conservative parties that have engaged in active anti-welfare measures, for example, the 1993 Klein government in Alberta and the 1995 Harris government in Ontario. The opportunity for anti-welfare action by Conservative governments is being broadened by the federal withdrawal from cost-shared programming.

The Reform Party in western Canada and Ontario and the Social Credit in Alberta and British Columbia have expressed a strong market orientation that has usually resulted in opposition to social programs and a willingness to engage enthusiastically in restraint policies. The 1983 Social Credit Bennett government in B.C. will long be remembered for the reputation it established for cutbacks and mass firings of civil servants. The rhetoric was of removing the state from areas of activity that should be left to families and to charitable institutions.

The Parti Québécois in Quebec has been preoccupied by the issues of separation. However, the policy statements and referendum campaigns of the party show an active concern for social policy issues. In the 1995 campaign virtually every women's group and social services group in the province were in the "Yes" camp. Federalism and the conservative social and economic policies of the "rest of Canada" were critiqued and rejected for the social policy direction of a sovereign Quebec.

The Courts

The courts played an important role in the early development of Canadian social policy in upholding provincial jurisdiction and thereby forcing the federal government either to seek constitutional amendments or to influence, rather than control, social policy through use of the spending power. However, it was not until the passage of the Charter of Rights and Freedoms in 1982 that the courts obtained the authority they now have. The Charter requires that the law and its administration be impartial and free from discrimination. Social policy, by contrast, is all about discrimination. Some people receive benefits while others do not. Some programs are only available to seniors while others are only available to children. Some relationships, for example, heterosexual marriage, are recognized by the state, while others are not. Some people, for example, Aboriginal peoples, have a special status. Some women become pregnant and have abortions, while others do not. In these many instances of discrimination, the courts have to judge whether the discriminations in social policy are "reasonable." The courts are not a law-making body, nor do they control expenditures. The power of the courts lies in their ability to strike down legislation or prohibit administrative actions that cannot be justified as reasonable. They can, of course, also award settlements to persons who have been discriminated against. The courts are thus an important instrument of social change in such areas as women's equality rights, abortion, gay and lesbian rights, and mandatory retirement. At some future point they could be much more active than they have been so far and strike down many more social policy provisions. Courchene sees a possible role for the courts "for creative destruction in the evolution of social policy"[9] – by which he means the wholesale removal of existing programs as discriminatory. Historically, however, the courts have not readily set aside the policy decisions of legislatures, so a wide use of the courts in striking down major social policy provisions seems improbable.

The Corporate Elite

In his analysis of social class and power in Canada, John Porter distinguished a series of elites: an economic elite; a labour elite; a political elite; a bureaucratic elite;

and an ideological elite composed of the media, higher learning, and clergy.[10] In Porter's study the corporate or economic elite was defined by studying the boards of directors of 183 corporations that dominated the Canadian economy. He found a pattern of interlocking memberships and shared family ties, private school education, Anglo-Saxon origins, and a capitalist value system. Clement's analysis of the corporate elite in the 1970s found a similar pattern, with a tendency toward greater concentration of power and more ties to American and multinational capital.[11] Later works and studies have confirmed the existence of an elite comprised of Canadian business leaders and multinational corporate representatives that collectively own or manage the major capitalist enterprises that dominate the Canadian economy. This elite group has acquired greater influence through its participation in the global economy. The corporate elite and its small business allies can be viewed as being usually hostile, or at best tolerant, toward social welfare institutions. Porter wrote:

> The Chamber of Commerce and the Canadian Manufacturers' Association are together organized corporate capitalism, if not at prayer, at least in an intense passion of ideology. At meetings and in briefs to governments the way to salvation which is presented is through competitive free enterprise. All measures toward welfarism are seen as the road to ruin. Higher profits, higher incomes, and lower taxes to provide initiative at the top are seen as essentials to social progress.[12]

During the period when social programs were being developed, the effects of the economic elite's influence on social welfare appeared to lie principally in their power to delay or divert the extent of the welfare transfer. The egalitarian approach to taxation proposed in the *Report of the Royal Commission on Taxation* (1966) triggered a period of intense lobbying by economic interests seeking to protect incentives and productivity. The subsequent amended Income Tax Act (1971) led away from the egalitarian thrust of the original proposals. The influence of the economic elite on specific measures, for example, pensions, also appears to have been substantial. The introduction of the Canada Pension Plan was marked by the opposition of the Canadian life insurance industry. Judy LaMarsh provided an entertaining account of a group of insurance company presidents visiting her with the intention of persuading her not to proceed with the legislation:

> We had no real meeting of minds at all, although the discussion was polite enough, because I could not understand their bland assumption that we would renege on our election promises, and they could not make me see that it would be better all round, and less disruptive of business, if we just forgot the whole thing.[13]

However, the effects of this campaign remain. Judy LaMarsh herself pointed out that the Canada Pension Plan was designed with the expectation that private insurance plans would be "stacked" over the government plan. This is another way of admitting that the government plan would provide a rather low level of benefit so that the interests of the private insurance industry would not be seriously hurt. In addition, the right of individuals to deduct life insurance premiums from their pre-tax earnings was retained, and subsequently the amount deductible was increased.

Since the 1970s the corporate elite has become more sophisticated and influential. It has supported the development of a significant research and policy analysis capacity. The Fraser Institute, the C.D. Howe Institute, and the Business Council on National Issues have a substantial research, analytic, publishing, and lobbying capacity. The C.D. Howe Institute's Social Policy Challenge series, for instance, comprises fourteen volumes covering every aspect of social policy reform from workfare to pensions, from Unemployment Insurance to the family, from demographics to Aboriginal policy. Although the Institute claims to present a diversity of viewpoints, the overwhelming authorship is by labour market economists who share the values of the corporate agenda. Other views that are published are introduced by the authors as "dissenting" and are treated as marginal. The corporate agenda has also been reinforced through the ties that have been drawn between the agenda and the global economy. McQuaig indicates that the Canadian business community has sometimes looked for bad news on the Canadian debt and deficit as a way, presumably, of reinforcing an internal agenda of social policy restraint and reform.[14] Ralph writes:

> The underlying goal is to "harmonize" the Canadian labour force with the demands of the global market place. In other words, the reviews are not just another round of cuts. They are about destroying the whole notion of social insurance and social rights and replacing it with a draconian corporate model based on forcing workers to "adjust" to Third World labour conditions. Both Liberal and Conservative federal governments (as well as provincial governments of all three parties) seem to have decided that the world economy globalization is inevitable and, for some, even desirable. Under threats of lowered credit ratings, and heavy pressure from corporate lobbies, they have all agreed to collaborate with business interests to help them stay afloat among the high stakes players of the international market place.[15]

The corporate agenda is an open one, and in the 1990s it is exercising a dominant influence on the direction of change.

The Political and Bureaucratic Elite

The political and bureaucratic elite is comprised of leading politicians, judges, and senior civil servants. The social background of this group is primarily upper middle class. Entry to its ranks formally depends on politics or merit, rather than money. However, Porter's analysis of the political and bureaucratic elite thirty years ago suggested that "the underprivileged classes have never produced a political leader at the federal level." One could have added that women were rare exceptions and ethnic origin was disproportionately Anglo-Saxon. Porter also found that Canadian politics is affected substantially by "avocationalism" (political careers are interstitial in business or legal careers rather than being vocations in their own right) and by the fact that the complex structure of federalism tends to convert potentially partisan political issues into issues of administrative politics between bureaucracies. In turn:

> Avocational and administrative politics leaves the political system relatively weak as a system of institutional power. With a political elite of substantially middle class origins the dynamics of social class which give rise to conservative and progressive social forces have never worked themselves out within the political system. Perhaps it is from looking at their politicians that Canadians get the impression that their society is a middle class one. Neither the corporate elite, nor the very wealthy, have much to fear from middle class politicians. It is more likely that the politicians hold the corporate elite in awe.[16]

Olsen, writing about the early 1970s, found some changes, particularly more Francophone presence. However, attitude changes were slight. The "middle class state elite sees itself in alliance with business, or at least not in any fundamental opposition to its general interest."[17] As a result, the bureaucratic and state elite is influenced relatively easily by the corporate elite and its agencies.

The political and bureaucratic elite is also sensitive to Canada's national standing in formal international assemblies. Canada has an established international reputation for living standards, social stability, human rights, support to the United Nations and other international agencies, relative openness to receive refugees, and peacekeeping. Canada maintains that reputation by support and adherence to United Nations conventions on such matters as human rights (including the Convention on the Rights of the Child) and racism. United Nations conventions do not have the force of law, nor do they require member governments to operate social programs.[18] The most the United Nations can do is monitor compliance by publishing reports on the records of member states. Canada's record of treatment of Aboriginal peoples is an example of a field where Canada has been sensitive as to how its actions are viewed at the international level.[19]

The influence of international financial agencies is also substantial. These agencies include the Organization for Economic Co-operation and Development (OECD), the International Monetary Fund (IMF), and the World Bank. These agencies monitor the world's economies from differing perspectives and for different reasons. However, they share a common free market economic set of interests and ideologies. The OECD provides parallel analysis and data on the economies of twenty-four market economies, principally in Europe and North America. Its view of Canada's fiscal performance mirrors that of the corporate elite and of the C.D. Howe Institute. The 1994 edition of the OECD Canada survey contains a section on social programs. It concludes:

> . . . Canadians were adversely affected by two major recessions and dislocation due to economic restructuring (a reference to NAFTA and to the global economy).

However, the current trend of expenditure on UI and social assistance cannot be sustained in the current fiscal environment. Furthermore, these programmes are no longer appropriately designed for current economic and labour market conditions. Indeed, they contain disincentives to work, which may contribute to a growing dependency on transfer income.[20]

Views held in the IMF and World Bank are similar. If Canada had to turn to the IMF for support for the Canadian dollar, one would expect that cuts to social programs would be high on the list of items to be conceded as a condition of support, just as has been the case with all other countries that have had to turn to these agencies for financial support. Tester writes:

> The logic behind the structural adjustment programs applied to third world countries is deceptively simple. As a condition of receiving ongoing financial support, debtor countries have to accept terms laid on them by the IMF. These measures include: reducing the cost of government, especially by reducing the size of the public service; terminating government subsidies for food, fuel, and other essentials; devaluing the currency to control imports and increasing exports. . . . According to some reports, Canada has been secretly advised by the IMF to handle the Canadian economy in the same way . . . .[21]

The political and bureaucratic elite is sensitive to messages of this type. They would like Canada to have a more positive international financial report card.

The Media

Ownership of the media (with the exception of the CBC) is by the Canadian corporate elite and by international corporations. This ensures that the perspective of the corporate elite on policy issues is always maintained. It does not mean that the views of the elite are presented on every occasion and in every article. At the day-to-day level of operation journalists and editors have freedom to operate and seek to present a broad array of points of view. However, it would be unusual for a major paper or television network to mount a sustained coverage of social policy issues from a pro-welfare perspective. On the other hand, all provide sustained coverage of corporate and business news, usually written from an informed and sympathetic position.

The National Council of Welfare's 1973 study, *The Press and the Poor*,[22] explored how the media treated poverty. The findings suggested that the media tend to maintain rather than alter contemporary attitudes toward the nature of poverty and social welfare. Several reasons for this tendency are suggested. The media are often monopolies – one-newspaper cities abound in Canada, for example. But the media are also expected to be responsible, to avoid the one-sided pursuit of partisan issues, and to present all sides of an issue. Where this task is done well, the result is to confirm existing understandings of issues. In addition, there are tendencies, not deliberate or malicious but inadvertent, to make media coverage of poverty shallow. These include the relatively "unimportant" nature of the community involved, the control of most information by bureaucracies hostile to the disclosure of their internal affairs, and the tendency to view the situation of the poor in "we-they" terms. Because of these tendencies, the media tended to reinforce existing stereotypes and misunderstandings. Given media ownership, it is not realistic to expect them to develop depth of critical analysis nor to play a critical role in presenting interpretations of issues contrary to the interests of their owners.

Government Human Service Organizations and Program Beneficiaries

The establishment of social welfare policy objectives and programs has required the development of major administrative and service organizations. Indeed, the presence of such organizations is seen as "a hallmark of modern society." These organizations have the task of translating the policies, values, and ideals of the welfare state into specific programs. They do the work of redistribution and provide the social services. On the one hand, they provide access to service, distribute benefits, and create special statuses; on the other, they deny access to service, maintain social control, and stigmatize their clientele. They are needed but they are rarely loved. Indeed, "The individual's loss of power to human service organizations is a fundamental characteristic of the welfare state."[23] Whereas the elected governments are invested with the formal powers of the state, the actual day-to-day operations and the power that derives therefrom are held by the organizations that do the work. The billions of dollars and the thousands of civil servants and professional social workers involved represent a substantial interest in their own right.

The division of powers between federal and provincial governments has increased the power and influence of the organizations that deliver benefits and services, having the effect of removing political decision-making with respect to policy from elected assemblies to intergovernmental negotiations between federal and provincial bureaucracies. The career civil servant works within the context of existing social welfare programs. The day-to-day dealings necessary for the conduct of the large shared-cost programs required the maintenance of working agreements and relationships. Individuals involved shared similar backgrounds, usually in social work or public administration, participated in career patterns that move from provincial bureaucracy to federal bureaucracy, and shared similar values and goals with respect to social welfare programming. At one time, during the 1960s and 1970s, these organizational interests provided an enduring and consistent force for social welfare reform. However, this influence has been weakened at both federal and provincial levels by staffing policies that have focused on management expertise rather than social policy knowledge in senior staff, accompanied by policies of moving senior staff between ministries. Both sets of staffing policies have made it more difficult for civil servants to develop and maintain a progressive influence on social policy.[24] Nevertheless, the government service organizations provide what Courchene refers to as "the inertial power of the status quo."[25]

The power is established at two major levels, employees and beneficiaries. Both levels are broad enough to have an impact on elections, particularly in some constituencies and particularly in areas of the country where the benefits of the regional redistribution that accompanies social welfare are strongest. In addition, for the employees their position is further strengthened by union membership, permitting collective action to be taken. There have been examples of successful political resistance to change in social programs, as when seniors opposed the de-indexation of Old Age Security proposed by the 1985 Mulroney government.

One proposal to reduce the costs of Canada's social programs is to reduce the wage levels in the public services generally and in the human service organizations in particular. Richards, one of the editors of the C.D. Howe series on social policy, is a major proponent of this approach:

> Identification of the public sector payroll as a source of spending reduction is warranted for three reasons. First, the wages of public and quasi-public employees are a large item; of the order of 15% of total program spending of Ottawa and 60% for the provinces. Second, the compensation advantage of public sector wages over comparable private sector wages has become unjustifiable given the need for budgetary restraint. Third, comparative compensation studies do not take into account the benefit of greater public sector job security.[26]

The problem of applying this strategy is recognized by Richards, who goes on to say that "Reducing the payroll is a tactic that will be intensely unpopular among public sector unions." Courchene, too, acknowledges that "these vested interests [employees and beneficiaries] are indeed powerful."[27] As governments, of all persuasions, get closer to elections they become much less likely to undertake any sudden action that would annoy voters. There is a tendency to defer any cutting until after the election. Thus, the time of greatest vulnerability to change in existing programs is limited to the first two years following an election.

A purely defensive posture in regard to social programs is not attractive to many social policy advocates, who in most cases spent a good deal of time criticizing programs for their policy shortcomings and for their bureaucratic administration. Ralph writes:

> The vision of fighting just to keep what we have is too narrow. People feel justifiably ambivalent about the social programs they use and pay for. It's hard to work up much enthusiasm for even the "good old days" of the Welfare State. We wanted a just, equal, safe and humane society. We got inadequate, demeaning welfare, UI and Workers' Compensation. We wanted an end to violence against women, and we got underfunded shelters and rape crisis lines. We wanted an end to racism, and we got small grants to competing ethnic minorities to fight among themselves and blame all whites.[28]

Nevertheless, the inertial power of the status quo is what the dominant corporate elite and their allies appear to think is the most likely reason they will not reach their goals of a radical pro-market restructuring of social welfare. This, more than anything else, leads them to want to reinforce their arguments by reference to Canada's deficit problems. Courchene writes:

> In the final analysis, it may well be wishful thinking on my part that the politics of social policy reform is do-able. But then the alternative is to run into the fiscal and financial "wall" and to turn over the restructuring, in part at least, to agents outside Canada.[29]

Organized Labour

The role of organized labour in social welfare has been an uneven one. The Canadian Labour Congress, in particular, has been proud of its support of the process of social reform:

> In the deliberations of labour conventions since 1898 there have been changes, sometimes in subject matter, sometimes in emphasis; but there has always been a persistent theme of concern with social issues which affect all citizens. The trade union movement, from its beginning until the present, has seen itself as a spokesman for ordinary working people in those matters.[30]

Social welfare, however, has not been a central concern of labour in Canada, which has concentrated most of its attention on the basic processes of labour organizing and wage and benefit negotiation. Nor has organized labour been immune from the sexism and racism found in Canadian society generally and in social policy in particular. Carniol concludes his sympathetic treatment of the labour movement and social work by saying:

> Coming from a history of hostility from employers and the state, the labour movement has had an uphill struggle. In addition to being put on the defensive by dominant economic structures, trade unions had incorporated the sexism and racism prevalent in Canadian life. Only in recent years has the labour movement become inclusive of women and people of colour.[31]

In fighting for a "family wage" and accompanying social policy provisions in UI and Workers' Compensation, the labour movement emphasized the financial dependency of women. Attention was primarily on the blue-collar industrial worker. The reality of the gender division of the labour force is that it now has two worker stereotypes – the male blue-collar worker and the female service worker – with a large wage differential between them. The single mothers in the service occupations are most vulnerable to living below the poverty line, whether employed or on social assistance, yet their cause has received less attention because women were assumed to be secondary earners rather than full labour force participants.

In turn, Canadian social welfare legislation has been less attentive to the relationship between social welfare and wages than in those Western countries, such as Australia, in which the labour movement has played a more substantial role in the development of minimum wages as a central feature of social welfare. Wage differentials between men and women are significantly less in Australia.

In the current unstable economic climate organized labour is primarily focused on job preservation and creation, particularly the preservation and creation of jobs in the manufacturing and public service sectors of the economy where unionization has been highest and where job losses are reducing union memberships. As noted above, the stance of organized labour has not gone unnoticed by those who are proposing radical changes in social program employment terms. A secondary objective of labour has been to preserve the existing structure and benefits of the UI program. These objectives make organized labour a significant contributor to the defence of existing programs and benefits. In addition, in recent years organized labour has given more attention to issues of women's equality and freedom from harassment or discrimination in the workplace.

The Higher-learning and Religious Elites

Porter identified two additional elite groups, a higher-learning elite and a religious elite. In 1965 Porter wrote that the higher-learning elite contributed little to social criticism and had little impact on the society outside its walls in English Canada. French-Canadian higher learning appeared to have a more dynamic relationship with the society of which it was part. However, such writers as Marcel Rioux[32] and Yves Martin[33] or, indeed, Pierre Trudeau, concentrated their attention on nationalistic issues rather than on issues of social class and inequality. Neither the English nor the French tradition was thus particularly productive with respect to the development of a distinct Canadian welfare ideology. However, the isolation of higher learning from social welfare programs was not complete, and since 1965 there has been substantial growth in informed academic analysis of social welfare. One school of thought has been characterized by the concern for liberal values and the pursuit of social justice; a second has been characterized by Marxist and structural analysis of welfare; a third has been characterized by economic analysis. Each of these schools of thought has well-defined positions on the current issues of social policy. However, they do not cohere into a single position; hence, the overall effect of the higher-learning elite is diminished.

The religious elite has also had a dispersed relationship to social policy. The influence of organized religion on electoral and regional politics has been substantial. On the Prairies, with the exception of Alberta, the Social Gospel of the Protestant churches, the agrarian populist sentiment, and the hostility to eastern business interests provided the context for the emergence of the one consistent supporter of welfare ideals in the Canadian political spectrum – the Co-operative Commonwealth Federation (now the New Democratic Party). The early leaders of the CCF-NDP, among them J.S. Woodsworth, Tommy Douglas, and Stanley Knowles, were drawn principally from the ranks of the clergy. The United Church, in particular, continues to be a source of progressive thought and action. In Alberta the same social forces, combined with fundamentalist rather than Social Gospel traditions, provided the context for the development of the Social Credit Party, which has tended to support individualism rather than welfare collectivism. In Quebec, the Roman Catholic Church viewed itself as the protector of nationalism and to this end sought and obtained control over the institutions of health, education, and welfare. It was not until the second half of this century that Quebec began the task of legislating the secular social institutions, responsible to state political processes, that are characteristic of Western industrialized societies. Thus, although the impact of churches on social welfare in Canada has been considerable, the influence has not been in one direction but has rather contributed to substantial differences in approaches to social welfare between different regions of Canada. At the national level, no unified influence exists.

The Welfare and Academic Lobbies

The pro-welfare think-tanks at the Canadian Council on Social Development, the National Council of Welfare, and the Caledon Institute provide an important research, analytic, and publishing capacity that matches the capacity of the Fraser Institute and the C.D. Howe Institute. They are also part of a wider network of social policy advocacy that includes associated national organizations like the National Anti-Poverty Organization and End Legislated Poverty, professional organizations like the Canadian Association of Social Workers, local community social planning councils and similar organizations, and university departments of social work and social policy. The strength of this chain is primarily intellectual. It has provided a stream of ideas as to how to improve social programs. The most recent product has been the focus on child poverty and the proposals for an expanded family or child benefit program. Parts of the chain are also effective organizers of public demonstrations and protests. At one time, during the 1960s and 1970s, it had the attention of governments. Now it has to fight for attention against the dominant position established by the corporate elite and their organizations. Parts of this chain are also vulnerable to government restraint or reprisal as they depend for funding on government programs.

The Feminist and Other Social Movements

The feminist social movement has been an important influence on social policy, particularly during the 1980s and 1990s, and its achievements in forging new fields of social policy and establishing new services, particularly at the community level, are impressive. At the national level the Canadian Advisory Council on the Status of Women sponsored a series of studies on the relationship between women's situation in employment, social policy, and poverty.[34] The more militant National Action Committee on the Status of Women (NAC) has provided organizational support to protest actions against government restraint and reform proposals at both the federal and provincial levels. The NAC has also been a strong advocate of women in the refugee and immigrant communities and has opposed measures that make immigration more difficult or more dependent on payments. An important contribution of feminism to social policy changes comes in the form of an expectation now that all social policy change will be subject to a "gender lens" review.

A "gender lens" review examines proposals from the perspective of their effects, positive or negative, on women and equity. Sumera Thobani, the NAC president, provides the following account of how she raised the need for such a review with Finance Minister Paul Martin:

> "What is the national interest? Patriarchy? Sexism?" She noted that NAC had held at least five meetings with Finance Minister Paul Martin and had asked him whether or not his department had conducted a gender analysis of the federal budget. "Quite frankly, Ms. Thobani, our department does not have the capacity for doing that kind of analysis", she quoted him as saying. She added that "any democratic government which is committed to the political partici- pation of women has a responsibility to be funding that kind of work."[35]

Other social movements, for example the gay and lesbian movement, also have notable accomplishments, both as service providers and as critics of existing ser- vices and advocates of change.

From a political perspective, a weakness of the social movements is that they are based on organizing people on sectarian lines for sectarian purposes. Each movement seeks its own objectives and common agendas are difficult to establish, or, if formed, contain so many items that the agenda as a whole becomes over- loaded with the specific issues of each group. How to unite the social movements in a common vision is of central concern to such writers as Brian Wharf,[36] Diana Ralph,[37] and Peter Leonard.[38] But until a solution is found the source of the strength of the social movements will also be a source of weakness. Individually, they can influence how social welfare changes, but they have little or no influence over the scope and resources of social welfare as a whole. Courchene and the corporate elite he speaks for appear to ignore them. One can read the social policy series of the C.D. Howe Institute from cover to cover without finding a social movement per- spective seriously incorporated into a policy proposal. In most cases they are not even acknowledged to exist.

Aboriginal Peoples

Whereas most of the parties to the conflict on the future role and substance of social welfare are giving primary attention to specific program objectives and issues, Aboriginal peoples are concerned principally with jurisdiction. The Aboriginal encounter with social welfare has been oppressive and destructive of Aboriginal culture from its nineteenth-century formulation in the Indian Act and in treaty negotiation to its present expression in federal and provincial programs. From an Aboriginal perspective there is no virtue to be found in the loss of an independent way of life and the substitution of social assistance; no virtue to be found in the removal of children and their placement as foster or adopted children in non- Aboriginal homes; no virtue in having replaced the elders by the wisdom of judges, lawyers, and social workers; no virtue in having introduced communities to alcohol and drugs and offered in return detoxification and counselling; and no virtue in generations of children going to residential school, only to return abused and poorly educated for either world.

Poverty is everywhere in the Aboriginal community. However, a result of its prevalence is that it loses some of its power to frighten and obtain conformity to social norms. The Aboriginal community is by far the most militant of the social movements, the only one prepared to challenge the Canadian state by armed action, and, along with the environmental movement, one of a few social movements prepared to defy courts and go to jail for political reasons.

The objective of Aboriginal militancy is control of social policy, that is, jurisdiction rather than specific reforms. Canadian governments at both the federal and provincial levels have indicated that social policy is "on the table" for negotiations on Aboriginal self-government, but what this means has yet to be clarified. It could mean something akin to provincial status for Aboriginal communities, in which case resources would need to be transferred to Aboriginal communities through a formula that worked like the federal-provincial equalization program. In addition, Aboriginal communities would have to be as free to spend those resources on their own objectives as are provincial governments. On the other hand, that social policy is negotiable could mean that the federal and provincial governments are prepared to expand the network of program management agreements that, in the fields of both social assistance and child welfare, have transferred administrative authority for provincial programs to Aboriginal communities, while maintaining policy and financial controls in the non-Aboriginal community. This policy is referred to by Fleras as "institutional assimilation," which now replaces the "cultural assimilation" of the 1960s and 1970s.[39] The resulting status of Aboriginal communities in this case is more like that of municipal than provincial governments.

Federal and provincial governments are also engaging in political action to co-opt the Aboriginal agenda and convert it into less militant and more acceptable forms. This includes vigorous suppression of the most militant groups, marginalizing their influence by ignoring their demands; funding the less militant Aboriginal groups; and conducting limited reforms, as in the management agreements. Will these techniques work as they have on other occasions? We do not know the answer. The struggle of Aboriginal peoples for social policy autonomy is a worldwide struggle that also embraces the post-colonial societies of Africa and Asia. It is impossible to read McPherson's *Social Policy in the Third World*[40] without being struck by how close the parallels are for Aboriginal peoples under both colonialism and post-colonialism. These links give particular significance to the international social movements of Aboriginal peoples.

The Political Process

There are two principal views concerning the distribution of power in society. The first is that power is concentrated in all societies in the hands of an elite.[41] The elite rulers of the society control all important decisions within the society, protect their own interests and power, and enjoy the benefits derived therefrom. In this view, power and the extent of the social welfare function are in the end determined by the corporate elite both within and outside Canada. Elections and electoral politics matter little, as the state and the elected politicians are, in truth, a front for more powerful elites. These elites are now engaged in a process of tightening the controls on labour, reducing the income of labour, and reducing the extent of social welfare in order to increase their own wealth and power. Furthermore, they have the power to impose this regimen on Canada, whether the rest of the society wants it or not.

This view contrasts sharply with the most widely held view of Western industrialized democracies – that they are characterized by a high degree of diffusion of power.[42] This diffuse or pluralist model suggests that society is organized into a series of competing interest groups. Each group is able to defend and to obtain some adjustments to its particular interests, and no group is in a position to impose unilaterally its interest on others. From this view the power of the corporate elite is regarded as significant but not overwhelming. The views of the corporate elite are dominant in the 1990s, but the interests of other groups also have to be considered. Governments remain in control of the political process and are not just puppets, fronting for corporate interests. Elections and electoral politics remain important.

Redistribution, Change, and Social Class Considerations

The changes being proposed for Canada's social welfare redistributive system have different relationships to different social classes. For the top 40 per cent of income-earners the present system provides few direct benefits. Those few that it does provide, for example, RRSP and RPP pension provisions and the child-care deduction, are entrenched in the tax system and are viewed by some as having been earned by employment income. The indirect benefits from the redistributive system and other social welfare policies are found in the general social order. These benefits are substantial. They include the privilege of living in a peaceable society and the assurance that if individual circumstances change, then they, too, will be treated with justice and fairness. Canada has repeatedly been assessed as one of the most desirable societies to live in. Redistribution plays a significant role in keeping it that way. People in these income groups also receive benefits from the universal service systems, e.g., medicare and education, and, by a process of institutional creaming, receive the best of treatment from these systems. In the 1990s, with regard to the distribution of income, these groups are more than holding their own and are capturing a larger share of pre-tax, pre-redistribution income. This means that they will have to give more back to the redistributive system to maintain the balance that has been achieved, let alone help in achieving any additional objectives. Are they prepared to recognize the broader public interest and the values of a just society?

The next 40 per cent of income-earners, including most children and most seniors, draw benefits from the upper tier of the redistributive system. Health and social services are very important components of their financial well-being. Although the programs are patchy and do not meet all needs, they are available as social rights and receipt of benefit is usually free of stigma. Programs at this level, particularly the UI and Workers' Compensation programs, are under critical scrutiny to make them "more efficient," meaning lower or more restricted benefits, and, for UI, to give greater attention to labour market effects. Unless these changes are matched by a much stronger and better targeted child benefit program the future for children is grim. For seniors, the concept of the OAS and CPP/QPP programs being available as social rights is being eroded. OAS is already subject to clawback provisions and these could be extended to CPP/QPP. The level of benefits provided by these programs is falling behind the levels achieved in the 1970s and 1980s. Courchene discusses "social insurance as the problem area."[43] The 40 per cent of income-earners in the third and fourth quintiles could provide significant resistance to the changes in government social policies that Courchene advocates. Will they use their votes in this way or will they vote, in disillusionment, for a smaller role for government and a larger role for private savings?

Finally there are the lowest 20 per cent of income recipients. For them the redistributive system is the major, sometimes the only, factor in their incomes. The programs at this level serve a disproportionate number of women and children, persons with disabilities, recent immigrants, and most Aboriginal people. The programs (social assistance, public housing, enforced dependencies, etc.) are definitely aimed at those below the poverty line, and the recipients are stigmatized and their benefits are subject to administrative discretion with only limited rights of appeal. In that the beneficiaries are covered by universal service transfer programs they tend to get the worst treatment – the poorest facilities, the least qualified professions, the inconvenience of long waiting periods.

For this group the period since the 1971 Senate Committee on Poverty report has been uneven. The gains made in some provinces were lost in others. The effect of the lack of a commitment to national objectives is very apparent. Even those standards that did exist under the CAP have been removed under the CHST. The House of Commons commitment to deal with child poverty is, in 1995, bereft of any substance. It seems that the federal objective of reducing the deficit is being applied in an arbitrary manner. The dollar reductions under the CHST are specified, the means of achieving them and the social costs that will be incurred are left to the provinces. One would think that support for social welfare should be widespread in this group. But is it? This is also where disillusionment at what has been achieved may be most directly experienced.

Crane conducted a study of public support for social programs in 1991 and 1992.[44] A questionnaire and interview technique was used with 106 randomly chosen heads of household from Vancouver and the Fraser Valley and with twenty-two organizational representatives.[45] Table 26 provides an example of Crane's results. Crane used a seven-point scale to record satisfaction.

The results showed that there was more support than opposition for social programs. Crane interprets his results to mean that the public would be willing to expand social programs and pay more for them. However, although there were more positive than negative responses, the largest response was in the "mixed" category, reflecting ambivalence, or even disinterest, rather than enthusiasm and

TABLE 26: *Satisfaction with the Number, Kinds, and Direction of Social Programs*

	Number of Programs		Kinds of Programs		Direction of Programs	
Satisfaction	No.	%	No.	%	No.	%
1. Extremely Dissatisfied	7	5.6	4	3.2	10	8.4
2.	5	4.0	10	8.1	32	18.5
3.	14	11.3	30	24.2	50	15.1
4. Mixed	43	34.7	40	32.3	44	37.0
5.	29	23.4	33	26.6	19	16.0
6.	16	12.9	14	11.3	5	4.2
7. Extremely Satisfied	10	8.1	7	5.4	1	0.8

SOURCE: John Crane, *The Public's View of Social Programs* (Vancouver: UBC Press, 1994), p. 172.

commitment. As a result, the social class and electoral politics of social policy are full of uncertainty and the future of social welfare is unclear.

The three major schools of thought that are active in the debate on the future of social welfare programs view the uncertainty in very different ways. The social welfare and poverty-oriented groups are very worried. Objectives such as a guaranteed income and an end to poverty, which seemed achievable in the 1970s and were deferred in the 1980s, now seem to be beyond consideration. There is also a feeling that the public is no longer interested in the ideas that have motivated a generation of social policy advocates.

The equity-oriented groups that look for some recognition of issues of relative disadvantage by gender, ethnic origin, class, ability, and sexual orientation see limited token changes that also seem vulnerable to backlash. They are also deeply concerned that the gains they have made are set in the context of an overall enterprise that is in decline. There is no evidence in the discussion of the redistributive system of fundamental rethinking toward the development of what Neysmith refers to as a "social-care model [that] would provide explicit recognition that care of vulnerable persons is not a family responsibility but rather that public services must be made available to people who need them as part of a social security system based on the rights of citizenship."[46]

However, the conservatives and labour market economists who form the third major contributor to the debate on the redistributive system look on the changes that have begun to occur with satisfaction. Courchene concludes his assessment of the CHST in the following way:

> The CHST has finally broken the political and jurisdictional tug-of-war on the social policy front. The entire system is now in motion. . . . These are tough times for social Canada and even for employed Canadians. I have tried to argue that the forces impinging upon Canada's social programs have been gathering steam for at least a decade. By ignoring their impact we have only made the ultimate adjustment that much more severe.[47]

This latter stream of thought, urged on by global economic restructuring that stands beyond the control of national governments, would appear to be in the ascendancy at present.

The separation of Quebec would change the politics of social policy in ways that appear ominous for redistributive social policy but are difficult to predict. Quebec, within Canada, has provided powerful support for fiscal equalization and financial redistribution. Historically, a Canada without Quebec, dominated economically by Ontario, Alberta, and British Columbia, would have probably been a less sympathetic place for social policy. In the current situation one would expect that the ascendancy of the conservative position would be confirmed and the influence of the remaining liberal and progressive forces reduced as Canada dealt with the economic issues that separation would create.

Notes

1. Canada, *Income Security and Social Services* (Ottawa: Queen's Printer, 1969).
2. Canada, *Report* of the Royal Commission on Dominion-Provincial Relations (Ottawa, 1940), Book II, p. 128. "These areas" refers to the Maritime and Prairie provinces.
3. The next three federal-provincial funding and policy mechanisms are referred to by Courchene as "fiscal federalism." For a much fuller and more technical account of how they work, see Thomas Courchene, *Social Canada in the Millennium* (Toronto: C.D. Howe Institute, 1994), ch. 4.
4. Constitution Act, 1982, Section 36(2).
5. Courchene, *Social Canada*, Table 14, pp. 86-87.
6. For a general discussion of conditional grant mechanisms, see Donald Smiley, *Conditional Grants and Canadian Federalism* (Toronto: Canadian Tax Foundation, 1973).
7. See Diana Ralph, "Anti-poverty Policy under NDP Governments," *Canadian Review of Social Policy*, 31 (1993).
8. Judy LaMarsh, *Memoirs of a Bird in a Gilded Cage* (Toronto: McClelland & Stewart, 1968), p. 49.
9. Courchene, *Social Canada*, p. 206.
10. John Porter, *The Vertical Mosaic* (Toronto: University of Toronto Press, 1965).
11. Wallace Clement, *The Canadian Corporate Elite* (Ottawa: Carleton University Press, 1986).
12. Porter, *The Vertical Mosaic*, p. 306.
13. LaMarsh, *Memoirs of a Bird in a Gilded Cage*, p. 90.
14. Linda McQuaig, *Shooting the Hippo: Death by Deficit* (Toronto: Viking, 1995), pp. 41-46.
15. Diana Ralph, "Fighting for Canada's Social Programs," *Canadian Review of Social Policy*, 34, (1994).
16. Porter, *The Vertical Mosaic*, p. 412.
17. Dennis Olsen, *The State Elite*, as quoted by Leo V. Panitch, "Elites, Classes and Power in Canada," in Whittington and Williams, eds., *Canadian Politics in the 1990s* (Scarborough, Ont.: Nelson, 1990), p. 186.
18. Y.N. Kly, "On the Meaning and Significance of the United Nations Convention on the Rights of the Child," *Canadian Review of Social Policy*, 27, (1991).
19. Andrew Armitage, *Comparing the Policy of Aboriginal Assimilation: Australia, Canada and New Zealand* (Vancouver: UBC Press, 1995), p. 229.
20. OECD, Economic Surveys, *Canada* (Paris: OECD, 1994), p. 114.
21. Frank James Tester, "The Disenchanted Democracy: Canada in the Global Economy of the 1990s," *Canadian Review of Social Policy*, 29/30 (1992).
22. Canada, *The Press and the Poor* (Ottawa: National Council of Welfare, 1973).
23. Y. Hasenfeld, *Human Service Organizations* (Englewood Cliffs, N.J.: Prentice-Hall, 1983), p. 1.
24. Richard Splane, "Social Policy Making in the Government of Canada: Reflections of a

Reformist Bureaucrat," in S. Yelaja, ed., *Canadian Social Policy* (Waterloo: Wilfrid Laurier University Press, 1987).

25. Courchene, *Social Canada*, ch. 6.

26. John Richards, "Living within Our Means," in Harris *et al.*, *Paying Our Way: The Welfare State in Hard Times* (Toronto: C.D. Howe Institute, 1994), p. 60.

27. Courchene, *Social Canada*, p. 197.

28. Ralph, "Fighting for Canada's Social Programs," p. 78.

29. Courchene, *Social Canada*, p. 200.

30. Canadian Labour Congress, *Labour's Social Objectives* (Ottawa, 1973).

31. Ben Carniol, "Social Work and the Labour Movement," in Brian Wharf, ed., *Social Work and Social Change in Canada* (Toronto: McClelland & Stewart, 1990), p. 137.

32. Marcel Rioux, *Quebec in Question* (Toronto: James Lewis and Samuel, 1971).

33. T.B. Bottomore, *Critics of Society: Radical Thought in North America* (New York: Random House, 1969), p. 113.

34. Canadian Advisory Council on the Status of Women, *Brief presented to the Commission of Inquiry on Unemployment Insurance* (Ottawa, 1986); CACSW, *Integration and Participation: Women's Work in the Home and the Labour Force* (Ottawa, 1987); CACSW, *Planning our Future: Do We Have to be Poor?* (Ottawa, 1988); CACSW, *Women and Labour Market Poverty* (Ottawa, 1990).

35. Sumera Thobani, in *7th Conference on Canadian Social Welfare Policy: Remaking Canadian Social Policy: Selected Proceedings* (Vancouver: Social Planning and Research Council of B.C., June 25-28, 1995), p. 25.

36. Wharf, ed., *Social Work and Social Change in Canada*, pp. 144ff.

37. Ralph, "Fighting for Canada's Social Programs," pp. 78-80.

38. Peter Leonard, "Knowledge/Power and Post-modernism: Implications for the Practice of a Critical Social Work Education," *Canadian Social Work Review*, 11, 10 (1994).

39. Augie Fleras, *The Nations Within* (Toronto: Oxford University Press, 1992), p. 225.

40. Stewart McPherson, *Social Policy in the Third World* (Brighton: Wheatsheaf Books, 1982).

41. Gaetano Mosca, *Ruling Class* (New York: McGraw, 1939); Vilfredo Pareto, *Mind and Society* (New York: Dover, 1935).

42. R.A. Dahl, *Pluralist Democracy in the United States: Conflict and Consent* (New York: Rand, McNally, 1967).

43. Courchene, *Social Canada*, p. 311.

44. John Crane, *The Public's View of Social Programs* (Vancouver: UBC Press, 1994).

45. The organizational sample was created to represent diverse points of view on social programs and included members from business, consumer, women's, and professional associations. *Ibid.*, p. 10.

46. Sheila Neysmith, "From Community Care to a Social Model of Care," in Baines, Evans, and Neysmith, eds., *Women's Caring: Feminist Perspectives on Social Welfare* (Toronto: McClelland & Stewart, 1991), p. 283.

47. Thomas Courchene, "Remaking Social Policy: Fiscal/Global Imperatives and the CHST," in *7th Conference on Canadian Social Welfare Policy.*

Chapter 8

THE DISCIPLINE OF

SOCIAL POLICY

The systematic study of social policy is usually called a field of study to which the disciplines of social work, sociology, economics, political science, public administration, women's studies, and others contribute. However, these disciplines also have a shared discourse among them and so the products of their work can also be referred to, as they are in Britain, as the discipline of social policy. This discipline consists of the body of knowledge, theory, and research concerning solutions to social problems. Within the discipline there are five discernible schools of theory and research, organized principally on ideological lines. These are the *liberal, conservative, socialist (also referred to as Marxist), feminist, and "anti-racist"* points of view referred to in Chapter 1. The differences between these viewpoints are seen not only in differences of opinion about the origin and solutions of social problems but also in the methods of critical inquiry, research, language, and knowledge base that each uses.

The Liberal School

The early products of the liberal school are synonymous with the work of the first social reformers who documented social problems and proposed pragmatic solutions to those problems. The results of their work were briefs to governments, submissions to charities, and similar activities. If homelessness was the problem, then shelters should be provided. If people were poor they needed jobs or money. If people were sick they needed health care. The approach was practical and the underlying assumptions were moral and reformist. The society in which the problems arose was taken as a given, capable of being improved by being made more fair, just, and equal. Facts on social problems were the principal contribution that could come from research. The facts were reviewed using liberal values, and conclusions and recommendations pointed the direction for change.

This school of thought and work remains a central feature of the discipline of social policy. The early data-gathering of reformers on such matters as poverty, employment, incomes, health, and housing conditions has been taken over by government service and statistical agencies as part of a government data base. The resulting information on issues relevant to social policy that has been developed is basically descriptive. Extensive demographic data, problem-oriented data, "service output" data, and comparative data exist.

The Canadian census provides a typical major source of descriptive demographic data on population, age distribution, location, migration, income, housing, land use, employment, etc. The census is supplemented by extensive survey data developed by Statistics Canada and by provincial departments of vital statistics covering such continuing subjects as births, marriages, divorces, deaths, and epidemiological illness patterns. Furthermore, the meaning of these data is explored through monographs that indicate historical trends and provide comparisons between provinces and countries. The reasons for selecting some subjects for information-gathering while neglecting others are principally historical, influenced by specific requests and policy initiatives. The influence of a research and statistical establishment is also evident in the attention typically given in such data to issues of historical comparability. Data from the census and from statistical agencies represent an essential beginning point for the analysis of quantitative aspects of social welfare but are typically insufficient in detail to be of immediate utility in assessing social welfare programs or institutions.

Based on this work, Canada has developed ongoing data series that are essentially descriptive of particular social problems. The social problems chosen for the development of such series are usually those that have been of social policy interest. Typical examples of such series are poverty lines, unemployment rates, crime and delinquency rates, and the consumer price index. These "social problem" series differ from general demographic data in that they are developed around some basic set of government policies and thus tend to have a normative thrust. For example, since the "War on Poverty," data have been gathered as a record of government progress, or lack of progress, in combatting the problem of poverty. Attempts in the 1970s to use these data to develop a comprehensive set of social indicators are generally seen as having failed, largely because of unresolved conceptual problems and value conflicts.[1] More limited and focused work has continued, however, as in the development of reports on specific subjects such as the status of children, women, elderly people, and visible minority groups.[2]

The third type of descriptive data, available in voluminous quantity, is the service output and service resource data typically published in annual reports by human service organizations. Internally within each organization there is extensive data-gathering primarily for management purposes. This detail is usually not readily available for external analysis, but from it a more restricted set of annual statistics is developed to describe, in general terms, the type and quantity of the services. Thus, a day-care service will report so many "child-days" of day care; a counselling service will indicate the total number of clients seen and the average number of appointments; and a prison will indicate the number of persons admitted, incarcerated, and discharged. Such annual reports also often describe the cost of such services, the personnel by whom they were rendered, and the physical resources used.

Data from this source are by-products of the bureaucratic/professional social welfare establishment. When viewed in this way, such data can be seen as important, indeed essential, to the operation of existing social welfare institutions. However, such data are not oriented to overall priority analysis (they basically assume the priorities that have shaped their own development); they are not a good source of criticism of the institutions that produce them (the data basically serve the interests of the producing institutions and do not recognize the critical views or viewpoints of service consumers); and they present a unified view of the social reality based on one point of observation. Furthermore, this information is incomplete and unco-ordinated. The output of smaller organizations, of which there are many, is difficult to assemble: definitions of services vary, and it is usually impossible to know whether a small number of people are being served by many agencies or whether each agency is serving different people. Thus, understanding the collective impact of social agencies on social problems usually requires extensive, and costly, studies that begin with the consumer.

Comparative data between countries or provinces are also difficult to assemble because of differences of definition between jurisdictions and organizations. Yet, comparisons between jurisdictions are an important source of information. The first reason for comparisons is to address the problem of perspective. The social policies of a jurisdiction are complex constructions, each of which reflects the issues that were prominent when the policy was introduced. It is easy to confuse the effects of a particular policy with changes taking place in demography, economics, or culture and ascribe either undue efficacy or undeserved failure to policy differences. The scholar is also frequently too close to the policies to be studied to have an independent way of looking at them. He or she is usually a member of the society being studied and usually has an interest in the subject because of an association with particular views or proposed reforms. The comparative method provides a partial answer to the problem of perspective by laying one set of actions alongside another. As a result, one can see that they are similar in some respects and different in others. If the similarities are sufficiently confirmed in numerous examples, then it begins to be possible to ascribe some of the differences to conditions that are unique to a particular society. Joan Higgins, in her discussion of the comparative method, writes that "Probably the most important reason for engaging in comparative research is that it encourages a distinction between the general and the specific."[3]

The second reason to use the comparative method is that it assists in searching for new prescriptions for the conduct of social policy. Change begins in many ways, sometimes through limited and local actions,[4] often through state or national initiatives, and sometimes through international action. Regardless of the origins of change, the practical conduct of social policy is determined by the interface between client groups and the police, social workers, teachers, clergy, and volunteers who actually work with them. These people, both clients and helpers, can in practical ways change their own situation and develop new ways of working together. Often these changes are suppressed in the name of existing policies, good order, and stable government, but sometimes they are allowed to grow and receive the formal endorsement of social policy authorities. These "mutations" of social policy occur at different rates in different countries, depending on local conditions. Not all succeed; indeed, many can be expected to fail. However, all are of interest to the student of social policy who searches for new prescriptions for old problems. The comparative method can thus be an orderly search for examples of previously unknown or unused approaches, together with evidence of their effects.

Bodies like the National Council of Welfare, the Caledon Institute, the Canadian Council on Social Development, and a great number of policy advocates take these basic data and use them in making their arguments that government should provide social welfare programs. None of these typical products of the liberal school of social policy study have an explicit theoretical base for the analyses of social conditions or for the solutions they provide. The closest that they offer to such a base is the type of statement of commonly agreed values with which this book began, which makes it appear that the making of social policy is a matter of common sense once the facts are known. A major weakness, from a practical point of view, is that this approach has difficulty accounting for why its efforts have not been more successful. If Canada is a generous and liberal society committed to ending child poverty, then why does it not enact the measures that would bring child poverty to an end? A major weakness from a more theoretical point of view is that this approach has taken too much for granted: capitalism; the nation-state; democracy; Western cultural supremacy; "progress"; a patriarchal family model; and an assumption that the solutions provided by policy advocates will work. These assumptions have come under searching examination and analysis by the other schools of policy thought.

The Conservative School

The conservative school of thought and study also has a long history. It is characterized not only by values of its own but by its use of economic analysis as its core discipline. The values emphasize the freedom of the individual, the freedom of the economic market, private ownership, and minimum government intervention. The role of government is, first, to protect those mechanisms that are essential to the operation of the marketplace, such as contracts and private ownership, and, second, to maintain public order by punishing crime and maintaining stability. The conservative school of thought contributed nothing to the early development of social policy. Instead, it constituted a continuing opposition that could always be relied on to justify the least possible forms of public intervention carried out in the most coercive way.

In the 1990s proponents of this school like to think of themselves as deeply concerned with issues of social policy from a hard-headed but not hard-hearted perspective. The Preface to Thomas Courchene's *Social Canada in the Millennium*, for example, proclaims that:

Like the country he so obviously cherishes, Courchene is a fascinating mix of talents and interests. He is an economist with a heart, a sub species that, despite what many people think, actually does exist. His professional credentials are impeccable. . . . The implacable logic of the economist's model persuaded him that the apparently perpetual poverty of Canada's poorer provinces may well be the result of generous federal transfers; these, he contends, encourage people not to move to other regions of Canada where they might do better.[5]

It is a logic that takes many familiar assumptions of the liberal school and reverses them.

Courchene sees the world with the clear unblinking focus that is modern economics' most compelling attribute: if you pay people who live in poor regions, they may stay there; if you provide generous unemployment insurance (UI), don't be surprised if unemployment rates rise; . . . These are the facts of life. . . . People do maximise and if we ignore that fact we are simply fooling ourselves.[6]

An example of the analysis provided by this school is contained in the volume in the C.D. Howe series on Unemployment Insurance. Christopher Green, a McGill University economist, examines the different unemployment rates of Canada and the United States. Earlier studies revealing the existence of a difference led to study of the reasons for the difference. Green analyses data on the use of Unemployment Insurance during the last two business cycles, showing that the use of Unemployment Insurance *rises* in periods of economic expansion when one would expect that it would *fall*. The reasons for this are alleged to be: "the positive feedback of regional extended benefits (Milbourne, Purvis, and Scoones, 1991), the tailoring of market behaviour to the parameters of the UI system (Card and Riddell, 1993), and the 'repeat user' syndrome (Corak, 1991, 1993)."[7] In other words, people are using the system as a support to their incomes. Use rises during periods of economic expansion as more people have enough contributions to qualify; use also rises as people find out how to get the maximum benefit to which they are entitled, and repeat use rises as people become familiar with the system. Whether or not one concludes that the existence of these behaviours is a reason for changing the UI program depends on the values with which one has begun the discussion. To the conservative economist it is obvious that anything that diverts the worker's attention from accepting and continuing in a job, however poorly paid, means that the economy as a whole is not getting the benefit of that person's labour. As a result we are collectively poorer and less competitive than other societies.

A major strength of this line of analysis is that it fits well with the anxiety that has been accompanying the global restructuring of the world economy and of Canada's place in it. The Canadian economy needs to be able to withstand international competition and Canadian workers have to be competitive with workers anywhere in the world. This line of argument always suggests lower welfare benefits, and thus costs, fitting well the need of governments to reduce total expenditures.

The development of evaluation models and experimental techniques, and their application to social policy issues, is another important activity of this school. The first major works of this type were undertaken in the United States in the 1960s during the War on Poverty. Later, in the 1970s, there was the negative taxation experiment in Manitoba, modelled on the American experiments conducted in New Jersey, Seattle, Denver, and Gary, Indiana.[8] The central question for the negative taxation experiments was whether expanded welfare programs, particularly programs more available to the working poor, resulted in a decreased work effort. The experiments took three to five years to complete. The conclusion was that work effort was not decreased by a guaranteed income, at least not under the conditions in which the experiments were carried out. Left unanswered was the question as to whether work effort might decrease over longer periods or if the negative tax program was made available to all. The result was significant in relation to the original objectives of research, but it was not significant vis-à-vis a decision to introduce a guaranteed annual income. By the time the results were known, social policy issues had lost priority on the agenda of governments and a decision not to proceed had already been reached on political and financial grounds.[9] In the 1990s experimentation with workfare programs is taking a similar form.

Finally, this school has made an important contribution to the development of cost-analytic techniques to social programming. These techniques include cost-benefit analysis, cost-outcome analysis, and planned program budget systems. These are the working tools of much day-to-day policy and program analysis conducted by government agencies, either internally or through contracts with consulting firms or individuals. The questions for this type of research are usually narrow and administratively oriented. How much will it cost to introduce a new system for administering benefits? How much could be saved by reducing welfare rates or what would be the cost of increasing them? What savings could be anticipated by contracting for services rather than providing them directly by government employees? These questions are posed and answered without reference to any general policy direction, yet, cumulatively, they have a substantial and continuing effect on the conduct of social policy, reinforcing a conservative approach to the use of resources and to habits of thought and action.

The Socialist School

The socialist school is also referred to as the Marxist or political economy school of policy analysis. Marx did not himself analyse social welfare (it had not been developed when he wrote), but he was as concerned with the problem of poverty as were the liberal social reformers. However, while the reformers saw the problem of poverty as being one to be solved by knowledge and the application of values, Marx saw the problem of poverty to be the result of the oppressive way that economic processes were organized in capitalist society. Mishra writes:

> Under the capitalist mode of production the basic structural elements through which wealth and poverty are generated and reproduced are: private ownership of the means of production; production for profit; private property and inheritance; and the allocation of incomes and resources through the market

mechanism. For Marx, these core institutions of capitalism and the underlying values constitute the very antithesis of a welfare society. Under capitalism incomes and life chances are distributed almost entirely through the impersonal market mechanism. . . . Coercion and competition rather than cooperation and solidarity lie at the root of capitalist social organization. For Marx, then, the values and norms of welfare cannot make headway in a society of this type.[10]

The Marxist analysis provides an explanation of why social welfare policies have not been successful; they have been carried out in a society in which continuing economic processes continuously undercut and undermine both the reforms themselves and the values on which they rest. Thus the Marxist is not surprised at the problems now faced by social welfare. Indeed, the more surprising event was that the welfare state was established at all. Nevertheless, once established, social welfare has been recognized as a sphere of activity distinct from capitalism that has required examination.

The analysis to which this perspective leads is historical, political, and theoretical. Economic and social processes are discussed in order to show how they contribute toward maintaining capitalism. Information on political contributions, elite relationships, and the ownership of major corporations and of the media, for example, is used to show how social control is maintained and fundamental social reform prevented. The history of social welfare programs is studied to set the expansion or contraction of programs in the general framework of capitalist economic and political processes. Piven and Cloward's *Regulating the Poor*[11] is an excellent example of this mode of analysis, purporting to show the relationship between welfare programs and the maintenance of public order and work incentives. Tester and Kulchyski, in *Tammarniit (Mistakes): Inuit Relocation in the Eastern Arctic 1939-63*, show how the process of introducing social welfare to the Inuit served larger Canadian processes of territorial control, resource development, and totalization (the cultural and institutional integration of minorities). The Preface begins:

> The 1990s are witness to a fundamental re-examination of the Canadian liberal welfare state which developed following the Second World War. . . . there is a growing tendency to question whether the welfare state could ever achieve its stated ideal of equality, while respecting the diversity among Canadian citizens. Recent history also suggests that the welfare state has ultimately failed to act as an effective buffer against the excesses of capitalist enterprise. Social workers and others are coming to understand that the welfare state is not the benevolent purveyor of egalitarian and humanist values that it was once held to be. Rather, it is increasingly recognized as something quite different – a source of oppression and racism, a regime which, because of its structures and biases, has often discriminated against women, children, and other marginalised groups.[12]

Despite the importance of this school as a source of analysis and academic criticism, the contribution of the school to the development of social welfare has been questionable. In part this is because its conclusions were often pessimistic as to both the possibilities for change and whether any change short of an unachievable revolutionary one is worthwhile. Even in defence of social welfare, the Marxist analysis tends to defeatism as the forces of the global economy appear to be overwhelming. The analysis provided confirmation of the power and established position of capitalism and of other structural forces, but writers from the school have difficulty applying their analyses to indicate what follows.

One application that is gaining adherents in the university schools of social work is the development of "structural" social work. Mullaly provides an example of this approach in his discussion of social reform processes that work, first, "within (and against) the system" and, second, "outside (and against) the system."[13] The structural social worker is always working "against" rather than "for" the system. The system is the capitalist state, including its social welfare services. The goals of structural social work are "(1) to provide practical, humanitarian care to the victims and casualties of patriarchal, liberal-capitalist society; and (2) to restructure society along socialist lines."[14] By work "within (and against) the system," Mullaly means all those social workers who are employed by government human service organizations. Mullaly provides strategies for this work, including getting service providers and users to recognize that the personal is political, empowerment, consciousness-raising, collectivization, and radicalizing the agency. The role of workers within the system is filled with contradictions and many are said to hold the "belief . . . that they must become guerrillas in the bureaucracy and undermine the agency at every turn from their political underground position."[15] Social workers working "outside (and against) the system" are less caught in these contradictions as they can serve their employer and their clients simultaneously. Here, too, the struggle is not an easy one, as "we, as North Americans, have been socialized into working and living in social institutions where hierarchy, specialization, and an overreliance on rules prevail."[16]

In the context of the problems faced by social welfare the thrust of the thinking of this school is, in the short term, toward preserving whatever can be saved in order to extract resources from capitalism through it, and, in the long term, toward abandoning social welfare and replacing it, along with capitalism, with a different form of society.

The Feminist Contribution

The work of feminists is pervasive in both the liberal and socialist schools of social policy but is not present in the conservative school. There are, of course, women contributors to the conservative school, but no body of academic writing in the conservative school is written with a critical consciousness of gender relationships.

The contribution of both liberal and socialist feminists to the discipline of social policy begins with critical awareness of the role played by the concepts of patriarchy, family, motherhood, and caregiving that were assumed in the establishment of social welfare policy.[17] These ideas were also connected to nationalism and, in a number of jurisdictions, particularly Quebec in Canada, with pro-birth family policies. The pro-birth policies were designed to encourage the continuity of both nation and race. Examples of these policies include the increased Family Allowance payment with family size that was a feature of Quebec's administration of Family Allowances, the "bébé-bonus" that replaced it,[18] and the opposition to birth control measures in general and to abortion in particular. The patriarchal policies assumed women were dependent on men and were designed to reinforce the position of men as "heads" of households. Examples include the "man in the house" rule used in the administration of social assistance, whereby if a man lives with a woman then household income determines eligibility, and the assumption made in UI benefits that they should be adequate to support a family. In addition, many social agency policies were based on assumptions about the availability of women for unpaid "caring" work in the home and in the community. Examples here include foster care policies based on payment only for the expenses of foster children, not the work of caring for them; the presumption that women are available to care for handicapped or elderly relatives; and the lack of a major commitment to child care.

Liberal and socialist (and radical) feminists[19] differ as to the solution to these issues in much the same way as there are differences between the liberal and socialist schools of social policy. The liberal approach is reformist. It begins with an examination of the sex-based assumptions and laws that have characterized social policy. All those policies that have assumed a difference of rights or entitlements between men and women need critical examination and reform. The biological difference between men and women must be recognized positively by measures to permit and support women in performing their biological role in reproduction, but this must be done in ways that do not lead to unnecessary sexual stereotyping. Thus, "maternity" leave should be replaced by "parental" leave, for although women bear children there is no need to assume that women alone can care for infants. All caring roles need to be recognized as work and need to be shared by both men and women.

The socialist and radical approaches attach more importance to structural factors, particularly capitalism (for socialists) and patriarchy (for radicals). The radical point of view sees women as oppressed as a class by men as a class. The oppression takes the form of male control over sexuality and reproduction. The power is rooted in male aggression, violence, and militarism. For some radical feminists these are biologically determined.

> One solution for many radical feminists is political separation, that is, campaigning, organizing, working separately from men. A further step for some is personal separatism, living and having relationships with women only, not out of personal choice, but out of political choice. . . . The recreation, protection and provision of a 'women's culture' for the nourishment of women only, then, has become the mainstream of today's radical feminism and writing.[20]

The influence of radical feminism on social policy has been substantial. Action on a series of issues – rape, family violence, abortion, sexuality, and reproductive technology – has been either determined by radical feminists or deeply influenced by the positions they have taken. Socialist feminists concentrate their attention on the connection between capitalism and patriarchy, particularly the analysis of women's role in reproduction as providing workers for capitalist exploitation. For socialist feminists the role of women is socially "constructed" within capitalism rather than being biologically determined. For socialist feminists "there can be no socialism without women's liberation, and no women's liberation without socialism."[21]

Feminists from both the radical and socialist schools have also been at the forefront in the critique of the internal culture of social welfare organizations. Most welfare organizations, and all government human service organizations, have been structured by men. Consequently, their organization and functions are characterized by:

- male dominance rather than gender equality;
- competition and independence, rather than co-operation and interdependence;
- hierarchy;
- rational control and an emphasis on technology;
- a separation of private and public, which results in compartmentalizing experiences;
- a devaluing of subjective experience.[22]

Women thereby experience organizations differently from men. In the organization as a whole and certainly in its "lower levels" of pay and status, women predominate, but they do not control the culture. At the management and executive levels men predominate and establish a culture in which being male is normal. On the other hand, being female causes problems regarding femininity, pregnancy, having caring responsibilities, dress, and harassment. To succeed in such organizations women are expected to "behave like men" and become "super women" with all the qualities of both genders.

The human service organizations established by feminists have sought to establish a democratic internal culture: all participate, including service users; decision-making is by discussion and consensus, rather than by hierarchical position and majority vote; leadership is agreed on and changeable, depending on the issues; terms of employment recognize caring responsibilities; all participants are safe from harassment. Achieving this vision has not been easy in the social movement service organizations and has been even more difficult in the government service organizations. Nevertheless, the goal of a more equal and democratic workplace for workers and service users represents an important challenge. If human service organizations cannot produce a more equal and equitable environment in their own sphere of activity, how can they expect to introduce these values to the wider community? If the transformation to a non-patriarchal or socialist society cannot be started somewhere, how can it be started at all?

The contribution of feminism to the discipline of social policy also includes the development and application of institutional ethnography as a research method. Institutional ethnography was championed by Dorothy Smith in order to develop a "sociology for women." Smith was concerned that sociology had developed a "gender subtext" because "it was thought, investigated and written largely from the perspective of men." Men had written from their standpoint "within the organizational order" while the experience of women had "generally been outside the organizational order which governs contemporary advanced capitalist societies." Institutional ethnography begins with the day-to-day experience of women, rather than with the "defining issues and problems as they have been established in the currency of the discipline." With a beginning point centred on the question "How does it happen to us as it does?" Smith advocates a co-operative research method done with participants as a "means of exploring and making public the social ground and organization of our common and divergent experience."[23] The effect of Smith's approach is seen in the way that it makes visible the whole of women's lives and does not concentrate attention on the features of interest to researchers, managers, policy-makers, or any other representatives of established authority.

When applied to social policy the effect of research conducted through this method is to open up a whole new territory for understanding women's lives that had been ignored in social policy research. Government social policy in all its forms has been constructed to maintain order and achieve common objectives. Smith points to the fact that the objectives of social policy have been largely the work of men and that the standpoints of both the liberal and conservative schools are those of an established ruling apparatus, particularly those of its managers. The vast majority of research is undertaken to explicate questions of either policy or management that are of interest to policy-makers or managers. It is thus inevitable that the voices of those people who are not policy-makers or managers are marginalized. In many cases they may not be heard at all; in others, their voices will have been filtered and distorted by the process of gathering and selecting the pieces that were deemed important. In all cases there has been some objectification of what are considered to be data. Children, men, women, lesbian, gay, black, First Nation – all have become statistics. Added up, compared, and analysed, their individual experiences have been taken from them and turned into a product on the basis of which policy-makers can decide on a course of action and managers, acting for them, can distribute money, goods, and services.

Smith and other researchers using institutional ethnographic methods are making other buried voices heard, and what they have to say is different from the official rendering of events that has dominated the development of the discipline of social policy. An example of how some of these principles are being introduced is provided by Callahan, Lumb, and Wharf's "Strengthening Families by Empowering Women."

The objective of the project was to determine if a new and distinctive approach to child welfare could be developed using the following guidelines. (1) Women centred; the project will be designed to address the concerns of mainly single parent women as they see them. (2) Concerned with the economic as well as the social concerns of parents. (3) Focused on front line workers. (4) Designed to involve clients, community workers and local residents in the development and delivery of the project and to expand opportunities for clients to work in groups together. (5) Developmental rather than prescriptive. (6) Focused on the process of change. (7) Designed to be replicated elsewhere and to inform policy development.

The study offered recommendations that would permit social workers and clients to work much more closely together in supportive rather than conflictual ways.

> One finding from this study is overwhelmingly important: single women and their children make up a very large proportion of the child welfare worker's caseloads, yet they were not considered when developing child welfare policy and programs. Often investigations proceed, assessments are made and services are offered in the same way as if there were two parents. Single parent mothers in this project argued forcefully that they have an enormously difficult job with few supports and resources. They want child welfare services to be reshaped to deal with their reality.[24]

The resulting service paradigm replaced the investigation of neglect by social workers with empowerment principles of co-operation between workers and clients in finding solutions to the problems faced by single mothers in caring for their children.

Although the application of institutional ethnography to social policy has been pioneered by feminists, the method can be applied by men or women and can be applied to assist in understanding the perspective of any and all social groups.

The Anti-Racist Critique

The anti-racist academic critique of social policy has been developed principally in the United States and Britain. In the United States all discussion of social welfare has a racial subtext. American blacks are markedly worse off than whites: "in 1990 the median income for white families was $36,915, for black families $21,423: 44.8% of black children lived in poverty compared with 15.9% of white children. . . ."[25] As a result, blacks participate at much higher rates in all social welfare programs. Although the origins of modern American social policy are usually equated with the depression and the New Deal, contemporary American social policy is dominated by questions of race. Racial judgements affect social policy in two ways: (1) directly, through the existence of outright prejudice against any measures that collectively take resources from whites and give them to blacks; (2) indirectly, as a result of the interaction between the general expectation that welfare users should be "worthy" and the stereotype of blacks "as irresponsible and as failing to try as hard as they could or should to deal with their problems."[26]

In Britain the anti-racist critique of social policy has developed on the basis of the experience of the post-war Caribbean immigrants with the British welfare state. Despite its professed egalitarian values, the welfare state was in the forefront of dispensing unequal treatment to immigrants in housing, schooling, and policing. At first the reason was attributed to a lag in the responsiveness of welfare institutions to new problems. In time, measures were changed so that outright barriers to providing benefits to immigrants were removed and Britain began to think of itself as a multicultural society. However, as Britain and Western Europe go through their own processes of economic restructuring and integration into the world economy there is a growing tendency to look at imported labour of non-European origin as unneeded. Welfare resources used to maintain this resource are thus being "wasted." Immigration should be stopped or, better still, reversed.[27] Fifty years after the initial importation of large numbers of Caribbean and East Indian workers, it is difficult to see the recurring pattern of discrimination as being based in any other factor than European white racism.

The anti-racist critique of social policy exposes the connections between racism and social welfare in both societies. In Canada the anti-racist critique informs the positions taken by both the First Nations and visible minority social movements in their own criticism of their experience of social welfare. As with the feminist school of social policy analysis, there are anti-racist critiques of social policy within both the liberal and socialist schools but not within the conservative school.

Both schools begin by recognizing the importance of "deconstructing" white racism. This means accepting the existence of white racism and understanding how social policy has worked to marginalize and oppress First Nation peoples and visible minorities while upholding white privilege. The situation of First Nations provides the clearest example as the statute under which they are defined, the Indian Act, had an explicit racial base in European superiority in religion, culture, lineage, and genetics. The "right" of the Canadian government to rule Indians was provided without question, for in European minds the superiority of the settlers and their institutions was established by God and proved by science through the work of nineteenth-century geneticists on the "survival of the fittest." In relation to visible minorities the Canadian experience parallels in some ways the British one. Immigration policy is seen as an economic tool with people's social policy rights being subordinate to the extent to which their labour (or capital) is needed.

The approach of the liberal school to these problems is reformist. The institutions of social welfare need to be adapted so that all Canadians have equal access based on a common citizenship. The interest of First Nations in developing their own social policies and managing their own affairs can and should be respected through revisions to the Indian Act that recognize First Nations as distinct peoples with internal rights of self-government. The approach of the socialist school is more structural. White racism is seen as an entrenched set of attitudes that are growing as economic restructuring is proceeding. There is doubt in this school as to whether liberal reform will take place and a continued apprehension that explicit racial discrimination will come to the fore as it has in the United States and Britain.[28]

Auspices and Control of Research

Social welfare research is a complex and technical exercise. The resources needed in terms of money, manpower, and access to information make research dependent on the establishments that dominate the social welfare enterprise. Thus, the liberal architects of social welfare and the conservative critics command most of the resources. They are both represented by substantial policy institutes, and governments conduct or sponsor research to extend and explore the perspectives they represent. In contrast, the socialist, feminist, and anti-racist critiques of social welfare are largely academic exercises conducted in universities and rarely used directly in the actual business of establishing social policy. Pal provides an analysis of the Canadian policy research industry, one branch of which deals with the examination of social welfare policy.[29] Table 27 applies Pal's dissection of Canadian policy research sectors to the social policy field.

TABLE 27: *Social Policy Research Auspices in Canada*

| State Sector – Federal and Provincial | | | Private Sector | |
Government	Quasi-Government	Profit	Non-profit	University

• central agencies
  – treasury
    boards
  – premiers'
    offices
• departments of:
  – social services,
  – health,
  – women's
    affairs
  – Aboriginal
    affairs
  – etc.
	• advisory
	  councils
	  – National
	    Council of
	    Welfare
	• Royal
	  Commissions
	  and task forces
	  – Aboriginal
	    Peoples
	  – Reproductive
	    Technology
	  – Child Care
	  – "Transitions"
	    (Ont.)
	  – "Making
	    Changes" (BC)
	  – etc.,
		• consulting firms
		  – Price
		    Waterhouse
		  – Coopers and
		    Lybrand
		  – etc.
		• pollsters
		  – Decima
		  – Goldfarb
		  – Leger & Leger
		• consultants
		  – a host of
		    individuals
		    both within
		    and outside
		    academe who
		    sell policy
		    contracting
		    services
			• institutes and
			  centres
			  – Canadian
			    Council on
			    Social
			    Development
			  – Caledon
			    Institute
			  – C.D. Howe
			    Institute
			  – Fraser
			    Institute
			  – Institute for
			    Research on
			    Public Policy
			  – etc.
				• institutes and
				  centres
				  – McGill
				  – Wilfrid
				    Laurier
				  – Manitoba
				  – Regina
				  – UBC
				  – Victoria
				  – etc.
				• individuals
				  – a host of
				    individual
				    academics and
				    research
				    students
				• policy
				  conferences

SOURCE: Categories from Leslie Pal, *Public Policy Analysis*, 2nd edition (Toronto: Methuen, 1992), p. 71.

The dominance of the liberal and conservative viewpoints is clear from the table. Together they must comprise nearly all research undertaken in the first four columns and more than half of the work undertaken in universities in the fifth column.

A major aspect of the conduct of research is that government and private-sector for-profit research is largely a hidden, secret process. The reasons for secrecy are numerous. The first is that the initial exploration of policy topics by government is often conducted to gauge the political advantages or disadvantages that would accompany a more public debate. The second is that the process of administering programs has become an increasingly complex technical exercise and program managers regard this territory as their own, not an arena in which public debate is needed or useful. Lastly, some policies need to be developed as part of a negotiating stance in areas of controversy, conflict, and change and are only revealed as needed in the negotiating process. Secrecy is, on occasion, breached. The frustrated individual report writer, when he or she sees that the work is being ignored, suppressed, or distorted, may seek alternate means of reaching the public. The fate of the "whistle-blower" is usually that he or she is dismissed, or in the case of an external contract, denied further contracts. By these means control is maintained over the development of the social policy enterprise as a whole.

The Nature of Social Policy Knowledge

The characterization of the discipline of social policy and the auspices of social welfare research developed in this chapter has given considerable attention to the purposes for which research is conducted and the major schools of inquiry. What has become of the allegedly "pure" scientific concern with knowledge *per se*? The realm of pure scientific knowledge, free of considerations of value and politics, would appear to be not only unknown to social welfare research but also unknowable. In social welfare, the nature of knowledge is always related to the values of which it is perceived and to the methodology by which it is produced. There is no such thing as value-free social welfare research. Given that social welfare values are themselves in contention, it is not surprising to find that social welfare research is an element in a contentious and political process. Each of the major schools has developed methods of inquiry of its own that serve to expand the knowledge of social welfare that it regards as significant.

The impact of the discipline of social policy and of social policy research on policy and practice is also uncertain. First, there is the contention between the schools of policy development and research. Each provides its own stream of ideas and develops its own sets of proposals, frequently in conflict with each other. However, one would be naive to assume research is only undertaken to establish facts and to make recommendations for change. Research can be undertaken for a variety of reasons: to "contain" social problems by diverting attention from immediate reform proposals and establishing a distance, in time, before reform is again on the public agenda; as a symbolic gesture, recognizing political alliances, past commitments, and good wishes; to establish social control over opponents by examining their weaknesses and harassing them in the process of inquiry; and to establish a veneer of objectivity disguising conclusions already established on ideological premises. In all cases it is important to probe the auspices of research as well as the methodology before reviewing the results.

Research reports, even if accessible, are fundamentally produced by an elite for an elite. More frequently than not, information is couched in technical language and contributes thereby to a condition of social mystification. Findings are often inadequately translated into their meaning for application and so the general reader is left without a clear understanding of the implications of policy proposals. The use of language is also frequently confusing because each school has its own lexicon. Consider the phrase "incentive to work":

- For the liberal this phrase means developing social programs so that people on social assistance have the opportunity to keep a substantial fraction of employment income.

- For the conservative this phrase means a reduction in social welfare benefits accompanied by workfare measures.
- For the socialist this phrase confirms ideologically that the function of welfare is to maintain capitalist control over labour.
- For the feminist the phrase provides a reminder as to how incentives to work have been widened to include an increasing number of mothers with children, while simultaneously reducing benefits to them and perpetuating their poverty.
- For the anti-racist critique "incentive to work" means developing policies under which blacks and immigrants can be forced to take work that no one else will.

Meanwhile, most participants in the social policy process, whether service consumers, members of the public, media writers, or elected officials, operate from direct impressions and belief (affected in obscure ways by past inquiry). Conversely, those who operate in the elite realm of research have no monopoly on knowledge. The methodologies of the disciplines and of inquiry not only bring precision; they also inevitably distort the varied state of human affairs by emphasizing patterns of similarity and consistency at the expense of individual variations and uniqueness. Each, in its own way, has self-fulfilling characteristics that confirm to the participants the correctness of their preconceptions.

Notes

1. See, for example, Raymond Bauer, *Social Indicators* (Cambridge, Mass.: MIT Press, 1966); Kenneth Land, "On the Definition of Social Indicators," *American Sociologist*, 6, 4 (November, 1971); Bertram Gross, ed., "Social Goals and Indicators for American Society," *The Annals of the American Academy of Political and Social Science*, 371 (May, 1967); Dorothy Walter, "Social Intelligence and Social Policy," in *Social Indicators* (Ottawa: Canadian Council on Social Development, 1972), pp. 7-8, 11-12.

2. Deborah Rutman and Andrew Armitage, "Counting on Kids: An Overview of 'State of the Child' Reports," *Canadian Review of Social Policy*, 31.

3. Joan Higgins, *States of Welfare* (Oxford: Basil Blackwell, 1981), p. 12.

4. Marilyn Callahan and Brian Wharf, *Demystifying the Policy Process: A Case Study in the Development of Child Welfare Legislation in British Columbia* (Victoria: University of Victoria, 1982). Callahan and Wharf trace the origins of reform to practitioner dissatisfaction at the resources and policies available to them, although in the end the practitioners' concerns are largely lost in senior-level political manoeuvres. In a similar vein, Asa Briggs, in an introductory essay in E.W. Martin, ed., *Comparative Development in Social Welfare* (London: George Allen and Unwin, 1972), p. 12, recognizes that "local action has . . . frequently preceded national action in the making of English social policy."

5. Thomas Courchene, *Social Canada in the Millennium*, Preface by Thomas E. Kierans, John Richards, and William Watson (Toronto: C.D. Howe Institute, 1994), p. xv.

6. *Ibid.*, p. xvi.

7. Christopher Green, "What Should We Do with the UI System?" in Green *et al.*, *Unemployment Insurance: How To Make It Work* (Toronto: C.D. Howe Institute, 1994), p. 10.

8. See Arnold Katz, "Income Maintenance Experiments: Progress Towards a New American National Policy," *Social and Economic Administration*, 7, 2 (May, 1973).

9. Richard Splane, "Whatever happened to the G.A.I.?" *The Social Worker*, 48, 2 (Summer, 1980).

10. Ramesh Mishra, *Society and Social Policy: Theories and Practice of Welfare* (London: Macmillan, 1981), p. 71.

11. Frances Fox Piven and Richard Cloward, *Regulating the Poor: The Public Functions of Welfare* (New York: Random House, 1972).

12. Frank James Tester and Peter Kulchyski, *Tammarniit (Mistakes): Inuit Relocation in the Eastern Arctic, 1939-63* (Vancouver: UBC Press, 1994), p. xi.

13. Robert Mullaly, *Structural Social Work: Ideology, Theory, and Practice* (Toronto: McClelland & Stewart, 1993).

14. *Ibid.*, p. 153.

15. *Ibid.*, p. 176.

16. *Ibid.*, p. 184.

17. Fiona Williams, *Social Policy: A Critical Introduction* (Cambridge: Polity Press, 1989), p. xii.

18. The "bébé-bonus" provides payments of $500 for the first baby, $1,000 for the second, and $8,000 for the third and subsequent babies born to Quebec mothers as an inducement to have children. The program is designed to combat the low annual birth rate of 1.6 births per 1,000 women of child-bearing age in Quebec. This rate is substantially less than the 2.1 per 1,000 necessary to sustain the existing population.

19. Fiona Williams (*ibid.*) uses an expanded list of six distinctions within feminist critiques of the welfare state: libertarian feminism, liberal feminism, welfare feminism, radical feminism, socialist feminism, and black feminism. The distinctions have been shortened here in the interests of space. The reader is encouraged to look at Williams's work to see the full range of feminist criticism and contribution.

20. *Ibid.*, p. 54.

21. *Ibid.*, p. 57.

22. Wendy Weeks, "Gender in the Social and Community Services: Implications for Management," *Human Services Management Network Conference* (Brisbane: Queensland University of Technology, April, 1992).

23. Dorothy Smith, "Institutional Ethnography: A Feminist Method," *Resources for Feminist Research*, 15, pp. 6-12.

24. Marilyn Callahan, Colleen Lumb, and Brian Wharf, "Strengthening Families by Empowering Women," unpublished research monograph, Victoria, School of Social Work, 1994, p. iv.

25. See Andrew Hacker, *Two Nations: Black and White, Separate, Hostile and Unequal* (New York: Charles Scribner's Sons, 1992), for a host of statistics on black-white inequality in the United States.

26. Paul Sniderman and Thomas Piazza, *The Scar of Race* (Cambridge, Mass.: The Belknap Press of Harvard University Press, 1993), pp. 113-14.

27. Lena Dominelli, *Anti-racist Social Work* (London: Macmillan, 1988), p. 11.

28. K. Victor Ujimoto, "Studies of Ethnic Identity and Race Relations," in Peter Li, ed., *Race and Ethnic Relations in Canada* (Toronto: Oxford University Press, 1990), pp. 225-26.

29. Leslie Pal, *Public Policy Analysis*, 2nd edition (Toronto: Methuen, 1992).

THE FUTURE OF

SOCIAL WELFARE

Despite the size of the social welfare endeavour its future seems less secure in the 1990s than it has since the 1930s. First, its guiding principles, the liberal values that inspired a vision of a more just and equal society and with which this book began, can be made to seem out of place when compared with the accomplishments of social welfare policy. Second, the values themselves are not held, or are only partly held, by those who are now making social welfare policy. Third, the threatened separation of Quebec would appear to intensify the pressure to restructure social policy while weakening support for redistribution.

In 1975 and 1988 the perspective taken by this book was that of embracing the liberal value base but submitting the accomplishments, programs, and organizations to critical analysis. Serious internal contradictions were seen then and have been confirmed by the repeated failure to obtain the basic reforms that seemed obvious from the liberal point of view. Instead, the shortcomings of social welfare in administrative costs, bureaucratization, and accomplishments have become more apparent, providing ammunition to both the conservative critics on the right and the socialist critics on the left. In 1995 Canadian social welfare policies are in the middle of a critical conservative reappraisal and are being changed to conform to the results of that appraisal. So it is fitting to begin a discussion of the future of social welfare with the conservative view of where we are going.

The Conservative Vision

The conservative vision is, on its own terms, filled with optimism for the future. The change taking place in the world economy through the globalization of economic activity and the revolution in information technologies is seen as irreversible. The expanded capitalist global economy and the decline of the nation-state are welcomed, and not just for the opportunity for making money that they represent. The triumph of economics over politics is seen as bringing with it a decrease in the likelihood of the global warfare that would destroy us all. It is seen as providing the basis for more equality between nations and peoples as the protectionist and colonial policies of the developed countries can no longer be employed to manage production processes and restrict the dispersal of incomes and wealth. It is seen as a world in which Canadians can participate, but in order to do so Canada needs an appropriate set of social policies. Courchene writes:

> Canada, in the millennium, will be largely defined by its social infrastructure. As a working "mission statement", as it were, I adhere to the notion that Social Canada's role is to provide for Canadians to develop and enhance their skills and human capital to enable them to become full participants in the emerging global/information society. . . . Canadians have made impressive postwar gains in social policy. . . . However, under the onslaught of what I have referred to as "restructuring imperatives", our postwar achievements now hang in the balance. In order to maintain a distinctive, made in Canada social infrastructure, we have little option but to filter our long-standing values of fairness, sharing and equity through the new realities of fiscal restraint, globalization and the information revolution.[1]

Courchene is optimistic about the future because this prescription for the review of social policy is being followed by governments, both federal and provincial. The conservatives are also optimistic because this is a time of opportunity for them. Long-standing opposition to the extension of social welfare that was expressed at every step in its development can now be "repackaged." In the repackaged form it appears to provide the answers that are needed to the issues of the day, first to the problems of the deficit, second to maintaining economic productivity, and third to the disillusionment with the accomplishments of the liberal social welfare state. The conservative position is based on a long-established view of the public welfare that draws its strength from some values shared with social welfare. The values of concern for the individual, faith in humanity, and faith in democracy are shared with liberalism. However, these values are set in a context that favours personal freedom over social justice and financial incentives over equity or equality.

Although the conservative values are held by the corporate elite and are developed through its institutions, they derive their strength, too, from the meaning they give to common experiences of all people. As was said of the British Conservatives:

> The strength of Thatcherism is its ability to ventriloquize the genuine anxieties of working-class experience. The declining economy and reduced living standards are explained by the expensive burden of public services as the economics of the State are reduced to the accountancy of the kitchen. . . . The ringing appeal to freedom has displaced any lingering enthusiasm for the musty attractions of social democracy, so readily identified with an enervating Statism.[2]

The election in Canada of Conservative governments that hold public positions once seen as extreme is one indicator of this shift. A second indicator is the increasingly conservative nature of Liberal government proposals, such as those made by

Finance Minister Paul Martin in the 1995 budget. A third is the way that even provincial NDP governments have been converted to conservative policies during their time in power. Out of office the NDP sounds as if governments can continue to spend their way out of recessions and the problems of the deficit are a capitalist plot to divert attention from the need for higher social spending. However, once they become governments they do not seem to be able to bring themselves to act on this rhetoric.

The conservative social vision is also relatively clear. Individual action is favoured over collective solutions; privacy is valued over the intrusion of social workers; risk and entrepreneurship are valued over the privilege of either union tenure or civil service security; selectivity, keeping intervention and costs as limited as possible, is valued over universalism; market incentives to move away from the Atlantic provinces to Ontario and the West are favoured over regional policies to preserve communities; open competition is favoured over all forms of affirmative social action for women, Aboriginal peoples, visible minorities, or other marginalized group; social integration through economic processes is favoured over all forms of separate community development; punishment of crime is favoured over structural change to reduce the causes of social alienation and crime.

Although moderate conservatives, conservatives "with a heart" such as Courchene, want to hold onto some parts of the heritage of Canadian social policy and reshape it to the new imperatives, it is clear that this is not the full conservative agenda. Walter Block, the senior economist of the Fraser Institute, is quoted as answering the question, "What services should the public sector provide?" by stating:

> Little or none. The classical liberal tradition, the tradition of Adam Smith, John Stuart Mill, and David Hume was that government was mainly for defence, judiciary. And when it tries to act in the public good it actually worsens the situation of the people that it is acting in behalf of. The Fraser Institute would certainly advocate the government as a safety net of last resort but not one of first resort as is all too popular in this province and this country.[3]

The commitment of conservatism to a continued reduction in all forms of social welfare alarms social welfare advocates. It suggests a "race to the bottom" between provinces and between nations to do the least. It suggests that the interests of the transnational corporations in the highest possible profits and the greatest freedom of action can and should determine the future of social welfare. As the conservative economists have control of the social agenda, the critical questions for other points of view are not where are we going, but where we will end and what visions can be developed as alternatives.

The Marxist/Socialist Vision

The Marxist/socialist writers of the political economy school of social policy analysis have little confidence in the social welfare institutions that have been established. They recognize the triumph of corporate capitalism as representing the sum of all their fears but differ as to whether anything can be done. The starkest vision is provided by Teeple. Social democracy and the liberal welfare state are dismissed as a product of economic conditions and national government authority that no longer exist.

> The social democratic left has become, in effect, part of the problem. It remained wedded to a notion of reformed capitalism until the 1980s and since then has produced little analysis of alternatives to neo-liberalism [a reference to what we have termed conservatism in this text]. Where it came to power, it has sooner or later introduced new right policies in the face of an electorate desirous of protecting the social security of the working class. . . . By accepting this agenda in theory and practice, social democracy has lost much of its credibility as a party representing the working population, and hypocrisy has become its hallmark.
>
> Social democracy as we know it has no future, because the conditions that gave rise to it are being transformed and because its policies and programs – the reforms of the nation-state era – were nothing more than what these conditions allowed or demanded.[4]

The work of the social movements is acknowledged as offering the seeds of an alternative, but:

> Both . . . resistance and . . . alternatives face enormous odds as long as the current system continues to provide a tolerable existence for the majority and second, control over the ideological and political systems remains a monopoly of the powers that be.[5]

Instead, the future can only hold a continuing process of economic concentration and political repression:

> . . . largely unfettered by political considerations, is a tyranny unfolding – an economic regime of unaccountable rulers, a totalitarianism not of the political sphere but of the economic.[6]

Not all writers of this school are as pessimistic as Teeple. Tester emphasizes the ecological limits to capitalism that are emerging.

> The evidence that global environments are threatened by the economic growth mindlessly celebrated by World Bank and IMF officials . . . is overwhelming. . . . Ultimately, the failure to deal with the failure of the global environment must leave national governments with the responsibility of protecting their own environments by regulating the activities of transnational and other corporate interests. . . . It is the democratic will of people to act against vested interests which threaten their well-being that is the key to solving these problems.[7]

Ralph, while not disagreeing with the direction of Teeple's argument, places more reliance on the social movements, strengthened by international connections between movements. Ralph makes three suggestions for the future.

(1) Prioritize building the popular base of our movements and connections between them, as well as people's movements elsewhere in the world. We are not strong enough now to have much impact on policies or even electoral outcomes. So we need to retrench and rebuild our bases. Because our main strength is people, we need to focus first on building and re-building grassroots groups and training participatory leaders. Our emphasis needs to be on building the movement, not on initially expecting to influence the TNC giants. (2) Research the opposition better. At this point, little is known about the BCNI [Business Council for National Issues] members, the shadow government behind Federal and provincial decisions. If we want to take back the initiative, we need to anticipate their next moves and their likely response to our tactics. We need to investigate their vulnerabilities. . . . We also can develop linkages with their employees and consumers elsewhere in the world. . . . (3) Plan strategically for the long haul, rather than reactively protesting each new injustice. . . . It will take a long time for us to turn around the twenty years of losses we've endured. . . . To win victories, we need to identify focused targets and aim our tactics at their vulnerable areas grounded in our areas of strength.[8]

Mullaly's structural social work tactics of working "within (and against) the system" and "without (and against) the system" that were referred to in the previous chapter are also parts of the future vision of the socialist/Marxist school. Mullaly sees these as strategies toward "the ultimate goal . . . the transformation of liberal-capitalist society to one that is more congruent with socialist principles."[9] In Mullaly's view this transformation will take place gradually through changes in the institutions of social welfare resulting from the work of structural social workers. There are few signs that this is about to happen. Indeed, all the structural forces that Mullaly analyses point in the opposite direction, toward the transformation of social welfare to a more conservative form. A major problem for Mullaly and for structural social work generally is the credibility of the view that a new form of social work practice will be able to achieve the objective of beginning the transformation of society.

If this transformation does not occur, the socialist/Marxist vision appears to accept that the institutions that have been developed, and the alliances they represent, are in a process of inevitable decline. In its place is the virtual certainty of much increased poverty and crime, along with political and racial violence. The United States represents the closest model of such a society, but the end model looks more like the Latin American models described by Campfens.[10] Perhaps then, when things get bad enough, some form of popular movement will come to the rescue, but not inevitably. Kaplan's bleak vision of the twenty-first century, based on what is happening in West Africa, Bosnia, and Iraq and on what can be foreseen for Los Angeles and Washington, D.C., has no such silver lining. In his stark essay on the twenty-first century, anarchy rather than tyranny predominates.

Nations break up under the tidal flow of refugees from environmental and social disaster. As borders crumble, another type of boundary is erected – a wall of disease. Wars are fought over scarce resources, especially water, and war itself becomes continuous with crime, as armed bands of stateless marauders clash with the private security forces of the elites.[11]

All of this *could* happen. The question is, will it? The direction of social welfare policy may be conservative, but how far and how fast will this trend go? The leap from a government decision to end the Canada Assistance Plan and replace it by the Canada Health and Social Transfer to a forecast of the problems of a society in which all institutions of welfare are in collapse is an enormous one. To base our actions today on the assumption that such a society is now inevitable is to accept the deterministic premises of the socialist/Marxist analysis.

The Communalist Visions

Community has always been a major concept for social welfare. In the 1990s, several different applications of the concept of community move toward establishing independent provisions for social welfare. The First Nations demand for self-government is one expression. The development of separate social service organizations by feminists, gays, lesbians, visible minorities, and religious organizations is a second. The community economic development process and social housing are others.

Each of these groups is asserting a community-based autonomy. The objective is control of the planning and implementation of their own social welfare. A major strength of each of these movements is that services are under community control and government is not involved in detailed management, local differences, or staffing matters. Government can concentrate its attention on the jurisdictional issue of who is being served and the fiscal issue of what resources can be provided. The social movements differ as to the degree of autonomy they can exercise and the extent of their objectives.

1. *The First Nations.* It seems that governments, both federal and provincial, are ready to negotiate with First Nations on the terms of First Nations independence in the development and operation of social welfare. There are no legal barriers to prevent a full assumption of responsibility. In a legal review prepared for the Royal Commission on Aboriginal Peoples, Hogg and Turpel[12] address all the essential issues to the exercise by First Nations of an independent jurisdiction.

> The authors suggest that the elements of the Charlottetown Constitutional Accord could be included in a political accord or accords, which could become the basis for self-government negotiations. . . . The issues that are examined include personal and territorial jurisdiction, concurrent and exclusive powers, the relationship of Aboriginal laws to federal and provincial laws, the administration of justice and the financing of self government. . . . The applicability of the Charter of Rights is also discussed and a recommendation made for the development of Aboriginal constitutions, which could include Aboriginal Charters of Rights.[13]

The barriers to First Nations self-government and their development and operation of independent social welfare provisions are political and developmental.

There are good reasons to think that both these barriers will be overcome in the near future. Neither the federal nor provincial governments are enamoured by the present arrangements, which provide for continued conflict with First Nations and criticism from all sections of Canadian society. Many First Nations have already developed a substantial administrative and professional capacity at the band and tribal council level. The principles for the establishment of equitable financial arrangements are already entrenched in the Canadian constitutional provisions for federal and provincial fiscal equalization and could be extended to First Nations.

2. *The feminist and other social movements.* The development by feminists and by other social movements of their own fields of social welfare policy and of their own social service organizations has been documented and discussed. There is every reason to think that this trend will continue. The development of diverse provisions within social welfare meets the needs of a more complex and plural society. It also places services directly in the community where they are located in immediate proximity to their users.

3. *Community economic development.* CED is another approach that contributes to social policy objectives by building the capacity of the local community to sustain itself in the economic environment created by the global economy, without becoming trapped by its corporate and economic values.

4. *Social housing.* Social housing has been developed by most of the social movements and by a host of local community non-profit and co-operative groups. Although federal support for new social housing projects is suspended, the development of social housing at the provincial level continues. In addition, there are opportunities to redevelop parts of the existing social housing stock and for changes in management practices to make the fullest possible use of the existing resource. Housing remains a critical component of social welfare, particularly for those groups most vulnerable to housing market discrimination. Social housing provides the physical setting for fulfilling important parts of the communalist model of the self-governing social community.

Each of these communalist visions is compatible with the conservative, socialist, and liberal ideologies and future visions. The moderate conservative finds them acceptable because they are compatible with overall conservative goals of fiscal restraint and reduced government. The socialist is enthusiastic for them as they represent a form of social organization independent of capitalism and that may yet become the basis for a different social order. The liberal shares both these reasons for supporting the communalist vision and respects, too, the way that they are serving the needs of a diverse and plural society. At the international level the communalist vision draws strength from international social movements, particularly the importance that such organizations have in Latin America, and the link to liberation theology.[14]

The Continued Strength of the Liberal Vision

The liberal vision continues to draw its strength from the pride that Canadians have in building a social order in North America that is safer and more just than that of the United States. The established liberal values with which this book began, which now include the values of a more plural, less homogeneous society, capture the essence of that difference. There are certainly signs of increasing ambivalence and disillusionment, but as Crane points out solid majorities still exist that support nearly all the existing social programs.[15] Although the critical voices and actions are stronger than they were in 1985, they are still not the defining force in establishing the character of social welfare in Canada.

The conservative vision, even in the moderate form proposed by Courchene, fails to provide such a definition. The contextual issues to which it draws our attention – the deficit, the global economy, and the information revolution – are all important. The values that it shares with liberalism of individualism, faith in humanity, and democracy produce some common ground. But the conservative vision fails because it provides insufficient attention to the other values that the social welfare services represent and the functions in society that they perform, functions that still appear to be important to the majority of Canadians in preserving a distinct social policy. The failures of the conservative vision are many.

1. *Poverty.* There is a failure to acknowledge the seriousness of the problem of poverty. The conservative proposals are bereft of goals that deal in any way with poverty, and in their silence they acquiesce to the expansion of poverty, the increase in homelessness, and the increasing disadvantage and oppression of all individuals and families in the lower 60 per cent of the income distribution, in particular the marginalization and oppression of single mothers, children, the handicapped, visible minorities, and Aboriginal peoples.

2. *Equity and diversity.* There is a failure to recognize the processes of domination that have led to women, lesbians, gays, visible minorities, and Aboriginal peoples being marginalized and oppressed. At every turn the conservatives oppose measures to counteract historic oppression and achieve social justice. The need for a society in which pluralism is an important value is not understood.

3. *Community.* The central role of the community and of community-based visions of social welfare is not appreciated. The silence condemns communities to the vicissitudes of the global marketplace.

4. *Unpaid work.* Unpaid work, principally caring roles carried out in the home, is invisible to the economist, yet the contribution of such work to collective well-being is essential. The conservative failure to value what is not paid for depreciates the contribution of all women and distorts the economists' understanding of social welfare.

These failures all point to the continued moral blindness of capitalism and of its advocates. In addition, the advocates of an unbridled capitalism are overlooking the history of capitalism. On several occasions in the past, capitalist accumulation and speculation have exceeded the regulatory and offsetting capacity of government to stabilize market behaviour. The result in each case has been not only social disaster but also serious internal problems for capitalism itself. The most devastating example in the Western developed countries was the Great Depression of the 1930s, but there has been no lack of the disruptions caused by massive inflation in all other parts of the world, where capitalism has been less regulated than it was in the West and less balanced by the existence of a developed social welfare system.

Heilbronner reviews the capitalist protest about the growth of government and concludes:

> If the great scenarios teach us anything, it is that the problems that threaten capitalism arise from the private sector, not the public. . . . all successful capitalisms, I further believe, will find ways to assure labour security of employment and income, management of the right to restructure tasks for efficiency's sake, and government as the legitimate coordinator of national growth.[16]

Looking to the twenty-first century, he continues:

> Two formidable self-generated problems are certain to disturb the capitalist world. One of these is the approach of ecological barriers. . . . These barriers imply a coming necessity to curtail industrial growth. . . . The second problem is the internationalizing tendency of capital that continues to outpace the defensive powers of individual governments. Thus capitalism itself encroaches on the political independence of nations in a manner that exposes the centre to the very forces that have sowed so much economic disarray on the periphery. . . . In so far as the malfunctions exist on a transnational scale, they require transnational political counter-force, and nothing of the kind exists.[17]

International capitalism will in the end need the institutions of social welfare policy for exactly the same reason that national capitalism did; they stabilize and make possible the continued capitalist enterprise.

The Marxist/socialist vision gains its strength from its ability to connect with the experience of service consumers, social workers, community advocates, and the social movements. By directing attention to structural forces it makes the movement toward a more conservative social order understandable. But as a guide to action it, too, has problems. The analysis is too deterministic and the conclusion too pessimistic. The alternative models of society are too distant or out of touch to command popular support. Applying the model can also lead to practical and ethical difficulties, particularly for those who work inside the system. Can one perform one's daily work for an employer and *always* be working "against the system"? If social workers believe that the interests of the consumers of service are *never* being served, surely they should leave and find other work where they can serve both their employer and the service consumers with integrity.

The communalist visions are an important part of the future of social welfare for all future scenarios, but the social movements and organizations that exist are not strong enough or developed enough to provide a realistic substitute for mainstream social welfare programs and services. In particular, all the communalist visions depend on the capacity of the state to carry the redistributive function of social welfare policy. Without this function they or their members would be much weaker than they are today, and in some cases they would not exist at all; yet the social movements have no way to perform this function for themselves.

The exception to this generalization is the Quebec sovereignist movement, a communalist vision on a scale that may have a mandate to establish a separate nation-state. Once established, the new state of Quebec would face all the issues of redistributive social policy for itself. During the 1995 referendum campaign there were many references to social policy and most social policy advocates within Quebec supported the establishment of a sovereign society. Such a society would have the ability to make its own internal redistribution of income and wealth. However, it would also be subject to the external pressures from the global economy that are affecting the development of social policy everywhere. An independent Quebec would be exposed to the direct influence of these external forces as it sought to establish itself within the North American Free Trade Agreement, the International Monetary Fund, and the United Nations and as it negotiated with Canada the terms of its separation and the division of responsibility for the national debt. The rejection of separation by the Cree people of northern Quebec could also become a major issue for both Quebec and Canada, raising the possibility of a change of territorial boundary. Thus, although separation would provide Quebec with a full mandate to operate its own social policy, it would not provide it with immunity from having to deal with the same issues that are causing the restructuring of Canadian social policy.

For both Canada and Quebec, together or separate, the liberal vision remains capable of guiding a collective response to the economic and social policy challenges of the twenty-first century. We must give attention to the economic issues but must not turn our backs on the social issues of our time. Both sets of challenges have to be dealt with together. The liberal believes that it is still possible to work "for the system" and "for the consumers of service." Facing the future means that a number of variables must be considered.

1. *Deficits.* Deficits must be dealt with at both federal and provincial levels of government. They have already grown too large and are crowding out the ability of government to support the functions of social welfare policy on which both economic and social policy depend. However, the job of balancing the accounts has to be done in a manner that is fair to all sections of Canadian society. It must not be done at the expense of the poor and it should not be done in a manner that burdens youth and families with children while allowing others to escape their responsibilities. Saskatchewan has shown the way to deal with the deficit through a combination of expenditure cuts and revenue increases.

2. *International capitalism and the global economy.* International capitalism and the global economy must be tamed and integrated into a world social order. Uncontrolled, the global economy, sooner or later, will be the architect of its own demise, and of ours, too. Canada should be at the forefront of efforts to create effective international institutions for this task.

3. *Poverty.* Poverty must not be overlooked. The deteriorating situation of single mothers and their children and the growing number of children in poverty comprise the central challenge for social policy. Social policy needs to be rebuilt from the bottom up, and the "bottom" means the standard of living that is afforded to those who are worst off. The structural factors reshaping our economy are increasing the need for social welfare redistribution. The total resources needed for such

a rebuilding are already committed, but their use has to change. Inevitably, some will be worse off than they are now, but this price cannot be delayed, nor can the future continue to be mortgaged. A revised approach to child benefits, preferably at the federal level, but if necessary at the provincial level, has to be enacted.

4. *Diversity.* Diversity must be provided for. The First Nations assertion of self-government and of social policy responsibility is essential to a rebuilding process that has already begun. The Canadian attempts to impose policy on First Nations and to integrate and assimilate First Nations, Metis, and Inuit have been recognized as mistakes. Canadians seem ready to rectify these mistakes by providing Aboriginal peoples with the legal and financial resources to govern themselves. A similar respect needs to be extended to all members of Canadian society. The influence of all the social movements is growing, as is their ability to organize and provide social services. These developments need to be supported because they are providing for better attention to the needs of service consumers.

5. *Equity.* Equity must be achieved in all the provisions of Canadian social policy. There is a need to reform and change policies that do not recognize the relationships of gay men and lesbian women. There is a need to have programs of affirmative action so that our public services encourage the participation of minorities. Women and racial minorities continue to need the support of human rights councils and workplace harassment offices to ensure that they are treated with dignity and respect.

6. *Coercion.* The use of coercion must be restricted. The coercive possibilities of social policy remain one of its most serious internal problems. There is no place in liberal social policy for workfare or for any other forms of coercion, except in those situations where the use of force by one person against another must be stopped.

Within this framework of imperatives, several issues have been identified by conservatives and liberals as requiring attention. Unemployment Insurance, Workers' Compensation, and the retirement sub-system are all due for thorough reappraisals. They were designed fifty years ago and the social circumstances that shaped them have changed. Each has provided benefits as entitlements. The entitlements have to be recognized in the process of reappraisal and change, but they cannot be an absolute barrier to change. Similarly, public-sector employment and wage levels have to be placed on the table for re-examination. Some parts of the public sector, for example, higher-income earners in the health and post-secondary education systems, seem to have done very well from the way that social policy has operated.

Politically, the process of decentralization of social policy from the federal government to the provinces continues. This means that influencing provincial governments is growing in importance, but it does not mean that we should forget the need for a national vision or national standards. Quebec has shown that it values such a vision and is prepared, if necessary, to pursue it on its own as a separate society. Canadians outside Quebec also value the social programs that have made Canada a more just society than the United States and one of the most desirable countries in the world to live in. With or without Quebec, Canada has now to remake that vision under the changed social and economic conditions and understandings that now exist.

Conclusion

These are not easy times for liberals. Goals no longer seem achievable and accomplishments seem flawed. Ethical dilemmas are frequent. Should one stay in the system and work to influence the form of the changes taking place, or should one leave? Can one still work for the consumers of service and for the social welfare system? Nonetheless, the notices of the demise of the liberal vision that have been filed by both the conservatives and the socialist/Marxist critics are at least premature and may not be needed at all. The next decade will tell the story. Perhaps the conservatives will be too powerful for their own good and the institutions of welfare will be reduced to a minimalist shell. Perhaps the socialist/Marxist critics will be proved right in their views and we will have moved closer to the tyranny, or anarchy, that is to follow. But in the meantime a voice is needed for the original ideals of the liberal social welfare agenda – an agenda strengthened by the recognition of the importance of diversity as a value, broadened in its understanding of equity, and approached in a manner that is within the economic and fiscal limits of Canadian society in the twenty-first century.

Notes

1. Thomas Courchene, *Social Canada in the Millennium* (Toronto: C.D. Howe Institute, 1994), p. 322.
2. David Bull and Paul Wilding, eds., *Thatcherism and the Poor*, Poverty Pamphlet 59 (London: Child Poverty Action Group, April, 1983), pp. 10-11.
3. John Crane, *Directions for Social Welfare in Canada* (Vancouver: UBC Press, 1994), p. 129.
4. Gary Teeple, *Globalization and the Decline of Social Reform* (Toronto: Garamond Press, 1995), p. 148.
5. *Ibid.*, p. 194.
6. *Ibid.*, p. 151.
7. Frank James Tester, "The Disenchanted Democracy: Canada in the Global Economy of the 1990s," *Canadian Review of Social Policy*, 27 (1991).
8. Diana Ralph, "Tripping the Iron Heel," in Jane Pulkingham and Gordon Ternowesky, eds., *Remaking Canadian Social Policy: Staking Claims and Forging Change* (Toronto: Fernwood, 1995).
9. Robert Mullaly, *Structural Social Work* (Toronto: McClelland & Stewart, 1993), pp. 125, 128.
10. Herbert Campfens, "Forces Shaping the New Social Work in Latin America," *Canadian Social Work Review*, 5 (1988).
11. Robert Kaplan, "The Coming Anarchy," *The Atlantic Monthly*, February, 1994.
12. Peter W. Hogg and Mary Ellen Turpel, "Implementing Aboriginal Self-government: Constitutional and Jurisdictional Issues," *Canadian Bar Review*, 74 (June, 1995). Article prepared originally for the Royal Commission on Aboriginal Peoples and printed with the permission of the Royal Commission.
13. *Ibid.*, Abstract, p. 197.
14. Campfens, "Forces Shaping the New Social Work," p. 19.
15. Crane, *Directions for Social Welfare*, p. 133.
16. Robert Heilbronner, *Capitalism in the Twenty-First Century* (Concord, Ont.: Anansi, 1992), p. 113.
17. *Ibid.*, p. 114.

GLOSSARY

The field of social welfare has an extensive terminology that is frequently confusing to the student. The source of confusion derives in part from the overlapping definitions of terms and in part because the meaning of terms is defined in two spheres – ideology and programs. Thus, a term can be used to indicate an idea. However, when the same term is used to refer to a program, the program is often only a partial fulfilment of the idea. The term's meaning is thus changed and, quite often, a new term will be coined to reassert the idea.

The purpose of this glossary is not to provide a definitive discussion of social welfare terminology (such a task would be a subject for a book itself); the purpose is more modest. The first objective is to indicate the meaning of terms as used in this book; the second is to indicate major meanings that the student may find in source materials; and the third is to indicate where terms have been used in Canada to describe operational programs – and the meaning of the term in such contexts.

Aboriginal peoples: Canada has three Aboriginal peoples, the Indian peoples, also known as First Nations, the Inuit, and the Metis.

Child welfare: Child welfare is a specific field of practice inclusive of a series of community-based and case-oriented measures designed to protect children. The primary services included are family support, homemakers, child and youth care, protection, foster care of children, and adoption.

The term is used in modified form as in the title Children's Aid Society. It is also used in some provinces as part of the title of a senior administrator in the provincial department of social welfare, as in Superintendent of Child Welfare.

Communalism: A theory or system of government in which communes or local communities, sometimes on an ethnic or religious basis, have virtual autonomy within a federal state. When applied to social welfare the focus is on the government of a community's social welfare functions, which may or may not be part of a larger process of self-government.

Community development: Community development refers primarily to a community self-help methodology.[1] The term is also used to refer to a program designed to apply the methodology in specified communities, as in the "community development program" of _____.

In some literature, the term is used to indicate the product rather than the methodology, that is to say, the development of the community. Such uses can only be found through inspection of the context.

Community economic development (CED): CED is the application of the community development process to the development and ownership of self-sustaining economic enterprises.

Corrections: Corrections is a field of practice inclusive of a series of measures designed to protect society from criminal behaviour and to rehabilitate those judged criminal. Corrections includes probation and parole programs.

Demogrant: A demogrant is a cash payment to an individual or family based solely on demographic characteristics (usually age). No recognition is given of differential needs. Old Age Security is a demogrant.

Feminism: The pursuit of equal political, economic, and social rights for women.

Field of practice: Field of practice refers to a subdivision of the totality of social work practice. Thus child welfare, corrections, mental health, etc. are fields of practice.

First Nations: The First Nations are the separate peoples who lived in Canada, south of the tree line, prior to European settlement.

Guaranteed income: Guaranteed income is a term that has had wide use and several different meanings. The primary use is to indicate a social objective, the provision of a guarantee of minimum income for individuals and families.

However, the term is also used to indicate the means for obtaining this objective. As there are several different means available, and as each of these may be referred to as a guaranteed income program, there is confusion in meanings. The different means include social insurance, social assistance, negative income taxes, and demogrants. Which method of income guarantee is intended by a particular author can usually be discerned from the context.

Human service organization: A human service organization is one having a mandate to protect, maintain, or enhance personal well-being. Human service organizations take many forms. This book makes a division between government service organizations and the social movement service organizations. Examples of government organizations include schools, welfare agencies, mental health services, correctional facilities. Examples of social movement service organizations include transition houses, rape and sexual assault centres, First Nations band offices and tribal councils, and HIV/AIDS services.

Income security: Income security refers to all programs in which a cash payment is made to beneficiaries. In some uses, as in this book, the term has an expanded meaning, including all those programs where tax expenditures, goods, or services are provided by government in order to distribute economic benefits more equitably than is achieved by the market economy.

Inuit: The Inuit are the Aboriginal people who lived north of the tree line prior to European settlement.

Metis: The Metis are the Aboriginal people who, following intermarriage of First Nations peoples with traders and settlers in the eighteenth and nineteenth centuries, founded a distinct society on the Prairies.

Negative income tax: Negative income tax refers to a proposed program of payments to individuals and families in which the amount of payment would be determined on the basis of an income declaration. The paying agency might be the relevant income tax department rather than a traditional welfare agency. The precise form of program envisaged by a particular author can usually be discerned from the context.

Social administration: Social administration refers to the planning and management of all aspects of social welfare. It is an activity engaged in by "social administrators," who are usually identified as being the senior officials of social welfare organizations.

In the British literature, "social administration" is used to indicate a field of studies. In turn, university departments are sometimes entitled Schools of Social Administration.

Social assistance: Social assistance refers to income security programs that use a "means" or "needs" test to determine eligibility for benefits. These programs are also referred to as *social allowance* programs. In the American literature, they may be referred to as *public assistance* programs. The term is also used as the title of specific income security programs. Thus, some provinces have a Social Assistance Act.

Social development: Social development is used to indicate the entire field of social welfare, with particular emphasis on change and on the future. The term has been used in a number of recent books and has had a variety of meanings. What a particular writer means, beyond a future orientation, has to be discovered from the context.

The term has also been used by a number of government departments, as in the Department of Health and Social Development; it also forms part of the title of the former Canadian Welfare Council, now the Canadian Council on Social

Development. These uses may or may not indicate change in the functions of the organizations concerned. That, too, can only be discovered by studying what they did and what they do. Changes in name are easier to accomplish than changes in substance.

Social indicators: Social indicators are a proposed set of time series statistics that, in total, would provide a representation of the social affairs of the society. Some social indicators already exist, for example, unemployment rate, but a comprehensive system of social indicators has not been possible.

Social insurance: Social insurance refers to income security programs in which eligibility for benefits is determined on the basis of a record of contribution and on the occurrence of a foreseen social contingency, be it unemployment, retirement, injury, or widowhood.

Social planning: Social planning refers to a professional activity carried out as part of social administration. The activity centres on the design and evaluation of social programs. In the American literature, particularly the writing of Alfred Kahn, the term social planning is used very broadly. In such use, it encompasses all parts of the process whereby social programs are introduced.

The term is also used in the title of a number of local bodies, such as the social planning councils. These are typically voluntary social welfare organizations that engage in studies of social needs and programs.

Social policy: Social policy is a broad term encompassing not only social welfare but other activities of government affecting social life. Marriage and divorce legislation and support to culture and the arts are examples of social policy that lie beyond the field of social welfare. The term is also linked with "economic policy." In this sense, it usually contrasts a concern for people with a concern for economic issues and growth. Shankar Yelaja identifies four key assumptions implicit in social policy. (1) The government has responsibility to meet the needs of the less fortunate members of society. (2) The state has a right to intervene in areas of individual freedom and economic liberty. (3) Governmental and/or public intervention is necessary when existing social institutions fail to fulfil their obligations. (4) Public policies create social impacts, the consequences of which become the moral obligation of some group to act upon.[2]

Social security: Social security is a term used to refer to programs. It has had a number of uses and some inspection of the context is usually necessary to understand the writer's meaning. In United Nations and most Canadian writings, the term refers to income programs plus social services. Thus, the total of both is referred to as "social security."

The existence in the United States of a major government department and a number of programs using social security as parts of their title further affects the term's meaning. These programs are all income programs and most use a social insurance technique. Thus the Social Security Act indicates a program of retirement benefits. As a consequence, "social security" in American writing frequently has the reduced meaning of income security and may have the even narrower meaning of "social insurance."

Social service: Social service is a broad term used to indicate the provision of services, other than income support. Thus adoption, day care, protection, and probation are all social services.

Social service worker: Social service worker is a term that has received increased usage as the social work profession has sought to restrict "social worker" to its own members. Social service worker has been used to cover not only professional social workers but all those who perform similar functions, for example, case aides and probation officers. The term indicates an occupational class.

Social utilities: Social utilities, a term introduced into wide usage through the writings of Alfred Kahn, refers to "a social invention, a resource, or facility, designed to meet a generally experienced need in social living."[3]

Social welfare: Social welfare is the term used in this book, and elsewhere, to describe the totality of the enterprise under study. There is a tendency to use it to describe the present rather than the future, hence the connection in meaning to the more future-oriented term "social development." There is also a tendency to use the term to indicate both intended and unintended consequences. Social welfare is what has been produced, warts and all. In earlier writing, social welfare has rather more of a future orientation than it has in contemporary use. The term is also used as part of the title of government departments, as in the Department of Social Welfare.

Social work: Social work refers to a professional skill used principally in social welfare. The skill can be applied to both individual and small-group activities, to communities, and to social administration.

Social work is also the name of a profession. In some provinces the title "Social Worker" is restricted to registered members of the profession. In others the term is used more loosely and employer job descriptions define employees as "social workers" even though they do not have professional credentials.

Voluntary agency: A voluntary agency is one in which the sponsorship is not government. The term is used to refer to at least three types of non-governmental organizations:

a. *The quasi-non-governmental agency*: privately incorporated but depending almost, if not entirely, on government support. Children's Aid Societies and children's treatment institutions are typical examples.
b. *The private-service agency*: which may be answerable not to a membership but

to itself, that is, to a paid professional staff and a self-perpetuating board of trustees. It is legitimized by the utility of its program rather than by its status as the representative organ of defined bodies of citizenry. A family service agency and the YMCA are typical examples.

   c. *The truly voluntary association*: resulting from action taken by private citizens on their own volition, not for profit, and outside the initiative and authority of government. Social movement service organizations provide good examples of this type of voluntary organization.

Welfare state: The welfare state is used to indicate a state in which there is a commitment to use resources primarily for the collective welfare. Originally, the "welfare state" was contrasted with the fascist "warfare state." In the immediate post-war period it was used to indicate that totality of legislation whereby social security (in its broad sense) was obtained, plus the commitment to maintain a focus on welfare into the future. In recent writing there has been less of a tendency to use "welfare state." Perhaps this is related to the fact that the earlier welfare states, primarily Britain, but also Sweden, are now viewed as being overly bureaucratized and stagnant.

Notes

1. See W. and L. Biddle, *The Community Development Process* (New York: Holt, Rinehart and Winston, 1965).
2. Shankar Yelaja, ed., *Canadian Social Policy*, 2nd edition (Waterloo, Ont.: Wilfrid Laurier University Press, 1987), p. 1.
3. Alfred Kahn, *Theory and Practice of Social Planning* (New York: Russell Sage Foundation, 1969), p. 178.

CHRONOLOGY

This annotated chronology is intended to provide the student with an overview of the sequence of development of legislation and institutions. It is not intended to provide a history of the development of Canadian social welfare institutions. Major sources used in the development of the chronology are the articles by Bellamy and Willard in the *Encyclopedia of Social Work*,[1] Guest's text, *The Emergence of Social Security in Canada*,[2] and the chronology of events between 1985-93 provided by Courchene.[3] Guest's work provides the best liberal treatment of the history of Canadian social welfare. A socialist/Marxist history has yet to be written.

Pre-1900

The development of Canadian social welfare provision is principally a twentieth-century phenomenon. Pre-1900 programming[4] included the following major features:

a. Limited municipal responsibility for the poor and indigent – responsibility assumed *only* for the sick, elderly, young, and women with dependent children, *only* after all the family financial resources have been exhausted, and *only* where local residence was clearly established.
b. Custodial institutions for the mentally ill and mentally retarded.
c. Custodial institutions for criminals, with some provision for the segregation of young offenders into reformatories.
d. Beginnings of major voluntary welfare organizations, principally in Toronto: Toronto Children's Aid Society (1891); Red Cross (1896); Victorian Order of Nurses (1897).
e. Early forms of workers' compensation legislation (1886).
f. Separate authority for services to Native peoples based on treaty obligations incurred by the Crown and, subsequently, on the Indian Act (1876).

1900-1920

During this period, there was a continuation of the pattern of programming noted for the pre-1900 period, with some expansion and modification. These changes include:

a. Growth of major voluntary welfare organizations. Children's Aid Societies were formed to serve other urban areas; the Toronto Family Service Agency was founded in 1914, the Canadian Mental Health Association in 1918, the Canadian National Institute for the Blind in 1918, the Canadian Council on Social Development in 1920, etc.
b. Segregation of juveniles in criminal proceedings was increased. The Juvenile Delinquents Act (1908) provided for juveniles to be charged as delinquent rather than as offenders and provided for a broad range of court dispositions.
c. A mothers' allowance program was introduced in Manitoba in 1916, providing for payments by the province to morally upright women with dependent children. Character references were required for eligibility. The program removed one category of destitute persons from dependence on municipal relief. Subsequently, many other categories were added (veterans, unemployed, elderly, etc.) and the whole relief function has been progressively transferred to provincial and federal governments.
d. Services to Indian people were provided through a church-state alliance, under which the churches accepted responsibility for the residential school system.

1920-1930

During this period, there was the first substantial involvement by the federal government in the field of income security. The federal involvement was a product not only of high regard for veterans but also of social unrest, including the Winnipeg General Strike. Returning veterans were not assured work and found a marked contrast between the society's rhetoric and their destitute circumstances. Principal events during this period included:

a. Various acts affecting World War One veterans. These included Returned Soldiers Insurance (1920), an act that provided for veterans to purchase private retirement annuities to a value of $5,000, Soldiers Settlement Act (1927), and War Veterans Allowances (1930), allowances being payable to veterans, widows, or orphans who by age or incapacity were unable to earn an income and had insufficient means. These federal programs were introduced on the basis of the federal responsibility for the armed services.
b. The Old Age Assistance Act (1927) was the first federal-provincial shared-cost program. An allowance was paid to the elderly on the basis of a means test. The provinces administered the program but were able to obtain 40 per cent of their costs from the federal government.
c. The Canadian Association of Social Workers was founded in 1928.

1930-1940

This period was dominated by the Great Depression. Millions of Canadians were unemployed and, on the Prairies, a period of drought destroyed farms and farm income. Many people turned to their municipalities for relief. However, the municipalities' source of income was principally the local property tax and the same circumstances that caused the need for relief payments also caused much tax delinquency. The result was municipal bankruptcy or near bankruptcy. Provincial governments were the guarantors of municipal bond indebtedness. As a result, the provinces had increasingly to assume responsibilities, including the "relief" responsibility from municipalities.

Some provinces, notably Saskatchewan, had the same problems in supporting relief payments as had been faced by municipalities: they lacked a sufficient income to cover their responsibilities as governments. In response, the federal government was increasingly involved in payments to the unemployed. As in the case of veterans' payments, the federal role was also a response to serious disorder. In Regina, workers on their way to Ottawa to protest inadequate programs were met with force by the RCMP. Principal actions by government included:

a. A series of unemployment relief measures enacted by the federal government. Between 1930 and 1935 these took the form of *ad hoc*, short-term acts, allowing federal funds to be used to provide relief. The emphasis was on work projects for the unemployed, including the establishment of labour camps. In southern Saskatchewan, the federal government took over the entire relief function through the establishment of the Saskatchewan Relief Commission.

b. In 1935, the federal government passed the Employment and Social Insurance Act, which was intended to institutionalize the federal unemployment role. The Act was challenged in the courts by Ontario and was eventually ruled *ultra vires* by the Privy Council in 1937.

c. In 1937 the federal government appointed the Royal Commission on Dominion-Provincial Relations (the Rowell-Sirois Commission). The Commission was charged with responsibility for "a re-examination of the financial and economic basis of Confederation and of the distribution of legislative powers in the light of the economic and social developments of the last 70 years" (since Confederation).

1940-1950

During this period the foundations of the modern structure of Canadian social welfare institutions were created. This was done, in part, through the reports of a series of inquiries related to the structure of social welfare in Canada. Principal inquiries that were reported during this period included the following:

a. The Royal Commission on Dominion-Provincial Relations reported in 1940.

A central conclusion was that "Not only national duty and decency, if Canada is to be a nation at all, but equity and national self-interest demand that the residents of these (impoverished) regions be given average services and equal opportunities. . . ."[5] The Commission proposed a federal unemployment program and a system of equalizing grants to the poorer provinces, but that the general responsibility for welfare should remain provincial.

b. The Committee on Health Insurance (Heagerty Committee) was appointed in 1942. The Committee proposed a reorganization of health services, including a full range of medical benefits: physician, dental, pharmaceutical, hospital, nursing, etc. Coverage was to be provided on payment of an annual $12 registration fee with financing from provincial and federal governments.

c. The House of Commons Advisory Committee on Post-War Reconstruction reported in 1943 (the Marsh Report). The Marsh Report suggested a twofold classification of income security risks: universal risks such as medical care and pensions; and employment risks, unemployment, disability, etc. Marsh's report shared ideas with the British Report on Social Insurance and Allied Services of 1942 (the Beveridge Report). A comprehensive set of income security proposals designed to protect national minimums was proposed.

d. The Dominion-Provincial Conference on Reconstruction, Proposals of the Government of Canada, 1945 (the Green Book proposals) presented formal proposals of the federal government "for establishing the general conditions of high employment and income policies, and for the support of national minimum standards of social services."

The results of these inquiries were twofold. General objectives for Canadian social welfare policy were established. In addition, some specific legislation was passed.

a. With the Unemployment Insurance Act, 1940, the provinces agreed to a constitutional amendment giving power to the federal government for Unemployment Insurance.

b. The National Employment Service (the forerunner of the Department of Manpower) was established in 1941.

c. The universal Family Allowances program was legislated in 1944 and introduced in 1945.

d. The National Housing Act was legislated in 1944, and the Central Mortgage and Housing Corporation was established in 1946.

e. Although there were no federal health insurance acts, some provinces began to provide specific types of health insurance, for example, hospital insurance acts in Saskatchewan (1947) and British Columbia (1949).

1950-1960

The decade 1950-1960 was a period of incremental extension in Canadian social welfare legislation. Important measures enacted included:

a. Income security provisions for the elderly and incapacitated were substantially revised. These revisions included universal Old Age Security payments (1951) beginning at age seventy; and a revised Old Age Assistance Act (1951) for persons aged sixty-five to seventy. A Blind Persons Act (1951) similar in its provisions to the Old Age Assistance Act was also legislated. In 1955, those federal cost-shared, means-tested programs were extended to the permanently disabled through the Disabled Persons Act.
b. In 1951 the Indian Act was amended so that provincial laws of general application, such as child welfare legislation, applied to Indians living on reserves.
c. In 1956, the Unemployment Assistance Act was passed whereby the federal government agreed to furnish 50 per cent of the costs of provincial social assistance payments.
d. In 1956, a federal Hospital Insurance Act was passed whereby the federal government agreed to share in the costs of provincial hospital insurance programs.

1960-1970

The decade 1960-1970 was a period of more substantial action than the preceding decade. During this period, action was taken to develop the social welfare institutions that had been foreseen during the 1940s. By the end of the decade, the only major fields in which the objectives of the 1940s had not been legislated were housing, particularly housing for low-income persons, and maternity allowances. In addition, new action was begun, centring on the subject of poverty. Finally, the issue of responsibility for social welfare was reopened during the series of federal-provincial conferences that followed Quebec's Quiet Revolution.

a. In 1961, the Royal Commission on Health Services (the Hall Commission) was appointed. In 1962, Saskatchewan enacted the first universal government medical care insurance program in North America. Despite a doctors' strike on its introduction, the program was generally regarded as successful. In 1964-65, the Hall Commission reported, advocating a universal medical insurance plan. In 1968, the federal Medical Services Act came into effect, whereby the federal government agreed to share in the cost of provincial programs of medical insurance. Despite initial provincial opposition, all provinces had enacted medical insurance legislation within three years.
b. In 1962, the Royal Commission on Taxation (the Carter Commission) was appointed. The subject of government payment programs to individuals (income security) was outside the terms of reference of the Commission. When it reported in 1966, the Commission asserted a principle of equity in the treatment of income, regardless of source. The Commission's proposals were the subject of a government White Paper, *Proposals for Tax Reform*, in 1969 (the Benson proposals). Revised income tax legislation, incorporating some but not all of the Carter Commission's proposals, was introduced in 1971 and came into effect in 1972.

c. There was substantial revision in provision for the elderly and incapacitated. The Canada Pension Plan, covering retirement, widowhood, disability, etc. through social insurance, was introduced in 1966. A companion plan, the Quebec Pension Plan, provided similar coverage in that province. In addition, the Old Age Security Guaranteed Income Supplement program (1966) was introduced. This program supplemented Old Age Security payments, ensuring that no elderly person's monthly income fell below a prescribed level.

d. The Canada Assistance Plan (1966) extended federal cost-sharing in provincial social welfare programs. The plan provided for a consolidation of previous cost-sharing programs, unemployment assistance, old age assistance, blind and disabled persons assistance, the inclusion of child welfare measures, and the inclusion of administrative costs.

e. The War on Poverty, begun in the United States in 1964, had an effect on Canadian social welfare programs. The objectives of the Company of Young Canadians (1965) showed similarities to those of the American Office of Economic Opportunity community action programs. The objectives of the Canada Assistance Plan, "the prevention and removal of the causes of poverty," are similar to the early War on Poverty declarations. In addition, careful study of poverty in Canada was begun. In 1968, the *Fifth Annual Review* of the Economic Council of Canada indicated that one in five Canadians lived in poverty. Also in 1968, the Special Senate Committee on Poverty (the Croll Committee) was appointed.

f. In 1968, the federal-provincial constitutional conference agreed to undertake a complete review of the constitution of Canada. Federal proposals on income security and social services were presented at a meeting in 1969. It was apparent, during the meeting, that the federal proposals (which basically affirmed the status quo) did not provide Quebec with the increased social policy responsibility that province sought.

g. In 1969, the federal government issued a White Paper on Indian affairs that would have led to the repeal of the Indian Act, the ending of separate legal status for First Nations, and the conversion of reserve lands to private tenure. The White Paper was rejected by First Nations, who began a sustained campaign for separate constitutional and policy recognition as independent nations within Canada.

1970-1980

The 1970s, in particular the first five years of the decade, were a period of major change and development in welfare programs. The future foreseen was characterized by expanded social welfare measures and restructuring of existing programs.

a. The process of constitutional review continued and proposals were presented to a federal-provincial conference on the constitution in Victoria (1971) that increased provincial jurisdiction over welfare. However, the increased authority was not adequate to satisfy Quebec and the proposals were rejected.

b. The Unemployment Insurance Act was amended in 1971, extending coverage to groups not previously covered, e.g., fishermen, and expanding coverage to include sickness and maternity leave. These changes, along with the previously enacted Canada Pension Plan, provided Canada a full range of social insurance coverage for the major insurable life contingencies foreseen by Marsh and Beveridge in the 1940s.

c. The concern with poverty continued with the publication of the Report of the Special Senate Committee on Poverty in 1971 (see summary of proposals at end of chronology). Concern with poverty was institutionalized at the federal level with the establishment of the National Council of Welfare and the publication by Statistics Canada of regular data on poverty.

d. The major federal initiative aimed at the design of a guaranteed income was initiated in 1971 with the federal proposal *Income Security for Canadians*. A two-level system was foreseen, one level for unemployable people and a second level, integrated with working income through wage supplementation, for unemployed but employable people. These proposals were published in 1973 in the *Working Paper on Social Security in Canada* (see summary of proposals at end of chronology), but no basic changes were enacted for both technical and financial reasons.

e. The personal social services were substantially expanded at the provincial level and major initiatives were undertaken to improve their integration and co-ordination. These initiatives took the form of an expanded provincial jurisdiction in relation to services previously provided by local government and private societies. There were also changes in inter-ministry jurisdiction to integrate services more closely and the introduction of new structures for the accountability of services to the local community. In most jurisdictions child welfare legislation was revised to reflect rights and due process. These changes were influenced by the British Seebohm Report (1968). However, they were not always consolidated, and legislation, such as British Columbia's Community Resource Board Act (1974), was both introduced and withdrawn again by the end of the decade.

f. The Canadian Council on the Status of Women was established in 1973, following a recommendation from the Royal Commission on the Status of Women.

1980-1990

The 1980s began with much uncertainty. The first referendum on the separation of Quebec was held; separation was defeated by a 60/40 margin. The federal income security review failed to produce a guaranteed income plan, and most provinces (Quebec is an exception) failed to reform personal social services in the manner foreseen. The welfare state was under conservative review in the United States and Britain on both ideological and financial grounds. Major events included:

a) Constitutional repatriation. Authority to amend the Canadian constitution was established in Canada in 1981. The constitutional documents included the Charter of Rights and Freedoms, incorporating fundamental civil rights into

the constitution. However, Quebec was not a signatory due to concerns about the amending formula and the federal spending power, as these impacted on provincial jurisdiction for language and social policy.
b) The Penner Committee on Indian Self-Government recommended that First Nations should be recognized as "a distinct order of government in Canada."
c) The Canada Health Act 1984 was passed to arrest the deterioration of universal medical coverage through the growth of provincial fee-for-service practices.
d) The Report of the Royal Commission on the Economic Union and Development Prospects for Canada (Macdonald Commission, 1985) refocused attention on the unfinished business of income security reform, arguing that a better system was needed to assist in the process of economic adjustment that would follow from a free trade agreement with the United States (see summary of proposals at end of chronology).
e) Registered Retirement Savings Plan and Registered Pension Plan contribution limits were raised as the first step toward increased tax expenditures to support retirement incomes.
f) The principles on which Quebec's full agreement to the Canadian constitution could be obtained were mutually agreed upon by the Prime Minister and the provincial premiers in the Meech Lake Accord (1987), wherein the federal government agreed to permit provinces to exclude themselves from federal-provincial shared-cost social programs in areas of exclusive provincial jurisdiction and receive financial compensation if they undertake initiatives compatible with the national objective. The Accord was never ratified by the provinces.
g) The Child Care Act (1988) was introduced to replace day-care provisions of the Canada Assistance Plan. It was never passed, and following the 1988 federal election was not re-introduced.
h) The Canada-U.S. Free trade Agreement was signed in 1988. Although the agreement made no mention of social policy, it established a trading and investment relationship that provided capital with increased freedom of choice as to which country to invest in, restricting the Canadian ability to develop taxation policies on corporations dissimilar to those in effect in the United States.
i) The House of Commons Resolution to eliminate child poverty by the year 2000 was passed unanimously (1989).
j) "Clawback" was imposed on Family Allowances and Old Age Security for incomes over $50,000/year (1989).

1990-

Canada's fiscal problems became more significant as industrial recession in central Canada between 1990 and 1992 reduced government revenues while raising government expenditures for social security.

a) In 1990 the full cost of Unemployment Insurance was shifted to employers and employees and government support from general revenue was ended. Expenditures under the Canada Assistance Plan were restricted to 5 per cent annual increases for Ontario, Alberta, and British Columbia. Canada Pension Plan contributions were raised.

b) Canada ratified the United Nations convention on the Rights of the Child (1991).

c) The Goods and Services Tax (GST) and the GST low-income rebate were introduced (1991).

d) In 1992 the Charlottetown Accord, which included recognizing a "distinct society" in Quebec and providing a framework for First Nations self-government, was defeated in a national referendum.

e) In 1993 Family Allowance payments, the child tax credit, and the child personal exemption were terminated and the Child Tax Benefit introduced.

f) Contributions to the CAP were raised each year from a maximum of $594.20 in 1990 to $806.00 in 1994: contributions to UI were raised each year from a maximum of $737.51 in 1990 to $1,245.24 in 1994.

g) The social housing budget was frozen at $2 billion (no new commitments) in 1993.

h) The Canada-U.S. Free Trade Agreement was expanded to include Mexico in 1993, and leaders of the three countries signed the North American Free Trade Agreement (NAFTA), with provision for other countries in the Americas to join in the future.

i) The Minister of Human Resource Development, Lloyd Axworthy, held a series of consultations on the future of social security and issued a discussion paper, *Improving Social Security in Canada*; at the same time the Minister of Finance, Paul Martin, held consultations based on the report, *Creating a Healthy Fiscal Climate*. Following the consultations the Canada Assistance Plan was replaced by the Canada Health and Social Transfer, and federal payments to the provinces were reduced (commencing in 1996). As Martin noted in the 1995 budget address, further cuts in Unemployment Insurance and pensions were also anticipated for introduction in 1996 and later years.

j) A Royal Commission on Aboriginal Peoples was appointed in 1992 but has not yet reported (1995).

k) The second referendum on Quebec independence was held on October 30, 1995. It was defeated by a margin of barely 1 per cent – 50.6 per cent to 49.4 per cent.

Major Reform Proposals

A number of major proposals bearing on the future of the Canadian income security system have been considered. The reports on these proposals are *Poverty in Canada*, the report of the Special Senate Committee on Poverty (1971); *Working Paper on Social Security in Canada* (1973); and *Report of the Royal Commission on the Economic Union and Development Prospects for Canada* (1985).

1. *Poverty in Canada.* This report from the Special Senate Committee on Poverty proposed a new income assistance program for which eligibility would be established on the basis of annual income as shown on the individual or family income

tax returns. This program was referred to as a negative income tax program with the following features:

- Single persons under forty were excluded.
- Benefit levels were at 70 per cent of poverty lines.
- Earned income was recaptured at the rate of seventy cents on the dollar.
- Income tax exemptions were increased and integrated with the negative tax system.
- Old Age Security, GIS, and Family Allowances were abolished.

The proposed negative income tax program was viewed as additional to other income security programs rather than as an alternative. Social assistance would continue to exist for some categories of applicant and the Canada Pension Plan and Unemployment Insurance would be retained.

2. *Working Paper on Social Security in Canada.* Although this contained detailed proposals, for example, to increase at that time Family Allowances to $20/month, it was not comprehensive. It stated a variety of principles and five strategies:

- an employment strategy, including work incentives, government job-seeking, and a community employment program;
- a social insurance strategy, consisting of expansion of existing plans;
- an income supplement strategy, including Family Allowances, income supplements for the working poor, income guarantees for the unemployed, and a residual social assistance program;
- a social aid employment service strategy, including such services as training, counselling, and day care;
- a federal-provincial strategy designed to secure minimums while providing for provincial flexibility.

These were seen as the beginning point for federal-provincial negotiations leading to a new income security system for Canada – similar to that proposed by the Special Senate Committee. However, lengthy negotiations did not produce federal-provincial agreement and the reform of income security was not achieved. While federal-provincial discussions were proceeding, a major experiment in income security programming was undertaken in Manitoba to pre-test the effects of the proposed guaranteed annual income on work incentive. The test was concluded and its results supported the conclusion that the guaranteed income would not reduce work incentives.

3. *Report of the Royal Commission on the Economic Union and Development Prospects for Canada.* The Macdonald Commission eloquently restated the case for major changes in the income security system. This case had been clearly made in the early 1970s, but by 1985 the weaknesses of the existing system were even more apparent:

- Many Canadians were still in poverty while payments go to many who are not.
- The system was too complex, with too many programs and too many people administering them.

- The system created serious work disincentives, both social assistance and Unemployment Insurance having effective 100 per cent marginal reduction rates on benefits.
- The system was inequitable – tax benefits increased with income.

The Commission considered the case for partial reform but concluded that major changes were both possible and necessary to correct the weaknesses of the present system.

The principal proposal was for a "Universal Income Security Program" to replace the Guaranteed Income Supplement, Family Allowances, child tax credits, married exemptions, child exemptions, federal contributions to social assistance payments, and federal social housing programs. The central features of UISP would be a universal minimum guaranteed rate of income, federally funded and administered. Payments of UISP would be reduced with receipt of other income at a rate that would maintain work incentives and integrate with income tax rates. Although the Commission made specific proposals for guarantee and tax-back rates, it also made it plain that these features should be flexible.

Notes

1. D. Bellamy, "Social Welfare in Canada," and J. Willard, "Canadian Welfare Programs," in *Encyclopedia of Social Work* (New York: National Association of Social Workers, 1965).
2. Dennis Guest, *The Emergence of Social Security in Canada*, 2nd edition (Vancouver: UBC Press, 1985).
3. Thomas Courchene, *Social Canada in the Millennium* (Toronto: C.D. Howe Institute, 1994), pp. 341-55.
4. For an account of pre-1900 social welfare provision, see R. Splane, *Social Welfare in Ontario 1791-1893* (Toronto: University of Toronto Press, 1965); T. Copp, *The Anatomy of Poverty: The Condition of the Working Class in Montreal 1897-1929* (Toronto: McClelland & Stewart, 1974).
5. *Report of the Royal Commission on Dominion-Provincial Relations* (Ottawa: King's Printer, 1940), Book II, p. 128.

BIBLIOGRAPHY

Adams, Ian, William Cameron, Brian Hill, and Peter Penz. *The Real Poverty Report*. Edmonton: Hurtig, 1971.

Armitage, Andrew. "Workfare in British Columbia: Social Development Alternatives," *Canadian Review of Social Policy*, 26 (November, 1990).

Armitage, Andrew. *Comparing the Policy of Aboriginal Assimilation*. Vancouver: University of British Columbia Press, 1995.

Austin, David, and Yeheskel Hasenfeld. "A Prefatory Essay on the Future Administration of Human Services," *Journal of Applied Behavioural Science*, 21, 4 (1955).

Baines, Carol, Patricia Evans, and Sheila Neysmith, eds. *Women's Caring: Feminist Perspectives on Social Welfare*. Toronto: McClelland & Stewart, 1991.

Bala, Nicholas, Joseph P. Hornick and Robin Vogl. *Canadian Child Welfare: Children, Families and the State*. Toronto: Thompson Educational Publishing, 1990.

Banting, Keith. *The Welfare State and Canadian Federalism*. Montreal: McGill-Queen's University Press, 1984.

Banting, Keith. "The Welfare State and Inequality in the 1980s," *Canadian Review of Sociology and Anthropology*, 24, 3 (1987).

Banton, Michael. *Racial Theories*. Cambridge: Cambridge University Press, 1988.

Battle, Ken, and Sherri Torjman. *Opening the Books on Social Spending*. Ottawa: Caledon Institute, 1993.

Bauer, Raymond. *Social Indicators*. Cambridge, Mass.: MIT Press, 1966.

Bella, Leslie, Penelope Rowe, and Deanne Costello. *Proceedings of Sixth Biennial Social Welfare Policy Conference St. John's, Newfoundland, June 27-30, 1993*. St. John's: School of Social Work, Memorial University, 1994.

Bella, Leslie. "Social Welfare and Social Credit: The Administrative Contribution to Alberta's Provincial Welfare State," *Canadian Social Work Review* (1986).

Bellamy, Donald. "Social Welfare in Canada," *Encyclopedia of Social Work*. New York: National Association of Social Workers, 1965.

Beveridge, William. *Social Insurance and Allied Service*. New York: Macmillan, 1942.

Bisoondath, Neil. *Selling Illusions: The Cult of Multiculturalism in Canada*. Toronto: Penguin Books, 1994.

Block, Walter. "The Case for Selectivity," *Canadian Social Work Review* (1983).

Bottomore, T.B. *Critics of Society: Radical Thought in North America*. New York: Random House, 1969.

Boulding, Kenneth. "The Boundaries of Social Policy," *Social Work*, 5, 12 (1967).

British Columbia. *Report of the Royal Commission on Family and Children's Law.* Vancouver, 1976.

British Columbia. *Interministry Child Abuse Handbook*, 2nd edition. Victoria, 1985.

British Columbia. *Liberating Our Children.* Victoria: Ministry of Social Services, 1992.

British Columbia. *Making Changes.* Victoria: Ministry of Social Services, 1992.

Bruce, Maurice. *The Coming of the Welfare State.* London: Batsford, 1961.

Cameron, Gary. "Social Work Research Centres," *Canadian Social Work Review*, 5 (1988).

Cairns, Alan, and Cynthia Williams. *The Politics of Gender, Ethnicity and Language in Canada.* Toronto: University of Toronto Press, 1992.

Caldwell, George. *Indian Residential Schools.* Ottawa: Canadian Welfare Council, 1967.

Caldwell, George, Jean Goodwill, Joanne Hoople, and Joseph Katz. "The Emerging Indian Crisis," *Canadian Welfare*, 43, 4 (1967).

Callahan, Marilyn, and Brian Wharf. *Demystifying the Policy Process: A Case Study in the Development of Child Welfare Legislation in B.C.* Victoria: School of Social Work, University of Victoria, 1982.

Canada. *Report of the Royal Commission on Dominion-Provincial Relations.* Ottawa: King's Printer, 1940.

Canada. *Report of the Royal Commission on Taxation.* Ottawa: Queen's Printer, 1966.

Canada. *Statement of the Government of Canada on Indian Policy.* Ottawa: Queen's Printer, 1969.

Canada. *The Measurement of Poverty.* Ottawa: Queen's Printer, 1970.

Canada. *Report of the Royal Commission on the Status of Women in Canada.* Ottawa: Queen's Printer, 1970.

Canada, Special Senate Committee on Poverty. *Poverty in Canada.* Ottawa: Queen's Printer, 1971.

Canada. *Report of the Royal Commission on the Economic Union and Development Prospects for Canada.* Ottawa: Queen's Printer, 1985.

Canada. *Report of the Commission of Inquiry on Unemployment Insurance.* Ottawa: Queen's Printer, 1986.

Canada. *Report of the Task Force on Child Care.* Ottawa: Queen's Printer, 1986.

Canada. *Agenda: Jobs and Growth – Creating a Healthy Fiscal Environment.* Ottawa: Department of Finance, 1994.

Canada. *Agenda: Jobs and Growth – Improving Social Security in Canada.* Ottawa: Human Resources Development, 1994.

Canada. *Social Security in Canada.* Ottawa: Human Resources Development, 1994.

Canadian Corrections Association. *Indians and the Law.* Ottawa: Canadian Welfare Council, 1967.

Canadian Council on Children and Youth. *Admittance Restricted: The Child as a Citizen of Canada.* Ottawa, 1978.

Carniol, Ben. *Case Critical.* Toronto: Between the Lines, 1987.

Carter, Novia, ed. *Social Indicators: Proceedings of a Seminar.* Ottawa: Canadian Council on Social Development, 1972.

Cassidy, Harry M. *Public Health and Welfare Organization in Canada.* Toronto: Ryerson, 1945.

Cassidy, Harry M. *Social Security and Reconstruction in Canada.* Toronto: Ryerson, 1945.

Clague, Michael, Robert Dill, Roop Seebaren, and Brian Wharf. *Reforming Human Services: The Experience of the Community Resource Boards in British Columbia.* Vancouver: University of British Columbia Press, 1984.

Clement, Wallace. *The Canadian Corporate Elite.* Ottawa: Carleton University Press, 1986.

Cochrane, Allan, and John Clarke, eds. *Comparing Welfare States: Britain in International Context.* London: Sage Publications, 1993.

Courchene, Thomas. *Social Canada in the Millennium: Reform Imperatives and Restructuring Principles.* Toronto: C.D. Howe Institute, 1994.

Crane, John. *Directions for Social Welfare in Canada: The Public's View.* Vancouver: School of Social Work, 1994.

Culyer, A.J. *The Economics of Social Policy.* London: Martin Robertson, 1973.

deMontigny, Gerald. *Social Working.* Toronto: University of Toronto Press, 1995.

Denholm, Carey, Roy Ferguson, and Allan Pence. *Professional Child and Youth Care.* Vancouver: University of British Columbia Press, 1987.

Dennis, Michael, and Susan Fish. *Programs in Search of a Policy: Low Income Housing in Canada.* Toronto: Hakkert, 1972.

Deschweinitz, Karl. *England's Road to Social Security.* London: Oxford University Press, 1943.

Dicken, Peter. *Global Shift.* London: Paul Chapman, 1992.

Djao, Angela. *Inequality and Social Policy.* Toronto: John Wiley & Sons, 1983.

Dominelli, Lena. *Anti-Racist Social Work.* London: Macmillan, 1988.

Dooley, Martin, *et al. Family Matters.* Toronto: C.D. Howe Institute, 1995.

Drover, Glenn. "Beyond the Welfare State: CASW Brief to the Royal Commission on the Economic Union and Development Prospects for Canada," *The Social Worker,* 51, 4 (1983).

Drover, Glenn, and Patrick Keirans. "Toward a Theory of Social Welfare," *Canadian Review of Social Policy,* 29/30 (Summer/Winter, 1992).

Drover, Glenn, and Patrick Keirans. *New Approaches to Welfare Theory.* Aldershot: Edward Elgar, 1993.

Drover, Glenn, and Alan Moscovitch. *Inequality: Essay on the Political Economy of Social Welfare.* Toronto: University of Toronto Press, 1981.

Economic Council of Canada. *Fifth Annual Review, 1968.* Ottawa: Queen's Printer, 1968.

Elliott, Jean Leonard, and Augie Fleras. *Unequal Relations: An Introduction to Race and Ethnic Dynamics in Canada.* Scarborough, Ont.: Prentice-Hall, 1992.

Etzioni, Amitai. *Modern Organizations.* Englewood Cliffs, N.J.: Prentice-Hall, 1964.

Fallis, George, *et al. Home Remedies: Rethinking Canadian Housing Policies.* Toronto: C.D. Howe Institute, 1995.

Ferguson, Evelyn B. "Liberal and Socialist Feminist Perspectives on Child Care," *Canadian Social Work Review,* 5 (1988).

Fleras, Augie, and Jean Leonard Elliott. *The Nations Within: Aboriginal-State Relations in Canada, the United States and New Zealand.* Toronto: Oxford University Press, 1992.

Galbraith, Kenneth. *The Affluent Society.* London: Penguin, 1958.

Galloway, Burt, and Joe Hudson. *Community Economic Development.* Toronto: Thompson Educational Publishing, 1994.

Galper, Jeffrey. *The Politics of Social Services.* Englewood Cliffs, N.J.: Prentice-Hall, 1975.

George, Vic, and Paul Wilding. *Ideology and Social Welfare.* London: Routledge and Kegan Paul, 1976.

Gonick, Cy. *The Great Economic Debate.* Toronto: James Lorimer, 1987.

Green, Christopher. *Negative Taxes and the Poverty Problem.* Washington: The Brookings Institute, 1967.

Green, Christopher, Fred Lazar, Miles Corak, and Dominique Gross. *Unemployment Insurance: How To Make It Work.* Toronto: C.D. Howe Institute, 1994.

Gross, Bertram, ed. "Social Goals and Indicators for American Society," *The Annals of the American Academy of Political and Social Science,* 371 (May, 1967).

Guest, Dennis. *The Emergence of Social Security in Canada,* 2nd edition. Vancouver: University of British Columbia Press, 1986.

Hammersley, Martyn, and Paul Atkinson. *Ethnography: Principles and Practice.* New York: Routledge, 1990.

Harris, Richard, John Richards, David Brown, and John McCallum. *Paying Our Way: The Welfare State in Hard Times.* Toronto: C.D. Howe Institute, 1994.

Hasenfeld, Y. *Human Service Organizations.* Englewood Cliffs, N.J.: Prentice-Hall, 1983.

Heilbronner, Robert *Twenty-First Century Capitalism: The Massey Lecture Series.* Concord, Ont.: Anansi, 1992.

Hill, Malcolm. "Free Trade and Social Policy: Are There Lessons for Europe?" *Canadian Review of Social Policy,* 29/30 (Summer/Winter, 1992).

Hillyard, Paddy, and Janie Percy Smith. *The Coercive State: The Decline of Democracy in Britain.* London: Fontana, 1988.

Hudson, Peter, and Brad McKenzie. "Child Welfare and Native Peoples: The Extension of Colonialism," *The Social Worker,* 49, 2 (1981).

Irving, Allan. "Canadian Fabians: The Work and Thought of Harry Cassidy and Leonard Marsh, 1939-45," *Canadian Journal of Social Work Education,* 7, 1 (1981).

Johnson, Andrew, Stephen McBride, and Patrick Smith. *Continuities and Discontinuities: The Political Economy of Social Welfare and Labour Market Policy in Canada.* Toronto: University of Toronto Press, 1994.

Johnston, Patrick. *Native Children and the Child Welfare System.* Toronto: James Lorimer, 1983.

Kahn, Alfred. *Studies in Social Policy and Planning.* New York: Russell Sage Foundation, 1969.

Kahn, Alfred. *Theory and Practice of Social Planning.* New York: Russell Sage Foundation, 1969.

Kahn, Alfred. *Social Policy and Social Services.* New York: Random House, 1983.

Kaim-Caudle, P.R. *Comparative Social Policy and Social Security: A Ten Country Study.* London: Robertson, 1973.

Kly, Y. "On the Meaning and Significance of the United Nations Convention on the Rights of the Child," *Canadian Review of Social Policy,* 27 (May, 1991).

Kymlicka, Will. *Multicultural Citizenship: A liberal theory of minority rights.* Oxford: Clarendon Press, 1995.

LaMarsh, Judy. *Memoirs of a Bird in a Gilded Cage.* Toronto: McClelland and Stewart, 1968.

Leman, Christopher. *The Collapse of Welfare Reform: Political Institutions, Policy and the Poor in Canada and the United States.* Cambridge, Mass.: MIT Press, 1980.

Lemon, Paul. *Deinstitutionalization and the Welfare State.* Rutgers, N.J.: Rutgers University Press, 1982.

Levitt, Kenneth, and Brian Wharf, eds. *The Challenge of Child Welfare.* Vancouver: University of British Columbia Press, 1985.

Li, Peter, ed. *Race and Ethnic Relations in Canada.* Don Mills, Ont.: Oxford University Press, 1990.

Lithwick, N.H. *Urban Canada: Problems and Prospects.* Ottawa: Central Mortgage and Housing Corporation, 1970.

Lubove, Roy. *The Professional Altruist: The Emergence of Social Work as a Career 1880-1930.* Cambridge, Mass.: Harvard University Press, 1965.

Macpherson, C.B. "The Real World of Democracy," *Massey Lectures, 4th Series.* Toronto: Canadian Broadcasting Corporation, 1965.

MacPherson, Stewart. *Social Policy in the Third World: The Social Dilemmas of Underdevelopment.* Brighton: Wheatsheaf Books, 1982.

Marsh, Leonard. *Report on Social Security for Canada.* Ottawa: King's Printer, 1943.

Marshall, T.H. *Class, Citizenship and Social Development.* Garden City, N.Y.: Anchor Books, 1965.

McQuaig, Linda. *The Wealthy Banker's Wife: The Assault on Equality in Canada.* Toronto: Penguin, 1993.

McQuaig, Linda. *Shooting the Hippo.* Toronto: Viking, 1995.

Midgeley, James. *Professional Imperialism: Social Work in the Third World.* London: Heinemann, 1981.

Mills, C. Wright. "The Professional Ideology of Social Pathologists," *American Journal of Sociology,* LXIX (1942).

Mishra, Ramesh. *Society and Social Policy: Theoretical Perspectives on Welfare,* Revised edition. London: Macmillan, 1981.

Mishra, Ramesh. *The Welfare State in Crisis*. Brighton: Wheatsheaf Books, 1984.

Mishra, Ramesh. *The Welfare State in Capitalist Society: Policies of Retrenchment and Maintenance in Europe, North America and Australia*. Toronto: University of Toronto Press, 1990.

Moran, Bridget. *Justa: A First Nations Leader*. Vancouver: Arsenal Pulp Press, 1994.

Moscovitch, Alan. *The Welfare State in Canada: A Selected Bibliography (1840-1978)*. Waterloo, Ont.: Wilfrid Laurier University Press, 1983.

Mullaly, Robert. *Structural Social Work: Ideology, Theory, and Practice*. Toronto: McClelland & Stewart, 1993.

Myrdal, Gunnar. *Beyond the Welfare State*. London: Duckworth, 1958.

Naidoo, Josephine. "Combatting Racism Involving Visible Minorities: A Review of Relevant Research and Policy Development," *Canadian Social Work Review*, 8, 2 (Summer, 1991).

National Council of Welfare. *Incomes and Opportunities*. Ottawa, 1973.

National Council of Welfare. *The Press and the Poor*. Ottawa, 1973.

National Council of Welfare. *Prices and the Poor*. Ottawa, 1974.

National Council of Welfare. *Poor Kids*. Ottawa, 1975.

National Council of Welfare. *Guide to the Guaranteed Income*. Ottawa, 1976.

National Council of Welfare. *The Hidden Welfare System Revisited*. Ottawa, 1979.

National Council of Welfare. *The Working Poor*. Ottawa, 1981.

National Council of Welfare. *A Pension Primer*. Ottawa, 1984.

National Council of Welfare. *Sixty-Five and Older*. Ottawa, 1984.

National Council of Welfare. *Better Pensions for Homemakers*. Ottawa, 1984.

National Council of Welfare. *Welfare in Canada: The Tangled Safety Net*. Ottawa, 1987.

National Council of Welfare. *Pension Reform*. Ottawa, 1990.

National Council of Welfare. *Poverty Profile 1980-1990*. Ottawa, 1992.

National Council of Welfare. *Welfare Reform*. Ottawa, 1992.

National Council of Welfare. *Incentives and Disincentives to Work*. Ottawa, 1993.

National Council of Welfare. *Welfare Incomes 1993*. Ottawa, 1993.

National Council of Welfare. *A Blueprint for Social Security Reform*. Ottawa, 1994.

National Council of Welfare. *Poverty Profile 1992*. Ottawa, 1994.

Organization for Economic Co-operation and Development (OECD). *OECD Economic Survey, 1993-4: Canada*. Paris, 1994.

Ontario. *Transitions: Report of the Social Assistance Review Committee*. Toronto: Ministry of Community and Social Services, 1988.

Pal, Leslie. *Public Policy Analysis: an Introduction*, 2nd edition. Toronto: Methuen, 1992.

Peattie, Lisa, and Martin Rein. *Women's Claims*. London: Oxford University Press, 1983.

Pinker, Robert. *Social Theory and Social Policy*. London: Heinemann, 1971.

Pinker, Robert. *The Idea of Welfare*. London: Heinemann, 1979.

Piven, Frances Fox, and Richard Cloward. *Regulating the Poor: The Public Functions of Welfare*. New York: Random House, 1972.

Porter, John. *The Vertical Mosaic*. Toronto: University of Toronto Press, 1965.

Quebec. *Report of the Commission of Inquiry on Health and Social Welfare*. Quebec City: Quebec Official Publisher, 1971.

Rawls, John. *A Theory of Justice*. London: Oxford University Press, 1973.

Rein, Martin. "Social Policy Analysis as the Interpretation of Beliefs," *Journal of the American Institute of Planners*, XXXVII, 5 (1971).

Rein, Mildred. *Dilemmas of Welfare Policy: Why Work Strategies Haven't Worked*. New York: Praeger, 1982.

Reitz, Jeffrey G., and Raymond Breton. *The Illusions of Difference*. Toronto: C.D. Howe Institute, 1994.

Richards, John, *et al. Helping the Poor: A Qualified Case for "Workfare"*. Toronto: C.D. Howe Institute, 1995.

Ricks, Frances, Brian Wharf, and Andrew Armitage. "Evaluation of Child Welfare: A Different Reality," *Canadian Review of Social Policy*, 25 (May, 1990).

Romanyshyn, John. *Social Welfare: Charity to Justice*. New York: Random House, 1971.

Ross, David. *The Working Poor: Wage Earners and the Failure of Income Security Policy*. Toronto: James Lorimer, 1981.

Ross, David, E. Richard Shillington, and Clarence Lochhead. *The Canadian Fact Book on Poverty*. Ottawa: Canadian Council on Social Development, 1994.

Salyzn, Vladimir. "Goals in Indian Affairs," *Canadian Welfare*, 42, 2 (1966).

Sarlo, Christopher. *Poverty in Canada*. Vancouver: The Fraser Institute, 1992.

Schellenberg, Grant. *The Road to Retirement*. Ottawa: Canadian Council on Social Development, 1994.

Seebaren, Roop. "Social Services in British Columbia: The Axe Falls," *The Social Worker*, 51, 3 (1983).

Shackleton, Doris. "The Indian as a Newcomer," *Canadian Welfare*, 45, 4 (1969).

Shewell, Hugh. "History and Social Policy: Understanding the Context of Canada's Native Indian Policies," *Canadian Review of Social Policy*, 25 (May, 1990).

Shragge, Eric. *Community Economic Development*. Montreal: Black Rose Books, 1993.

Sim, Alex R. "Indian Schools for Indian Children," *Canadian Welfare*, 45, 2 (1969).

Smedley, Audrey. *Race in North America*. Boulder, Colorado: Westview Press, 1993.

Smiley, Donald. *Conditional Grants and Canadian Federalism*. Toronto: Canadian Tax Foundation, 1973.

Smiley, Donald, ed. *The Rowell-Sirois Report*. Toronto: McClelland and Stewart, 1963.

Sniderman, Paul M., and Thomas Piazza. *The Scar of Race*. Cambridge, Mass.: The Belknap Press of Harvard University, 1993.

Splane, Richard. *Social Welfare in Ontario, 1791-1898*. Toronto: University of Toronto Press, 1965.

Splane, Richard. "Whatever Happened to the G.A.I.?" *The Social Worker*, 48, 2 (1980).

Stanbury, William. "Poverty Among B.C. Indians Off Reserves," *Canadian Welfare*, 50, 1 (1974).

Teeple, Gary. *Globalization and the Decline of Social Reform*. Toronto: Garamond Press, 1995.

Tester, James Frank. "The Disenchanted Democracy: Canada in the Global Economy of the 1990s," *Canadian Review of Social Policy*, 29/30 (Summer/Winter, 1992).

Tester, James Frank, and Peter Kulchyski. *Tammarniit (Mistakes): Inuit Relocation in the Eastern Arctic 1939-63*. Vancouver: University of British Columbia Press, 1994.

Titmuss, Richard M. *Commitment to Welfare*. London: George Allen and Unwin, 1968.

Titmuss, Richard. *The Gift Relationship*. London: George Allen and Unwin, 1968.

Torjman, Sherri, and Ken Battle. "Child Benefit Primer: A Response to the Government Proposal," *Canadian Review of Social Policy*, 29/30 (Summer/Winter, 1992).

Trist, Eric. *The Relationship of Welfare and Development in the Transition to Post-Industrialism*. Ottawa: Canadian Centre for Community Studies, 1967.

Trute, Barry, and Linda Campbell. "The Child and Family Services Research Group," *Canadian Social Work Review*, 5 (1988).

United Kingdom Home Office. *Report of the Committee on Local Authority and Allied Personal Social Services*. London: HMSO, 1968.

United Nations. *Universal Declaration of Human Rights*. New York, 1948.

Vaillancourt, François. *Income Distribution and Economic Security in Canada*. Toronto: University of Toronto Press, 1985.

Vanderbergh, Nancy, and Lynn Cooper. *Feminist Visions for Social Work*. New York: National Association of Social Workers, 1986.

Warren, Roland. *The Community in America*. New York: Random House, 1963.

Watson William, John Richards, and David Brown. *The Case for Change: Reinventing the Welfare State*. Ottawa: Renouf, 1994.

Wharf, Brian. *Toward First Nations Control of Child Welfare*. Victoria: University of Victoria Press, 1988.

Wharf, Brian, ed. *Social Work and Social Change in Canada*. Toronto: McClelland & Stewart, 1990.

Wharf, Brian, ed. *Rethinking Child Welfare in Canada*. Toronto: McClelland & Stewart, 1993.

Whittington, Michael, and Glen Williams. *Canadian Politics in the 1990s*. Scarborough, Ont.: Nelson, 1990.

Wilensky, H.L., and C. Lebeaux. *Industrial Society and Social Welfare*. New York: Macmillan, 1965.

Willard, J.W. "Canadian Welfare Programs," *Encyclopedia of Social Work*. New York: National Association of Social Workers, 1965.

Williams, Fiona. *Social Policy: A Critical Introduction*. Cambridge: Polity Press, 1989.

Wineman, Steven. *The Politics of Human Services: Radical Alternatives to the Welfare State*. Montreal: Black Rose Books, 1984.

Wolfensberger, W. *The Principle of Normalization in Human Services*. Washington: National Institute on Mental Retardation, 1972.

Woodsworth, David. "Agency Policy and Client Roles," *The Social Worker*, 37, 4 (1969).

Woodsworth, David. *Social Security and National Policy*. Montreal: McGill-Queen's University Press, 1977.

Yelaja, Shankar, ed. *Canadian Social Policy*, 2nd Edition. Waterloo, Ont.: Wilfrid Laurier University Press, 1987.

Young, Crawford, ed. *The Rising Tide of Cultural Pluralism: The Nation State at Bay?* Madison: University of Wisconsin Press, 1993.

INDEX